MacBook®

PORTABLE GENIUS
2nd EDITION

MacBook®

PORTABLE GENIUS
2nd EDITION

by Brad Miser

Wiley Publishing, Inc.

MacBook® Portable Genius, 2nd Edition

Published by
Wiley Publishing, Inc.
10475 Crosspoint Blvd.
Indianapolis, IN 46256
www.wiley.com

Copyright © 2010 by Wiley Publishing, Inc., Indianapolis, Indiana

Published simultaneously in Canada

ISBN: 978-0-470-56064-8

Manufactured in the United States of America

10 9 8 7 6 5 4 3 2 1

For general information on our other products and services or to obtain technical support, please contact our Customer Care Department within the U.S. at (877) 762-2974, outside the U.S. at (317) 572-3993 or fax (317) 572-4002.

Wiley also publishes its books in a variety of electronic formats. Some content that appears in print may not be available in electronic books.

Library of Congress Control Number: 2009938253

WILEY

About the Author

Brad Miser has written more than 40 books helping people get more out of their technology faster and easier. In addition to *MacBook Portable Genius, 2nd Edition,* Brad has written *Teach Yourself Visually MacBook, iPhoto '09 Portable Genius, MacBook Pro Portable Genius, 2nd Edition, MobileMe for Small Business Portable Genius, My iPhone, Teach Yourself Visually MacBook Air, My iPod touch,* and *Special Edition Using Mac OS X Leopard.* He has also been co-author, development editor, or technical editor on more than 50 other titles.

Brad is or has been a solutions consultant, the director of product and customer services, and the manager of education and support services for several software development companies.

In addition to his passion for silicon-based technology, Brad enjoys his steel-based technology in the form of motorcycles whenever and wherever possible. Originally from California, Brad now lives in Indiana with his wife Amy; their three daughters, Jill, Emily, and Grace; a rabbit; and a sometimes-inside cat.

Brad would love to hear about your experiences with this book (the good, the bad, and the ugly). You can write to him at bradmiser@me.com.

Credits

Senior Acquisitions Editor
Stephanie McComb

Executive Editor
Jody Lefevere

Project Editor
Jama Carter

Technical Editor
Brian Joseph

Senior Copy Editor
Kim Heusel

Editorial Director
Robyn Siesky

Editorial Manager
Cricket Krengel

Vice President and Executive Group Publisher
Richard Swadley

Vice President and Executive Publisher
Barry Pruett

Business Manager
Amy Knies

Senior Marketing Manager
Sandy Smith

Senior Project Coordinator
Kristie Rees

Graphics and Production Specialists
Beth Brooks
Jennifer Henry
Andrea Hornberger

Proofreading
Penny L. Stuart

Indexing
Potomac Indexing, LLC

The probability that we may fall in the struggle
ought not to deter us from the support of a cause
we believe to be just; it shall not deter me.

—Abraham Lincoln

Acknowledgments

My emphatic thanks goes to Stephanie McComb because she is the one with whom this project had its genesis and who allowed me to be involved. Jama Carter deserves lots of credit for keeping the project on track and on target; I'm sure working with me was a challenge at times. Brian Joseph did a great job of keeping me on my toes to make sure this book contains fewer technical gaffs than it would have without his help. Kim Heusel transformed my stumbling, bumbling text into something people can read and understand. Lastly, thanks to all the people on the Wiley team who handle the other, and equally important, parts of the process, such as production, sales, proofreading, and indexing.

On my personal team, I'd like to thank my wife Amy for her tolerance of the author lifestyle, which is both odd and challenging. My delightful daughters Jill, Emily, and Grace are always a source of joy and inspiration for all that I do, and for which I'm ever grateful.

Contents

chapter 4

What Can I Do on a Local
Network?   94

Sharing Files   96
  Sharing your files with others   96
    Configuring Sharing user
      accounts   96
    Configuring file sharing   97
    Setting sharing permissions
      for folders and files from the
      Finder   100
  Accessing files shared with you   101
    Using the sidebar to access
      shared files   102
    Accessing shared files using
      a URL   103
  Sharing files with Windows PCs   105
    Sharing files on a MacBook
      with Windows PCs   105
    Accessing files from a
      Windows PC   106
    Sharing files on a Windows PC   107
    Accessing files shared on a
      Windows PC using a Mac   108
  Sharing Screens   109
    Sharing your MacBook with
      other Macs   109

Sharing another Mac on a local
  network   111
Sharing Printers   114
  Sharing USB printers connected
    to a base station   114
  Sharing printers connected to a Mac 115
Sharing an Internet Connection   115

chapter 5

How Do I Take Advantage of
MobileMe?   118

Obtaining a MobileMe Account   120
    Configuring a MobileMe account   121
    Logging in to your MobileMe
      Web site   122
Working with iDisks   124
    Configuring and managing
      your iDisk   124
    Using your iDisk   126
    Sharing files on your iDisk   128
Synchronizing Data   133
Using MobileMe Web Applications   136
    Using the MobileMe email
      application   136
    Using the MobileMe Contacts
      application   140
    Using the MobileMe Calendar
      application   141
    Using the MobileMe Gallery
      application   142
    Using MobileMe to host a Web site 142

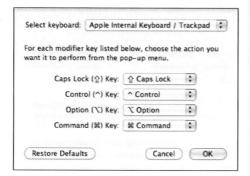

How Do I Store and Maintain
My Data? 286

How Can I Protect My MacBook? 306

chapter 15

How Can I Run Windows
Applications? 336

chapter 16

How Do I Solve MacBook
Problems? 350

Introduction

From its distinctive white case, amazing display, and inviting design, the MacBook is amazing technology that looks as great as it works. Running Mac OS X Snow Leopard and including lots of amazing software, MacBooks let you do more out of the box more easily than any other computer. In fact, MacBooks do so much, it is easy to overlook some of the great things they can do. That's where this book comes in.

While you probably already know how to turn your MacBook on, you might not know how to use Spaces to create virtual working spaces on the desktop so that you can keep many applications and windows open at the same time and move among them easily. While you likely know how to use the trackpad to point to objects on the screen to select them, you might not know how to create your own keyboard shortcuts for just about any command in any application that you use. While you have probably thought that you need to back up your important data, you might not have actually done it. And, while you've surfed the Web, you might not have taken advantage of all that being connected does for you, from file sharing locally to communicating with people around the world easily and inexpensively.

The purpose of this book is to provide a resource for you when you are wondering how to do something better, how to do it more easily, or even how to do it at all. You'll find that each chapter is organized around a question. Within each chapter are answers to its question; these answers are task-focused so you learn by doing rather than by just reading. The steps you'll find are very specific and, hopefully, quite complete; if you start at Step 1 and work through each step in sequence, you'll end up someplace you want to go. Thus, the book's title of *Portable Genius*; it is intended to be your companion to guide you on your in-depth exploration of your MacBook. Once you've been through a topic's steps, you'll be prepared to go even further by extending what you've learned to other tasks.

The book is designed to provide a broad range of topics in which most MacBook users will be interested. There's no particular order to the topics in this book so you can jump to any chapter without having read the preceding ones. To get started, I recommend that you take a look at the table of contents and decide which question you want answered first. Turn to the appropriate page and off you go!

How Can I Use
My Desktop Space
Efficiently?

Your MacBook desktop is the area that is displayed on its screen. Although the size of the screen is fixed, you can maximize the size of your desktop on that screen. Like a physical desktop, you place things (in this case, windows) "on top" to focus your attention on them and use their content. As you work, your desktop naturally becomes cluttered with windows for applications, documents, and system tools. Keeping control of all these windows can help you make the most of your MacBook's desktop space. The good news is that it's a lot easier to keep your MacBook desktop neat and tidy than it is a real desktop, and you don't even need a dust rag.

Maximizing Desktop Space

MacBooks have a 13-inch display. This is a good size for portability, but more display space is always better for maximum efficiency while you work. Fortunately, you can maximize the amount of information you see on your MacBook's screen by configuring its display. For even more working room, you can attach and use an external display. For the ultimate in desktop space, you can connect your MacBook to a projector. When you are using an external display or projector, you can have the same image displayed on the MacBook display and the external device, or you can expand your desktop over both displays.

Configuring the MacBook's display

While the physical size of the MacBook screen is fixed, the amount of information that can be displayed on it (its resolution) is not. Setting the appropriate resolution, which determines the amount of information that is displayed on the screen, is a matter of choosing the largest resolution that you can view comfortably with no eyestrain. Here's how to find your individual maximum resolution:

1. **Open the System Preferences application.**

2. **Click the Displays icon.** The Displays pane appears (see figure 1.1).

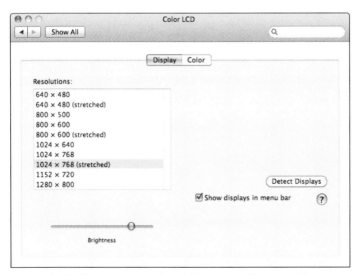

1.1 Use the Displays pane to maximize the amount of room you have on your desktop that's comfortable for you to view.

3. **Click the Display tab if it's not selected already.** In the Resolutions pane, you see all the resolutions that are supported by your MacBook's display. Resolutions are shown as

the number of horizontal pixels by the number of vertical pixels, as in 1024 × 768. Larger values have a higher resolution. Some resolutions are stretched so that they fill the screen (the MacBook has a widescreen format display).

4. **Click a resolution.** The screen updates to use the resolution you selected.

5. **Drag the Brightness slider to the right to make the screen brighter, or to the left to make it dimmer.**

6. **Add the Displays menu to the menu bar by selecting the Show displays in menu bar check box.**

7. **Hide the System Preferences application by pressing ⌘+H.**

8. **Open several windows on the desktop.**

9. **If you can see the information on the screen comfortably, move back into the System Preferences application and select a higher resolution.**

10. **Look at the open windows again.**

11. **If you can still see the information comfortably, repeat Steps 9 and 10 until the information gets too small to read comfortably or you reach the maximum resolution.**

12. **If the information in the windows is too small to read comfortably, move back to a lower resolution.**

Genius

You can quickly change resolution by opening the Displays menu and selecting the resolution you want to use. On this menu, you see a number of recent resolution settings you've used. You can change the number of recent resolutions displayed on the menu by selecting Number of Recent Items and then choosing a number between 0 and 10. You can also open the Displays Preferences pane by selecting Displays Preferences.

Adding an external display

One truth of working with computers is that you can never have too much screen space to work with. In addition to making your document and windows larger so you can see more of their contents, more screen space helps you work more efficiently because you can have more windows open at the same time.

As you learned in the previous section, one way to gain more display space is to make the resolution as large as you can comfortably view it to maximize the number of pixels on the screen and, thus, the amount of information displayed there. At some point you'll reach a maximum amount of information on the screen due to the maximum resolution of the MacBook (currently 1280 × 800) or because the information at a higher resolution becomes too small for you to view comfortably.

To add more screen space to your MacBook (which can support many displays and resolutions), you can connect an external display. You can use this display in two ways: It can become an extension of your desktop so that you can open additional windows on it just as if it was part of your MacBook's built-in display; or you can use video mirroring, which means the same information appears on both displays.

When choosing an external display, the two most important considerations are size and cost. Larger displays are better because they give you more working space. Larger displays also tend to be more expensive, although that depends on the specific brand you choose. In most cases, if you choose the largest display you can afford from a reputable manufacturer, such as Apple, ViewSonic, or Samsung, you'll be in good shape.

To add an external display, you connect it to the MacBook's Mini-DVI port. To do this, you need a Mini-DVI to DVI adapter that converts the Mini-DVI connection to a standard DVI connector used on most modern displays.

Attaching an external display to a MacBook is easy:

1. **Connect one end of the display's video cable to the Mini-DVI port to DVI adapter and the other end to the DVI port on the display.**
2. **Plug the Mini-DVI to DVI adapter into the Mini-DVI port.**
3. **Connect the display to a power source.**
4. **Power up the display.**

Once an external display is connected to your MacBook, you can configure it with the following steps:

1. **Open the System Preferences application.**
2. **Click the Displays icon.** A Displays pane opens on the MacBook's display and on the external display. The name of the pane on the MacBook's internal display is Color LCD, while the name of the pane on the external display is the name of the display. Also notice that the Displays pane on the primary display (by default, the MacBook's display) contains the Arrangement tab.

Genius

If the second display doesn't become active, click Detect Displays in the Displays pane. This should activate it.

3. **Click the Arrangement tab on the Displays pane on the MacBook screen (see figure 1.2).** You see an icon representation of each display. The display marked with the menu bar at the top is the primary display, which by definition is the one on which the menu bar appears. The Dock also appears on the primary display.

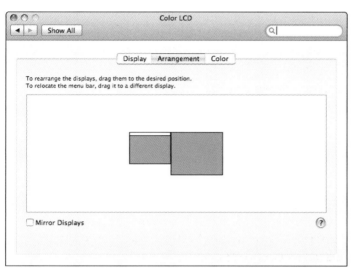

1.2 On the left is the MacBook display, while on the right is the external display; the menu bar is on the primary (MacBook) display.

4. **Drag the external display's icon so it is on the left or right side of the MacBook display's icon, to match the physical location of the display compared to the MacBook.**

5. **If you want the external display to be the primary display, drag the menu bar from the MacBook display's icon onto the external display's icon.** When you release the trackpad button, the menu bar jumps to the external display. Windows that were open on the MacBook's display move onto the external display and vice versa.

6. **Select the Displays pane for the external display.**

7. **Choose the resolution for the external display by selecting it on the list of available resolutions.**

8. **If the Refresh rate menu appears, choose the highest rate available.**

9. **Quit the System Preferences application.**

You can now use the space on the external display like you use the internal display. To place a window on the external display, drag it from the MacBook's display onto the external display. You can move windows, the pointer, and other items from one display to the other just as you can move them around the MacBook's internal display. You can configure windows on each display so that you can see many windows at the same time. For example, you might want your primary documents open on the external display and your email application open on the MacBook's display.

The menu bar remains on the primary display, so if you do most of your work on the external display, you might want to make it the primary display to make menu access easier.

Genius

If you click the Gather Windows button on the Displays pane, each pane is moved onto the primary display.

If the resolutions are significantly different between the two displays, you see a big change in appearance when you move a window between them. You might have to resize a window on one display that was the right size on the other.

To stop using the external display, disconnect it from the MacBook. If it was the primary display, the MacBook's display becomes the primary. Any open windows on the external display move onto the MacBook's display.

The next time you connect the external display, you don't need to reconfigure it; your last configuration is remembered so you can just connect the display again and get to work with the extra elbowroom.

Running with the Lid Closed

If you use Bluetooth devices, configure the MacBook so that those devices can wake the computer (see Chapter 12). Close the MacBook's lid so that it goes to sleep. Use the keyboard or mouse to wake it up. The internal display remains off, but the external display wakes up when the computer does.

To restore the internal display, simply disconnect the external display, or open the MacBook, open the Displays menu, and choose Detect Displays. The internal display becomes active again.

Using a projector

If you make presentations, conduct training, or just want a really big display, a projector is the way to go. With it, you can broadcast your MacBook's display to very large sizes for easy viewing by an audience. Using a projector is similar to using an external display so if you can work with one of them, you can work with the other.

Obtaining a projector is a bit more complicated than a display and is usually more expensive. Among the many things to consider when obtaining a projector are the following:

- **Size.** A smaller projector is easier to carry with you, and as you move through airports and such, this is very important. Smaller projectors of the same quality are more expensive than larger projectors, so you need to find a balance between portability and price.

- **Resolution.** There is more variability in the resolution of projectors than for displays. At the lower end of the price range, you'll find projectors that are capable of only 800 × 600 resolution. Many Mac applications can't even run at a resolution this low. The least resolution you should consider for a projector is 1024 × 768 (also called XGA). Higher resolutions are better but also more expensive.

- **Brightness.** The brightness of projectors is specified in lumens. Projectors with higher lumen ratings are generally able to throw larger and brighter images farther. How many lumens you need depends on a lot of factors, most of which are probably beyond your control (such as the brightness levels where you'll be using the projector if you travel with it).

- **Throw range.** This measures the closest and farthest distances at which the projector can be used.

- **Video interface.** Like displays, the options for projectors include DVI or VGA. However, most projectors provide a number of other input options such as component, composite, and S-Video. These are important if you will also be using the projector with other sources, such as a DVD player.

- **Bulb life.** Like all other bulbs, the bulb in a projector will eventually fail and need to be replaced. Unlike bulbs for lights, you can expect to pay hundreds of dollars for a replacement bulb for a projector, so you should try to get one with a long bulb life.

- **Cost.** You should expect to pay $800 or more for a good-quality projector that has at least 1024 × 768 resolution.

Genius

If you are using an unfamiliar projector, set the MacBook resolution to a relatively low value, such as 1024 × 768. If the projector doesn't display, reduce the resolution to see whether it starts displaying. Once it displays, increase the resolution until the projector is no longer capable of displaying the image.

Using a projector is very similar to using an external display. You connect a projector to the MacBook using a Mini-DVI to DVI or Mini-DVI to VGA adapter and then use the Displays pane to set the projector's resolution.

Caution   Some projectors automatically select the appropriate input source while some don't. If the projector isn't projecting an image, use its source menu to select the source to which your MacBook is connected. You can also use the Detect Displays command on the Displays menu or on the Displays pane of the System Preferences application to see if that restores an image on the projector.

However, in most cases, you want to use video mirroring so that the image being projected is the same as you see on the MacBook's desktop; this is the usual arrangement for presentations and

such, because you can stand in front of and face the audience, and view the MacBook display while the audience sees the same image through the projector.

You can activate video mirroring in a couple of ways:

- Open the Displays pane of the System Preferences application, click the Arrangement tab, and select the Mirror Displays check box.
- Open the Displays menu and select Turn On Mirroring (see figure 1.3).

When you turn video mirroring on, the projector takes on the same resolution as the MacBook's internal display.

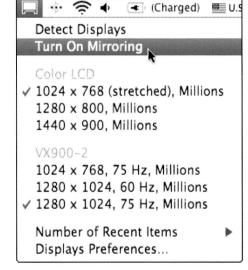

1.3 After you connect your MacBook to a projector, use the Turn On Mirroring command to have it display the same content that you see on the internal display.

Setting Desktop Preferences

You can configure your desktop so it appears the way you want it to. You can control some of the icons that appear on it by default, and you can configure the image that fills your desktop.

Setting Finder desktop icon preferences

By default, icons for your MacBook's hard drive, external hard drives, DVDs and CDs, and servers appear on the desktop. This is okay if that is your preference, but they take up space on the desktop that isn't necessary because you can get to these elements more easily by opening a Finder window and using the sidebar.

Genius It's easy to forget sometimes that the folders and files you see on the desktop are determined by the contents of the Desktop folder within your Home folder. If you want to keep a folder or file but don't want it to take up space on your desktop, simply move it into a different folder within your Home folder. In addition to having a neater appearance, this also helps you work more efficiently because you'll have an easier time finding folders and files than when they are scattered on your desktop.

To hide these icons, perform the following steps:

1. **Choose Finder ⇨ Preferences.** The Finder Preferences dialog box appears.

2. **Click the General tab if it isn't selected already.**

3. **Deselect the check boxes for the icons that you don't want to see on your desktop.** For example, to hide the icon for the MacBook's hard drive, deselect the Hard disks check box (see figure 1.4). As you deselect the check boxes, the related icons disappear from your desktop.

1.4 If you deselect the four check boxes in the Show these items on the Desktop section, your desktop immediately becomes less cluttered.

Configuring desktop pictures

I confess that this section has nothing to do with efficiency. However, there's more to life than being efficient. Because you stare at your desktop so much, you might as well have something interesting to look at, which is where desktop pictures come in.

You can set any image to be your desktop picture. The images you can use as your desktop include the default images that are included with Mac OS X, image files you create or download from the

Internet, and, best of all, photos from your iPhoto library. You can also configure your MacBook so that the desktop picture changes over time to keep it even more interesting.

To configure your desktop pictures, perform the following steps:

1. **Open the System Preferences application.**

2. **Click the Desktop & Screen Saver icon.** The Desktop & Screen Saver pane appears.

3. **Click the Desktop tab.** The Desktop picture tools appear. On the center-left side of the pane are the sources of images from which you can select pictures for your desktop. These are organized by source, including Apple (default images), iPhoto (images from your iPhoto library), and Folders (your Pictures folder plus any others you add).

Genius

When your MacBook is connected to an external display, the Secondary Desktop pane appears on that display. You can use that pane to set the desktop pictures on the external display as you can for the internal display. You can have the same desktop picture settings or completely different images and display options there.

4. **Expand the source of images you want to work with by clicking its Expansion triangle.** The contents of that source appear. For example, if you expand the Apple source, you see its folders. If you expand the iPhoto source, you see Events, Photos, photo albums, and so on.

5. **Select a source of images in the left pane of the window.** Thumbnails of the images in that source appear in the right pane of the window. For example, if you select the Nature folder under the Apple source, you see thumbnails of the nature images included by default.

6. **Click the image that you want to apply to the desktop.** The image fills the desktop and you see it in the image well at the top of the Desktop pane (see figure 1.5).

7. **If the image you selected isn't the same proportion as your current screen resolution, use the pop-up menu that appears just above the thumbnail pane to choose how you want the image to be scaled to the screen.** For example, choose Fit to Screen to have photos scaled so that they fit the screen, Fill Screen to have photos scaled to fill the screen, Tile to have images that are smaller than the desktop to fill the desktop space as tiles, and so on.

8. **If the image doesn't fill the screen, click the Color button that appears to the right of the menu when it can be used.** The Color Picker opens.

9. **Use the Color Picker to choose the background color that appears behind photos when they don't fill the desktop.**

1.5 I've selected the Aurora image as my desktop picture.

10. **To change the desktop picture automatically, select the Change picture check box.** This causes the images in the source selected on the Source list, such as Nature, to be applied to the desktop according to your settings.

Note

When you configure the picture to be changed automatically, the image in the image well is replaced by the recycle symbol.

11. **On the pop-up menu, choose how often you want the picture to change.** The options include at different time intervals or when different events occur.

12. **If you want images to be selected randomly instead of by the order in which they appear in the source, select the Random order check box.** A new image from the selected source is applied to the desktop according to the timing you selected.

13. **To have the menu bar be translucent so you can see the desktop picture behind it, select the Translucent menu bar check box.** When this option is not selected, the menu bar becomes a solid color.

14. **Quit the System Preferences application.** Enjoy your desktop!

Genius You can use any folder as a source of desktop pictures by clicking the Add (+) button located at the bottom of the source list. Use the resulting dialog box to move to and select the folder containing the images you want to use. After you click the Choose button, that folder appears as a source on the list and you can work with it just like the default sources.

Working with the Dock

The Dock is an important part of your desktop space. By default, it appears at the bottom of the desktop, but you can control many aspects of its appearance, where it is located, and, to a great degree, how it works. The Dock is organized into two general sections. The area to the left of the application/document separation line (the white, dashed line that looks like a highway dividing line that is a few icons to the left of the Trash icon) contains application icons. On the right side of this line, you see icons for documents, folders, minimized Finder or application windows, and the Trash/Eject icon.

When folders appear on the Dock, by default they become stacks. When you click a stack, it pops up into a fan or appears as a grid (depending on how many items are in the folder) so that you can work with items it contains (see figure 1.6). You can disable this feature for any folder so that it behaves more like a normal folder (more on that shortly).

The Dock performs the following functions:

1.6 Clicking a folder's (stack's) icon on the Dock causes it to fan out.

● **Shows running applications.** Whenever an application is running, you see its icon on the Dock. A small glowing light is located at the bottom of every running application's icon. Application icons also provide information about what is happening with those applications. For example, when you receive email, the Mail application's icon changes to indicate the number of messages you have received since you last read messages.

- **Enables you to open applications, folders, minimized windows, and documents quickly by clicking the related icon.**

- **Enables you to quickly switch among open applications and windows by clicking the icon for the item you want to bring to the front.**

- **Gets your attention.** When an application needs your attention, its icon bounces on the Dock until you move into that application and handle whatever the issue is.

- **Enables you to control an application and switch to any windows open in an application.** When you perform a secondary click (one way to do this is to Ctrl+click) on the icon of an application, a pop-up menu appears. When the application is running, this menu lists commands as well as all the open windows related to that application. When the application isn't running, you see a different set of commands, such as the Open command you can use to open the application.

- **Enables you to customize its appearance and function.** You can store the icon for any item (applications, folders, and documents) on the Dock. You can control how the Dock looks, including its size, whether it is always visible, where it is located, and which applications, folders, and documents appear on it.

Two icons on the Dock are unique and are always on the Dock: the Finder and the Trash. When you click the Finder icon (anchored on the left end of a horizontal Dock or at the top of a vertical one), a Finder window opens if none is currently open. If at least one Finder window is open, clicking the Finder icon brings the Finder window you used most recently to the front.

The Trash icon is where all folders and files go when their time is done. When the Trash contains files or folders, its icon includes crumpled paper so that you know the Trash is full. When you select an ejectable item, such as a DVD, the Trash icon changes to the Eject symbol. You can drag a disc or other ejectable item onto that icon to eject the disc, disk, or volume.

Unless an application is permanently installed on the Dock (in which case the icon remains in the same position), the icon for each application you open appears on the right (or bottom) edge of the application area of the Dock.

Unlike open applications, open documents don't automatically appear on the Dock. Document icons appear on the Dock only when you add them to the Dock manually or when you have minimized a document's window. Remember that when you open an application's menu in the Dock (secondary click), you see a list of all the windows open in that application.

When you minimize a window, by default, the window moves into the Dock using the Genie Effect, during which it is pulled down into the Dock. You can change this so that the Scale Effect is used instead. This looks like the window is being quickly scaled down while it is placed on the Dock. Minimized windows are marked with the related application's icon in the lower-right corner of the Dock icon so you can easily tell from which application the windows come.

Note

When you hide an application, its open windows do not appear on the Dock. The hidden application's icon continues to be marked so you know that the application is running. You can open a hidden application's Dock menu to jump into one of its open windows.

When you quit an open application, its icon disappears from the Dock (unless you have added that application to the Dock so that it always appears there). Minimized windows disappear from the Dock when you maximize them or when you close the application from which a document window comes.

Genius

To move between applications quickly, press ⌘+Tab or ⌘+Shift+Tab. The Application Switcher appears. Click an icon to move into the associated application, or keep pressing the keys to cycle through the list; when you release the keys, you move into the selected application.

Configuring and using Dock icons

The Dock gets even more useful when you organize it to suit your preferences. You can move icons around the Dock, add more applications to it, remove applications that are currently on it, and add your own folders and documents to it so that they are easily accessible.

To add an application's icon to the Dock, simply drag it from a Finder window and drop it onto the location on the Dock where you want it to be stored (see figure 1.7). (Application icons must be placed on the left side of the dividing line.) When you add an application icon to the Dock, an alias to the application is created; like the default application icons, you can click the icon to open the application and perform a secondary click on its icon to open its Dock menu.

1.7 Because I frequently use Firefox, I've added its icon to my Dock.

You can rearrange the application icons that are installed on the Dock by dragging them to the location where you want them to reside. Like installing a new icon, when you move an existing icon between two others, they separate so you can place the icon where you want it.

Note

The Dock has two icons that you can't move at all: Finder and Trash/Eject. Other than these two endpoints, you can change all the other icons on the Dock as much as you like. You can't change the location of the dividing line; it moves to the left or to the right, based on the number of icons on each side of it.

You can remove an application icon from the Dock by dragging it up onto the desktop and releasing the trackpad button. When you do this, the icon disappears in a puff of digital smoke and no longer appears on the Dock. Because the icons on the Dock are aliases, removing them doesn't affect the applications that those aliases represent.

When you place a folder's icon on the Dock, it becomes a stack. A stack has some special characteristics, which is why it isn't just called a folder (however, you can configure a stack to behave like a folder). Two stacks are installed on your Dock by default: the Downloads and Documents stacks. You can add any other folders to the Dock just as you add applications to the Dock; simply drag their icons onto the Dock and drop them where you want them to be placed (folders and documents have to be placed on the right side of the dividing line). You can also reorganize stack icons by dragging them around on the Dock. And, as you can probably guess, you can remove stacks from the Dock by dragging their icons up onto the desktop.

Stack icons sometimes take on the icon of the most recent file that has been placed into them. For example, if you last downloaded a disk image file, the Downloads stack icon is the icon for a disk image. When you place an image into your Pictures folder and have that folder installed on your Dock, its icon is a thumbnail of the last image you placed in it.

When you click a stack's icon, its contents fan onto the desktop if there are a few of them, or open into a grid if there are many. You can access an item on the fan or grid by clicking it. You can open the folder's contents in a Finder window by clicking Open in Finder.

As mentioned earlier, you can also configure how an individual stack's icon behaves by using its contextual menu. Perform a secondary click on the stack's icon and its menu appears (see figure 1.8).

The options you have include:

- **Sort by.** Choose the attribute by which you want the items in the stack to be sorted. For example, choose Date Added to have the most recently added content appear at the bottom of the fan (if the stack is set to fan, of course).

- **Display as.** Select Stack to have the icon look like a stack or Folder to replace the stack icon with the folder's icon. The only difference is that when you select Folder, you always see the folder's icon on the Dock, as opposed to the icon of the most recently added item, which is what you see when Stack is selected.

- **View content as.** Select Fan to see the default fan layout for the stack (until it contains too many items, at which point it uses the grid instead). Select Grid to have the folder's contents appear in a grid. Select List to display the contents in a list that looks similar to a mini-Finder window (see figure 1.9); this is very useful for folders that contain subfolders because you can select a folder to move into it on another hierarchical menu. Select Automatic to have the Mac OS select the view that is most appropriate, based on the folder's contents.

- **Options.** Choose Remove from Dock to remove the icon from the Dock. Choose Show in Finder to open a Finder window showing the folder's contents.

- **Open.** Choose this command to open the folder on the desktop.

1.8 Stacks have many configuration options.

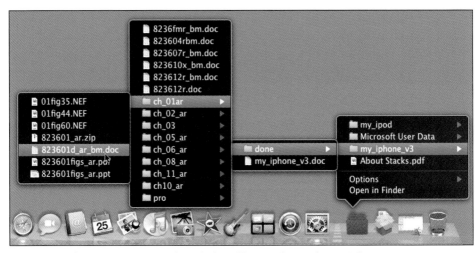

1.9 Viewing a folder icon as a List makes it behave like a Finder window in Columns view.

Note The third type of Dock icon is for windows you have minimized (by double-clicking a window's title bar for example). You can move a minimized window icon within the folder side of the Dock, but its location is only temporary (it remains there only until you maximize or close the window). If you drag a minimized window from the Dock, it snaps back to the Dock. You remove minimized windows from the Dock by maximizing or closing them.

Configuring appearance and behavior

The Dock offers several behaviors you can change to suit your preferences. You can also change various aspects of its appearance, as follows:

1. **Choose Apple menu ⇨ System Preferences.**

2. **Click the Dock icon.** The Dock pane appears.

Note All Dock settings are specific to each user account (see Chapter 2). One user's Dock settings do not affect any other user's Dock configuration.

3. **Drag the Size slider to the right to make the default Dock larger, or to the left to make it smaller.** This impacts only the size of the Dock when no applications that aren't installed on it are open and no windows are currently minimized. The Dock changes size automatically as you open applications and minimize windows, but this setting does change its starting size.

4. **Select the Magnification check box if you want to magnify an area of the Dock when you point to it.** This can make identifying items easier, especially when many items are on the Dock or when it is small.

5. **If you use magnification, drag the Magnification slider to the right to increase the level of magnification, or to the left to decrease it.**

6. **Select the position of the Dock on the desktop by clicking Left, Bottom (default), or Right.**

Note When your MacBook is connected to an external display, the Dock always appears on the primary display.

7. **On the Minimize using pop-up menu, select Genie Effect to have windows pulled down to the Dock when you minimize them, or Scale Effect to have them shrink down into the Dock.**

8. **By default, application icons bounce as the application opens; if you don't want this to happen, deselect the Animate opening applications check box.**

9. **If you want the Dock to be hidden automatically when you aren't pointing to it, select the Automatically hide and show the Dock check box.** If you set the Dock so that it is hidden except when you point to it, you can use more of your display. When this behavior is enabled and you point to the Dock's location, it pops onto the desktop and you can use it. When you move off the Dock, it is hidden again.

Genius

You can turn Hiding on or off by pressing Option+⌘+D.

Working with the Sidebar and Toolbar

Much of the time that you are working on your desktop will involve Finder windows. Two areas of Finder windows that you will use frequently are the sidebar and the toolbar. You can use these features as they are, but you can also customize them to make your desktop space more efficient.

Using and configuring the sidebar

The Finder's sidebar makes it easy to get to specific locations; in many ways, the sidebar is similar to the Dock. It comes with a number of default locations, but you can add items to or remove them from the sidebar so that it contains the items you use most frequently.

The sidebar is organized into sections (see figure 1.10). DEVICES includes disks and other devices (including iPods and your iDisk) that are mounted on your MacBook. SHARED items include those you are accessing on a network. PLACES contains folders and files. SEARCH FOR displays saved searches.

Using the items on the sidebar is simple (which is why the sidebar is so useful). Simply click the icon with which you want to work. What happens when you click depends on the kind of icon you clicked. The potential outcomes are:

- **Devices.** When you select a device, the contents of that device are displayed in the Finder window. For example, when you click a hard drive's icon, you see its contents.

- **Shared folder or drive.** When you select a shared network resource, you see the tools you can use to log in to that resource or you see the contents of the resource if your MacBook is configured to log in to it automatically.

- **Folder.** If the icon is a folder located in the PLACES section, you see the folder's contents in the Finder window.

- **Document.** If the icon is a document located in the PLACES section, the associated application launches and you see and work with the document's contents.

- **Application.** If the icon is an application located in the PLACES section, the application launches.

- **Search.** If you click an icon located in the SEARCH FOR section, the search runs and you see the results of the search in the Finder window.

1.10 Use the sidebar to quickly move to items that you want to view in a Finder window.

You can customize the sidebar so that it has the content you want. Here's how:

1. **Choose Finder ⇨ Preferences.** The Finder Preferences window appears.

2. **Click the Sidebar tab (see figure 1.11).**

3. **Select the check box for each item that you want to appear on the sidebar.**

4. **Deselect the check box for any items that you don't want to appear on the sidebar.**

5. **Close the Finder Preferences window.**

6. **Open a Finder window.**

7. **To remove an item from the sidebar, drag it from the sidebar and release the trackpad button when you've moved it off the sidebar.** It disappears in a puff of smoke. Like the Dock, when you remove something from the sidebar, it's not removed from the computer. The item remains in its current location on your MacBook, but it is no longer accessible from the sidebar.

8. **To add something to the sidebar, drag it from a Finder window or desktop onto the sidebar.** As you move the item onto the sidebar, a blue line appears on the sidebar at the location to which you've moved the item.

9. **When you're over the location in which you want to place the item, release the trackpad button.** The item's icon is added to the sidebar, and you can use it just like the default items.

10. **To change the order of items in the sidebar, drag them up or down the list.** As you move an item between others, they slide apart to show you where the item you are moving will be. (You can only move items around within their sections.)

1.11 You can determine the kinds of resources that are available on your sidebar by setting the appropriate preferences.

Using and configuring the toolbar

The toolbar appears at the top of the Finder window and contains buttons and pop-up menus that you can use to access commands quickly and easily. It includes a number of default buttons and pop-up menus, but you can configure the toolbar so that it contains the tools you use most frequently.

When you open a Finder window, the toolbar appears at the top of the window. The default tools on the toolbar (as grouped from left to right) are:

- **Back/Forward buttons.** These buttons move you along the hierarchy of Finder windows that you've moved through, just like Back and Forward buttons in a Web browser.

- **View buttons.** You can change the view of the current window by clicking one of the View buttons. For example, to see the window in List view, click the second button in the View group (its icon has horizontal lines).

- **Quick Look/Slideshow button.** When something in the window is selected and you click this button, you see a quick view of the item (such as a thumbnail of an image file) or a slide show if you have selected multiple items.

- **Action pop-up menu.** This menu contains a number of useful contextual commands (meaning the specific commands on the menu depend on the item or items you have selected). These commands are the same as those that appear when you perform a secondary click on an item.

- **Search bar.** You can search for items on the desktop by typing text or numbers into the Search bar. As you type, items that match your search term appear in the Finder window.

Genius

You can hide the sidebar and toolbar by clicking the Hide Toolbar/Sidebar button located in the upper-right corner of Finder windows. To restore these elements, click the button again. The Status bar at the bottom of the window is also controlled by this button; it appears or disappears when the toolbar and sidebar do.

You can place the tools you prefer on your toolbar by performing the following steps:

1. **Open a Finder window.**

2. **Choose View ⇨ Customize Toolbar.** The Toolbar Customization sheet appears (see figure 1.12).

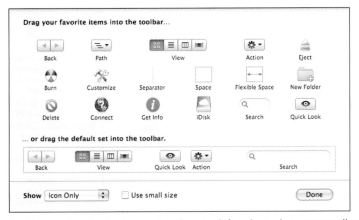

1.12 Use the Toolbar Customization sheet to define the tools on your toolbar and to organize them.

3. **To remove a button from the toolbar, drag its icon from the toolbar onto the desktop.** When you release the trackpad button, the selected button disappears in a puff of smoke. The button continues to be available on the sheet if you want to add it again later.

4. **To add a button to the toolbar, drag it from the sheet and drop it on the toolbar at the location in which you want to place it.** When you release the trackpad button, the selected button is added to the toolbar.

5. **When you finish customizing the toolbar, click Done.** The Toolbar Customization sheet closes and you see your customized toolbar.

Genius

To return the toolbar to its default state, open the Toolbar Customization sheet and drag the default set of buttons onto the toolbar.

Working with Exposé

As you work on documents, move to Web sites, check your email, choose tunes to listen to, and all the other things you do while using your MacBook, you can accumulate a lot of open windows on your desktop. This is a good thing because it makes it easy to multitask so that you don't have to stop one activity to start another. The downside is that it's easy to lose track of where a specific window you want is located, or you might have a hard time getting back to the desktop.

Exposé is the Mac OS X feature that helps you manage screen clutter from open windows. It has three modes:

- **Hide all open windows**
- **Reduce all open windows to thumbnails**
- **Reduce an application's windows to thumbnails**

Each of these options has specific uses, and you access them in slightly different ways.

Hiding all open windows

This mode is useful when your desktop is so cluttered that you are having a hard time finding anything. When you activate it, all the open windows are hidden so that you can work on the suddenly uncluttered desktop. To clear away all your windows in one sweep, press F3 or press the keyboard shortcut (in most cases, the default is Fn+F11; you learn how to set this later in this section). All the windows are moved off the screen, leaving an uncluttered desktop for you to work on. If you look carefully at the now shaded edges of the desktop in figure 1.13, you see the edges of the windows that have been moved off to the side.

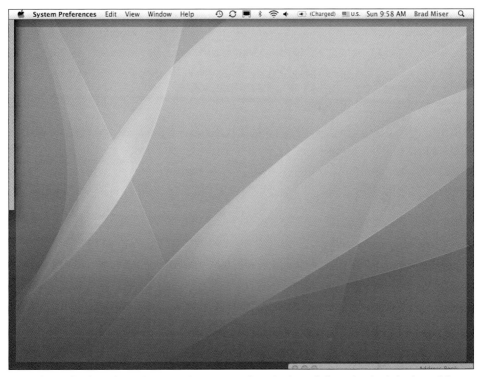

1.13 Where, oh where, have all my windows gone? (If you look carefully at the shaded edges of the screen, you'll see them.)

You can return your desktop to its cluttered condition by pressing the keyboard shortcut (Fn+F11 in most cases) or clicking anywhere in the shaded borders of the desktop. The windows slide back onto the visible part of the desktop where you can use them again.

Showing thumbnails of open windows

This technique is useful when you have a lot of open windows and you want to move into a specific one. You can reduce all your windows to thumbnails and then move into the window you want to use by clicking it. Press the keyboard shortcut (Fn+F9 by default) to shrink all open windows down so that they all fit on the desktop. Each thumbnail is labeled so you can more precisely tell what it is when several windows look the same (such as document windows).

When you point to a window, the window is highlighted in blue (see figure 1.14). To move into a window, click its thumbnail. The window becomes active and moves to the front so you can use it. The rest of the windows resume their former places and are moved into the background.

1.14 Reducing all open windows to thumbnails is a great way to find and jump into a specific window (here, I'm pointing to the Address Book window).

Genius

When you have windows showing with Exposé, press the Tab key to quickly move through sets of windows that are associated with each open application. Press ⌘+Tab to open the Application Switcher bar, showing all open applications. While holding the ⌘ key down, press Tab to move to the application you want to focus on; when you release the ⌘ key, the windows are shown for the application you selected.

Showing thumbnails of an application's open windows

This mode is similar to the previous one, except that instead of showing all open windows as thumbnails, it shows only the windows in the current application as thumbnails. Use this mode when you are working with multiple windows within the same application and want to jump to a specific one.

Press the keyboard shortcut (Fn+F10 by default) to shrink down all open windows for the current application so that they all fit on the desktop; each window is labeled with its title. When you point to a window, the window is highlighted in blue. To move into a window, click it. The window becomes active and moves to the front so that you can use it. The rest of the open application windows move into the background.

Note

When you activate Exposé for an application, its icon on the Dock is highlighted to help you know which application you are working with.

Configuring Exposé keyboard shortcuts

You can customize how you activate Exposé by performing the following steps:

1. **Open the System Preferences application.**

2. **Click the Exposé & Spaces icon.** The Exposé & Spaces pane appears.

3. **Click the Exposé tab.**

4. **To cause an Exposé action when you point to a corner of the desktop (to create a hot corner), use the pop-up menus located next to each corner of the desktop thumbnail at the top of the pane to select the action you want to happen when you point to that corner (see figure 1.15).**

5. **Use the All windows, Application windows, and Show Desktop pop-up menus to configure the keyboard shortcuts for those actions.**

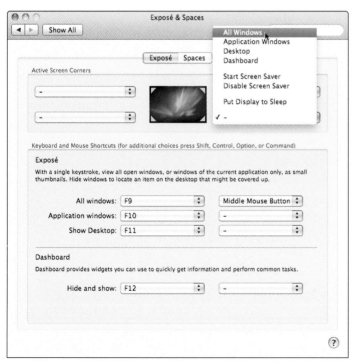

1.15 You can activate Exposé when you point to a corner of the screen by configuring the pop-up menus located on each corner of the display's thumbnail.

27

6. **Use the pop-up menu to the right of each of those menus to select if you want a secondary or middle mouse click (three- or more button mouse) to activate the related Exposé action.**

7. **Quit the System Preferences application.** The new keyboard shortcuts for Exposé take effect.

Genius

To add keyboard modifiers to the shortcut keys or hot corners, press a key, such as the ⌘ key, while you have a menu open. The symbols for the keys that you press are shown next to the function keys. If you select one of these combinations, you need to hold the same modifier keys down when you click the appropriate function key to activate the command.

Working with Spaces

As you use your MacBook, it's likely that you'll develop sets of tasks that you work on at the same time. For example, you might use Word to create text and a graphics application to write a book. These kinds of activities invariably involve a lot of windows. While you can use Exposé to manage these windows, it's not so efficient, because you can only focus on one window at a time and it can still take some work to get to the windows you want to use.

With Spaces, you can create collections of applications and their windows so that you can jump between sets easily and quickly. For example, if you have several Internet applications that you use, you can create an Internet space for those applications, such as an email application and Web browser. To use your Internet applications, just open that space and the windows are all in the positions you last left them. You might have another space that contains Address Book, iCal, and your email application. You can use these applications just by switching to their space. Spaces make moving to and using different sets of windows fast and easy, and improve the efficiency with which you work.

You can have as many spaces as you need, so there's really no limit to how you can configure your desktop.

Creating Spaces

To get started with Spaces, first create each space, using the following steps:

1. **Open the System Preferences application.**

2. **Click the Exposé & Spaces icon.** The Exposé & Spaces pane appears.

3. **Click the Spaces tab.** The Spaces pane appears.

4. **Select the Enable Spaces check box.** Spaces become active. At the top of the pane are thumbnails of the spaces you'll be configuring. By default, four spaces are available; you can add more if you need them. Each space is assigned a number that you use to identify that space.

5. **Select the Show Spaces in menu bar check box.** This puts the Spaces menu on the Finder menu bar, which makes it easier to work with your Spaces without going into the System Preferences application.

6. **Click the Add (+) button just above the pop-up menus at the bottom of the application list in the center pane of the window.** The Applications pop-up menu appears.

7. **Add the application you want to add to the space by doing one of the following:**

    - If the application you want to add appears on the menu, select it.

    - If an application you want to add doesn't appear on the menu, select Other. The Applications sheet appears. By default, the Applications folder, where most applications are stored, is shown. Move to and select the application you want to add to the space, and click Add.

Genius

You can select multiple applications at the same time by holding the ⌘ key down while you click on each application.

On the Spaces pane, you see the applications on the application list in the Application Assignments column. The space to which the applications are assigned is shown in the Space column. By default, all applications are assigned to Space 1.

8. **Open the Spaces menu for the first application on the list.**

9. **Choose the number of the space in which you want to include that application (see figure 1.16), or choose Every Space to include it in all spaces.** After you make a selection, the space number is shown on the menu for that application, and the selected space's icon at the top of the window is highlighted.

Genius

To sort the list of applications by space number, click the Space column heading. This is a more effective view because you see the applications organized by the spaces within which they are contained.

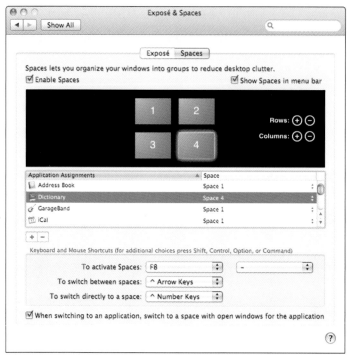

1.16 The space shown for each application is the one in which that application
will be included (here, I've added the Dictionary application to Space 4).

10. **To add two more spaces in a row, click the Add (+) button next to the word Rows in
the thumbnail section of the window; to add two more spaces in a column, click the
Add (+) button next to the word Columns in the thumbnail section of the window.**
Two new spaces appear in the thumbnail section, and the corresponding spaces are
available for application assignment. The numbers of the previous spaces are adjusted
according to whether you added new spaces in rows or in columns. Any space assignments are also adjusted so that the applications remain in their current spaces, even if
the space number changes.

Genius

I wouldn't go crazy with the number of spaces at first. Start with the default four and
work with them until you determine you need more spaces. If you create too many
spaces, you'll reduce the benefits you get because then you'll have to manage lots of
spaces, too.

11. **On the To activate Spaces menu, choose the keyboard shortcut you want to use to
activate Spaces; if you want to assign this command to a secondary or middle mouse-
click, use the pop-up menu near the right side of the pane.** The default keyboard

shortcut is F8, but you can choose any function key or function key and modifier key, such as ⌘ or Shift. (Because F8 is programmed to control iTunes, you need to hold the Fn key while you press F8.)

12. **On the To switch directly between spaces pop-up menu, choose the modifier keys with the arrow keys to move among your spaces.** The default is Ctrl+arrow.

13. **To set the modifier key that you use to jump directly to a space by its number, open the To switch directly to a space pop-up menu and choose the modifier key you want to use.** The default is Ctrl+number (of the space you want to jump to).

14. **If you don't want to move into a space with which an application is associated when you use that application, deselect the When switching to an application, switch to a space with open windows for the application check box.** When this is selected and you use an application, you automatically jump into a space that has open windows for that application. With the check box deselected, the space is ignored.

Genius

To delete spaces, click the Remove (–) button next to the Rows or Columns text. The spaces are removed and the applications that were assigned to them remain on the list, but they become assigned to the space adjacent to the ones you deleted.

Using Spaces

After you configure your spaces, you can start using them. If you expect that moving to a space causes all of the applications it contains to open, I hate to disappoint you, but spaces only impact running applications. However, this does make some sense because you'd use a lot of your MacBook's resources if all the applications in each space opened when you moved into that space. To use Spaces, do the following:

1. **Open the applications associated with your spaces.** As each application opens, the Spaces Manager briefly appears on the screen and the box associated with the space is highlighted in white.

2. **To move to a different space, press the Spaces activation key (the default is Fn+F8).** The desktop is hidden and the Spaces Manager appears (see figure 1.17). Here you see thumbnails of each of the spaces you have configured. Within each space, you see the windows that are open in that space.

3. **To move into a space, click it.** The open applications associated with that space appear, and you can work with them.

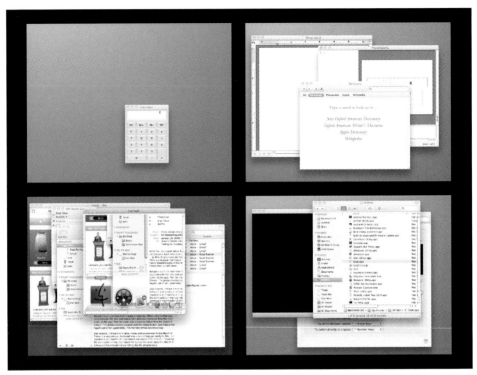

1.17 Here are the thumbnails for each of the four spaces I have configured.

4. **To jump directly to a space, press the keyboard shortcut for switching directly to a space, which by default is Ctrl+*number*, where *number* is the number of the space you want to move into.** The open applications associated with that space appear, and you can work with them.

5. **To move between spaces without using a space's number or clicking a space's thumbnail, press the keyboard shortcut for switching between spaces, which by default is Ctrl+*arrow*, where *arrow* is one of the arrow keys on the keyboard.** The Spaces Manager palette appears, and each box on the palette represents one of your spaces.

6. **While holding the Ctrl key down, press an arrow key to move to the space you want to enter.** As you press an arrow key, an arrow appears in the palette to show you in which direction you're moving.

7. **When the appropriate space is highlighted with the white box, release the trackpad button.** The open applications associated with that space appear.

Following are some other Spaces tips:

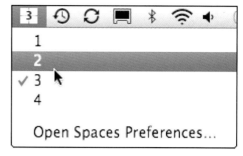

1.18 The Spaces menu enables you to jump into a space by selecting its number.

⊚ **You can use the Spaces menu on the Finder menu bar to manage your spaces (see figure 1.18).** At the top of the menu, you see the number of the space in which you are currently working. When you open the menu, you can select a space number to jump into it or select Open Spaces Preferences to move to the Spaces pane in the System Preferences application.

⊚ **You can't add the Finder to a space, but it is associated with the space under which a Finder window is currently open.** When you click the Finder's Dock icon, you jump into that space and can use that Finder window or open others as needed.

⊚ **Keep in mind that you can enable and disable Spaces whenever you want without impacting your Spaces configuration.** Sometimes, it's more efficient to disable it for a period of time, such as when you want to use a couple of applications that are in different spaces at the same time.

⊚ **When you open an application that is not included in a space, you remain in the current space.** Any applications not associated with a space can be used within any space, just like applications that are assigned to Every Space.

Working with the Dashboard

The Dashboard is actually an application that is a collection of mini-applications called widgets. By default, the Dashboard application is always running so that its widgets are always available to you. Unless you remove it from the Dock, the Dashboard's icon is located to the immediate right of the Finder icon on the Dock (or below the Finder icon if you use a vertical Dock).

By default, you can activate the Dashboard in the following ways:

⊚ Press F4 (default).

⊚ Click the Dashboard icon on the Dock.

⊚ Open the Dashboard Dock icon menu and choose Show Dashboard.

⊚ Double-click the Dashboard's icon in the Applications folder.

⊚ Double-click a widget's icon.

When you activate the Dashboard, the widgets that are configured to open when it is activated appear (see figure 1.19). You can then use those widgets or see their information.

When you finish using widgets, deactivate the Dashboard again by pressing F4 or by clicking on the desktop outside of any open widget. All the widgets disappear, the Dashboard closes, and you return to your desktop.

1.19 When you open the Dashboard, you get instant access to a set of widgets.

Setting the Dashboard keyboard shortcut and hot corner

Like Exposé, you can set the hot corners used to open or close the Dashboard by performing the following steps:

1. **Open the System Preferences application.**

2. **Click the Exposé & Spaces icon.** The Exposé & Spaces pane appears.

3. **Click the Exposé tab.**

4. **To open the Dashboard by pointing to a corner of the desktop (set a hot corner), use the pop-up menu located next to each corner of the desktop thumbnail at the top of the pane to select Dashboard for the corner you want to make the hot corner.**

5. **To change the Dashboard keyboard shortcut, open the Hide and show pop-up menu and choose the function or modifier keys you want to use; or use the menu to the right of that one to set the shortcut to be a secondary or middle mouse click.**

Configuring the Dashboard

One of the nice things about the Dashboard is that you can configure the exact set of widgets that you want to use and how those widgets appear on the screen. Here's how to customize your Dashboard:

1. **Press F4 to activate the Dashboard.** The widgets that are currently configured to open appear.

2. **Click the Add (+) button in the lower-left corner of the screen.** The widget bar opens and you see all of the widgets that are currently installed on your MacBook. At the bottom of each widget's icon on the widget bar you see the widget's name. Widgets are shown in alphabetical order from left to right; browse the widgets by clicking the left- or right-facing arrows at each end of the bar. Each widget open on the screen contains the Close (x) button that indicates you are in Dashboard management mode (see figure 1.20).

3. **To add a widget to your Dashboard, drag its icon from the widget bar onto the screen at the location where you want it to appear.** The widget appears on the screen with a cool rippling effect.

4. **Move the open widgets around the screen so they are in the position you want them to be when you activate the Dashboard.**

5. **Close any widgets that you don't want to open when you activate the Dashboard by clicking their Close button (the "x" located in the upper-left corner of each widget's window).** The widget disappears from the Dashboard but remains on the widget bar.

Genius

You can add multiple instances of the same widget to the Dashboard. Each time you add a widget, a new version of that widget is added to the Dashboard. This is useful for widgets that you configure with specific information, such as a location (the Weather widget is a good example).

1.20 The widget bar at the bottom of the Dashboard shows all the widgets that are installed on your MacBook.

You can use the Widgets Manager to configure your widgets. It is not shown by default, but you can open it using the following steps:

1. **Open the Dashboard if it isn't open already.**

2. **Click the Add (+) button located in the lower-left corner of the window.** The widget bar appears.

3. **Click the Manage Widgets button.** The Widgets Manager, which is actually a widget in itself, appears (see figure 1.21).

Following are some ways you can use the Widgets Manager:

1.21 Use the Widgets Manager to work with your widgets.

- **The list shows all of the widgets that are installed under the current user account.**

- **You can disable a widget by deselecting its check box.** This causes the widget to be removed from the Dashboard (if it's been added there) and to be removed from the widget bar. This doesn't actually remove the widget from your computer, however. You can restore a widget by selecting its check box again.

- **Widgets marked with a red circle with a hyphen in its center are available only under the current user account.**

Note Many widgets, such as the Weather and World Clock widgets, require an Internet connection to work. Others, such as the Calculator, don't.

Configuring widgets

To see if a widget has configuration options, move the pointer over the widget in which you are interested. If it has options, the Info button appears; this button is usually a lowercase "i", sometimes inside a circle, sometimes not. The location of the button varies, and sometimes it is hard to see, so just watch closely when you hover over a widget.

When you click the Info button, the widget's configuration tools appear (see figure 1.22). You can use those tools to make the widget work or look the way you want it to. When you finish, click Done and the widget is updated accordingly.

You should always check out the Info options for any widgets that you use because they will probably make those widgets even more useful to you.

Installing more widgets

The Dashboard includes quite a few widgets, but there are thousands of widgets available on the Apple widget Web site that you can download and install. Here's how to do it:

1. **Open the Dashboard.**

2. **Open the widget bar.**

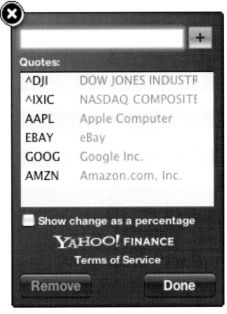

1.22 You can configure the stocks that the Stocks widget tracks for you.

37

3. **If the Widgets Manager isn't installed on your Dashboard, click the Manage Widgets button.** The Widgets Manager appears.

4. **In the Widgets Manager, click More Widgets.** Your default Web browser opens and takes you to the Apple widgets Web page (see figure 1.23).

5. **Browse or search until you find a widget you want to try.**

6. **Download the widget.** In most cases, the widget is downloaded directly and you're prompted to install the widget after it's been downloaded. If this is the case for a widget you download, skip to Step 8.

1.23 Got widgets?

7. **If the file is downloaded to your Downloads folder, move to and open it.** Widget files have the file extension .wdgt. If you don't see this extension, you might have to double-click the file you downloaded to expand it.

8. **Click Install at the prompt.** You move to the Dashboard and see the new widget that you installed.

9. **Click Keep to keep the widget or Delete to get rid of it.** If you click Keep, it is installed on your Dashboard. If you click Delete, it is not installed on your Dashboard.

10. **Configure and use the new widget.**

Creating your own Web widgets

While you have to do some basic programming to create a widget like those you see on the Apple widget Web site, you can create your own widgets by capturing parts of Web sites that then appear as widgets on your Dashboard. Follow these steps:

Note

You have to use Safari to create Web widgets.

1. **Open Safari.**

2. **Move to a Web page containing information or tools that you want to capture in a widget.**

3. **Do one of the following:**

   - Click the Add this page to the Dashboard button on the Safari toolbar (it looks like a pair of scissors cutting paper).

   - Choose File ➪ Open in Dashboard.

   A selection box and capture toolbar appear (see figure 1.24).

4. **Make the selection box enclose the part of the page that you want to be a widget by dragging the box to the general area you want to capture, clicking the trackpad button to lock the selection box, and then dragging its resize handles to enclose the part of the page you want as a widget.**

Genius

Depending on how the Web page is constructed, you may see certain parts of the page selected as you move over them. If they are the widget you want to create, it's a good idea to allow this automatic selection to achieve the best results.

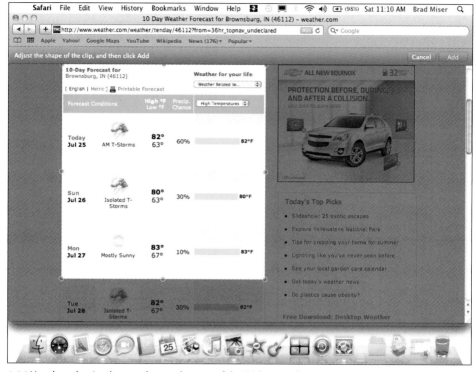

1.24 Use the selection box to choose the part of the Web page that you want to capture in a widget.

5. **Click the Add (+) button on the tool-bar.** The Dashboard opens and the part of the page you selected becomes a widget (see figure 1.25).

6. **Click the new widget's Info button.**

7. **Use the resulting tools to select a theme.** The theme determines the border of the widget.

8. **If the clip has audio and you want it to play only while the Dashboard is open, select the Only play audio in Dashboard check box.**

9. **Click Done.**

10. **Place the widget on your Dashboard.**

1.25 I captured a forecast from Weather.com as a widget.

The Web capture selection tool captures a static portion of the Web page, based on what you select. If the information changes on the source Web page, it might shift what's shown in the widget you create. You'll need to re-create the widget to fix any problems that result.

To get rid of a Web capture widget, open the Dashboard and then open the widget bar. Then click the Close button for the widget. Unlike other widgets, when you close a widget you've captured, it's gone forever.

Note If the widget isn't exactly what you want it to be, you need to recapture it. You can't edit the widget on the Dashboard.

How Do I Manage User Accounts?

Mac OS X is a multiuser operating system, meaning that your MacBook is designed to be used by multiple people. Each person has his own user account that includes a Home folder for storing files; system preferences for things like Dock configuration, the desktop picture, and screen resolution; application preferences; and security settings. When a user logs in, Mac OS X configures itself based on that user's specific preferences and, in effect, becomes personalized. Understanding how to create and manage user accounts is an important part of getting the most out of your MacBook.

Working with User Accounts

You use the System Preferences application to create and manage most of the user accounts on your MacBook. Before jumping in there, understand that there are a number of different types of user accounts:

- **Administrator.** Administrator accounts are the second-most powerful type of user account; when logged in under an Administrator account, you have complete access to the System Preferences application to make changes to the operating system, such as to create and manage user accounts and change network settings. Administrators can also install software at the system level, where it can be accessed by other users. The user account that you create the first time you started your MacBook is an Administrator account.

   Standard. Someone logged in under a Standard user account can only make changes related to that specific account. For example, someone using a Standard user account can change her desktop picture and application preferences, but can't install applications or create other user accounts.

Note

By default, your MacBook uses the Automatic Login feature; this logs in the default user account (the one you created when you first started your MacBook unless you've changed it) automatically as soon as you start up your computer, which can disguise the fact that you are accessing a user account.

- **Managed with Parental Controls.** The Mac OS X Parental Controls feature enables you to limit the access that a user has to various kinds of content, such as email and Web sites. When you manage this kind of account, you determine specific types of content, applications, and other areas that the user can access. People using this type of account are prevented from doing all actions not specifically allowed by their Parental Control settings.

- **Sharing Only.** This type of account can only access your MacBook to share files across a network and has no access to the operating system or other files that aren't being shared.

- **Group.** Access to folders and files on your MacBook is determined by each item's Sharing and Permissions settings. One of the ways you can assign privileges to an item is by configuring a group's access to it; a group user account is a collection of user accounts and is used only to set access privileges. You create a group, assign people to it, and then use the group to set access permissions for files and folders.

Authentication

Some tasks, such as creating or changing user accounts, require that you confirm that you have access to an Administrator user account. This is called authentication. When you work with an area of the System Preferences application that requires this, the Authentication status Lock icon is visible in the lower-left corner of the window. If the Lock is closed (the text next to it says "Click the lock to make changes.") and some buttons or commands are grayed out/inactive, you need to authenticate before you can perform an administrator action. If the Lock is open (the text next to it says "Click the lock to prevent further changes."), you are authenticated and can proceed with the action you want to perform.

1. **To authenticate, click the Lock icon.** The Authentication dialog box appears and the full name associated with the current account is entered in the Name field. If the full name isn't for an Administrator account, change it to be an Administrator account's full name (for example, Brad Miser) or the account name for an Administrator account (such as bradm).

2. **Type the account's password, and click OK.** You are authenticated as an Administrator and can return to the pane of the System Preferences application you were working with; the Lock icon is now open and you can perform administrative actions.

Root. Mac OS X is built on the UNIX operating system and so has an extensive security architecture that specifically controls what each user account can do and the resources that user can access. The Root user account is a unique user account that bypasses all the limitations that are inherent to the other types of user accounts (even Administrator user accounts). When you log in under the Root user account, the system doesn't limit anything you try to do. Because of this, the Root user account is the most powerful kind of user account and is also the most dangerous because you can do things that might damage the system or files that it contains. You typically only use the Root user account during troubleshooting tasks. Unlike the other user accounts, you don't administer the Root user account using the System Preferences application. You learn how to use the Root user account at the end of this chapter.

Creating Administrator or Standard user accounts

The following steps show you how to create a new Administrator or Standard user account:

1. **Choose Apple menu ⇨ System Preferences**.

2. **Click the Accounts icon.** The Accounts pane opens (see figure 2.1). In the list on the left side of the window, you see the current user accounts. The user account under which

45

you are logged in appears at the top of the list, and its details appear in the right pane of the window along with the tools you use to configure that account. At the bottom of the user list are the Login Options button and the Add (+) and Remove (–) buttons.

2.1 Use the Accounts tool in the System Preferences application to create and manage user accounts on your MacBook.

3. **Authenticate yourself if needed.**

4. **Click the Add (+) button.** The New Account sheet appears.

5. **On the New Account pop-up menu, choose Standard to create a Standard user account or Administrator to create an Administrator account.** After it is created, you can change a Standard user account into an Administrator account or vice versa.

6. **Type a name for the account in the Full Name field.** This can be just about anything you want, but usually a person's actual name works best. The Full Name is one of the names that a user types to log in or authenticate the account (if it is an Administrator account). Mac OS X creates an account name, based on the full name you type.

7. **Edit the account name if you want to change it.** This name appears in a number of places, such as in the path to the user's Home folder and in the URL to that user's Web site on the MacBook. It's a good idea to keep the account name short, and you can't include any spaces or special characters in it.

8. **If you want to create a password yourself, type it in the Password box and skip to Step 12; if you want to use the Password Assistant to help you create a password, click the Key icon.** The Password Assistant appears (see figure 2.2).

Genius

9. **Choose the password's type from the Type pop-up menu.** There are a number of options, such as Memorable and Letters & Numbers. After you choose a type, the Assistant automatically generates a password for you and enters it in the Password field on the New Account sheet.

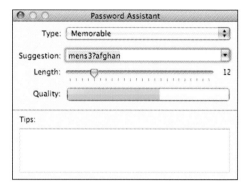

10. **Drag the slider to the right to increase the length of the password, or to the left to decrease its length.** The longer a password is, the more secure it becomes. A good password should include numbers or special characters to make it harder to crack. As you make changes to a password, the Quality gauge shows you how secure the password is.

2.2 The Password Assistant helps you create secure passwords.

11. **When the password shown on the Password Assistant is what you want to use, leave the Password Assistant open and click back in the New Account sheet.**

12. **Retype the password in the Verify field and type a hint about the password in the Password hint box.** This hint helps a user log in to his account when he can't remember the correct password.

13. **Click Create Account.** The user account is created and appears on the list of accounts. You are ready to customize it by adding an image and configuring other elements.

Note

An image, such as a photo or other graphic, can be associated with user accounts; these user account images appear in various locations, such as the Login window. Mac OS X automatically chooses an image for each user account from the default images it has. You can leave this image as is, or you can use the following steps to customize the user account with an image of your choice:

1. **Move to the Accounts pane of the System Preferences application and authenticate yourself (if needed).**

2. **In the Accounts list, select the user account with which you want to associate an image.**

3. **Click the image well, which is the box located to the left of the Change or Reset Password button.** (When you select the account currently logged in, the button is Change Password; when you select a different account, the button is Reset Password.)

4. **To choose one of Mac OS X's default images, select an icon from the pop-up menu; to create your own image, click Edit Picture.** If you select an icon, the menu closes, the image is associated with the user account, and you can skip the rest of these steps. If you click Edit Picture, the Edit Picture sheet appears (see figure 2.3).

5. **Choose the user's image by doing any of the following:**

   ◦ Drag a file containing the image you want to use from the desktop onto the image on the sheet. The file's image replaces the image currently shown there.

   ◦ Click Choose, select a file containing the image you want to use, and click Open. The image you select replaces the current image.

   ◦ Click the Camera icon to take a photo for the image with the MacBook's iSight camera. The photo you take replaces the current image.

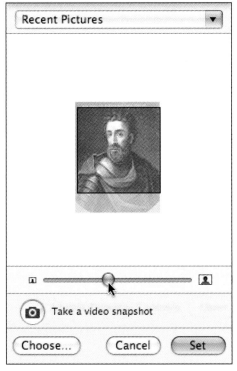

2.3 An image you associate with the user account appears in several locations, such as the Mac OS X Login window.

6. **Set the portion of the image that is displayed by dragging the slider to the right to include less of the image or to the left to include more of it.** The portion of the image

that will be displayed is shown within the selection box; the part of the image outside of the box and grayed out will not appear.

7. **Drag the image inside the box until the part you want to be displayed is contained within the box.** You may need to use the slider in conjunction with this step to get the image "just right."

8. **Click Set.** The Edit Picture sheet closes and you see the image you configured in the image well on the Accounts pane.

If the user has a MobileMe account, type her MobileMe username in the MobileMe username box. This associates the MobileMe account with the Mac OS X user account. This is optional, and the user can log in to her MobileMe account after she logs into her Mac OS X user account. (To learn more about MobileMe, see Chapter 5.)

Lastly, if you selected the Standard account type but change your mind, select the Allow user to administer this computer check box. This changes the account's type to Administrator.

The user account you created appears on the list of accounts and is ready to use (see figure 2.4).

2.4 Following good practice, I've created a troubleshooting account on my MacBook.

Limiting access with Parental Controls

The Mac OS X Parental Controls feature enables you to limit the access a user has to functionality and content, including the following:

- **Simple Finder.** When you limit users to the Simple Finder, they can only access their own documents and specific applications that you choose.

- **Selected applications.** You can use Parental Controls to create a list of applications to which the user has access.

- **System functions.** You can prevent users from administering printers, burning CDs or DVDs, changing their passwords, or changing the Dock.

- **Dictionary.** You can hide profanity in the Mac OS X Dictionary application.

- **Web sites.** You can prevent users from visiting specific Web sites.

- **Email and iChats.** You can specify the people with whom the user can email or chat.

- **Time Limits.** You can determine when the user is able to access her user account.

Using Parental Controls is a two-step process. First, create the user account that you want to limit; you can use Parental Controls with accounts of the Standard or Managed with Parental Controls types. (The only difference between these two types is that a Manage with Parental Controls type is set for restrictions from the start while you have to select an additional check box for a Standard account.) Second, configure the controls you want to use with the account; each of these controls is covered in its own section.

Creating Managed User Accounts is similar to creating Standard or Administrator user accounts. Just choose Managed with Parental Controls from the New Account pop-up menu. When you are done with the creation process, you see that the Enable Parental Controls check box is selected. To set limits on a Standard user account, select the account and select this check box (when you do so, the account's type becomes Managed instead of Standard).

You are now ready to use the Parental Controls pane to configure the restrictions the user account has. There are two ways to start this process:

- **Open the System Preferences application and click the Parental Controls icon.** Select the user account that you want to limit (only accounts of the Managed type are shown) on the list of accounts in the left part of the window.

- **Open the System Preferences application and click the Accounts icon.** On the Accounts pane, select the user account you want to manage and click the Open Parental Controls button.

After you open the Parental Controls pane with the appropriate user selected, you can configure that user's limitations by using the tabs at the top of the pane.

Restricting system resources

You can determine the Finder's behavior, the applications a Managed user can use, and access to certain system functions by clicking the System tab.

1. **Click the System tab.** The System controls appear (see figure 2.5).

2. **To enable the Simple Finder for the user, select the Use Simple Finder check box.** When the user logs in, he sees a very simple desktop. The Dock contains only three folders; when the user clicks a folder, it opens on the desktop and the user has access to the applications that you enable and to documents that he creates. Within Finder windows, everything opens with a single click.

3. **To limit the access of the user to specific applications, select the Only allow selected applications check box.**

4. **Deselect the check boxes for the categories or individual applications that you don't want the user to be able to use, and select the check boxes for the categories or individual applications that you do want the user to be able to use.**

5. **Select the check boxes at the bottom of the pane to allow (or deselect them to prevent) access to selected system actions, such as administering printers or burning CDs or DVDs. If you selected the Simple Finder option in Step 1, the Can modify the Dock option is disabled.**

2.5 Use the System tab to configure a user's access to various system resources, such as applications.

Restricting content

You can limit the user's access to various kinds of content by performing the following steps:

1. **Click the Content tab.** You see the Content controls in the pane (see figure 2.6).

2.6 If you don't want the user to access profanity in the Dictionary or selected Web sites, use the Content controls.

2. **To prevent profanity from appearing in the Mac OS X Dictionary, select the Hide profanity in Dictionary check box.**

3. **Limit the user's access to Web sites by doing one of the following:**

   - **Select the Try to limit access to adult websites automatically option, then click Customize.** On the resulting sheet, add the URLs you want the user to be able to visit to the top pane by clicking the upper Add (+) button and typing the URL, or block access to specific sites by clicking the lower Add (+) button and typing the URLs you want to block. Then click OK. The user can visit the sites you added to the allow list and can't visit sites you enter on the prevent list. Access to other sites (such as "adult" Web sites) may be blocked, too.

- **Select the Allow access to only these websites option.** When you choose the second option, the list of allowed Web sites (bookmarks) appears at the bottom of the pane. To add a site to the list (so the user is able to visit it), click the Add (+) button at the bottom of the list, choose Add bookmark, create a bookmark you want to add to the list, and click OK. To organize the bookmarks on the list, click the Add (+) button at the bottom of the list and choose Add Folder; name the folder and then add bookmarks to it. To remove a bookmark from the list so that a user can't access the related Web site, select the bookmark and click the Remove (–) button.

Limiting email and chats

Another area of activity that you can limit for a Managed user account is email and chatting. You can define specific email addresses and chat accounts with which the user can communicate. To provide more flexibility, you can set up a notification that you receive when someone not on the approved list attempts to communicate with the user; on the notification, you can choose to allow the contact, in which case the person is added to the approved list, or you can choose to reject it, in which case the communication is blocked.

In the Mail & iChat tab (see figure 2.7), you can limit email and chats by selecting the Limit Mail or Limit iChat check boxes.

2.7 Use the Mail & iChat tab to control the people with whom a user can email or chat.

To define the people with whom the user can email or chat, click the Add (+) button. The Contact sheet appears, as shown in figure 2.8.

Enter contact information on the sheet manually by typing first name, last name, and email or chat address; then choose Email, AIM, or Jabber from the pop-up menu to identify the type of address you entered and click Add. You add a contact from your Address Book by clicking the downward-facing triangle next to the Last Name box, selecting the contact you want to add to the list, and clicking Add; all the addresses for the contact you select are added to the allowed list.

If you want to receive a permission email when someone not on the list is involved in an email exchange, select the Send permission requests to check box and type your email address.

2.8 Configure the Contact sheet to allow the user to communicate with someone via email or chat.

Caution

Setting time limits

You can use the Time Limits tab to limit the amount of time for which the user can use the MacBook. When a time limit is reached or when the time is outside of an allowed window, the user can't log into his user account, or if he is currently logged in, he is logged out after a brief warning that allows him time to save open documents. Here's how to set time limits:

1. **Click the Time Limits tab (see figure 2.9).**

Note

When a user has been logged out because of time limits, a red circle with a hyphen in it appears next to the user's name in the Login window. The time at which the user can log in again is also shown.

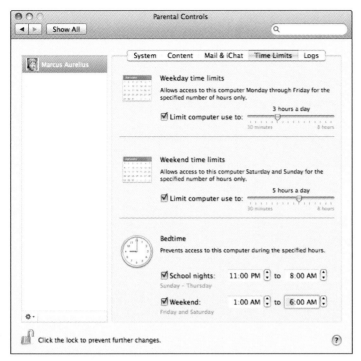

2.9 Using a MacBook can be a lot of fun; use the Time Limits to make sure it doesn't replace other important activities.

2. **To set the amount of time for which the user can be logged in on weekdays and/or weekends, select the Weekday time limits or Weekend time limits check box and set the time limit using the related slider.**

3. **To prevent the user from being logged in to the user account for specific periods of time Sunday to Thursday, select the School nights check box and enter the time period during which user activity should be prevented using the two time boxes.**

4. **To prevent the user from being logged in to the user account for specific periods of time on Friday and Saturday, select the Weekend check box and enter the time period during which user activity should be prevented using the two time boxes.**

Note
Time limits apply only to the managed user account. If the user can log in under another user account, he'll be able to continue to use the MacBook regardless of the limits set on his own account.

Checking Up on Managed Users

On the Logs tab, you can view a managed user's activities, such as Web sites visited, Web sites blocked, and applications used. To see user activity, click the Logs tab. In the Log Collections list, select the kind of activity you want to see, such as Applications. In the right area of the pane, you see the activity related to that category. For example, when you choose Applications, you see a list of all the applications the user has accessed. To see each instance of application used, click the expansion triangle next to the application's name. Under its icon, you see each date and time that the application was used, and the amount of time it was used. You can use the pop-up menus at the top of the pane to configure the information shown as when you choose One week on the Show activity for pop-up menu to see the activity under the user account over the past week. When you select an application or activity, click the Allow or Restrict buttons to change the permissions for that application or activity, or click the Open button to open the application or Web site.

Setting Login Items for a user account

Any application added to the Login Items list for a user is automatically opened when a user logs in to her account. For example, if a user opens Safari and Mail every time she uses the MacBook, you can add these applications to the user's Login Items so that they open when the user logs in to her account. Here's how you can make life easier for users (including yourself):

1. **Log in under the user's account (you can set Login Items for your own account by logging into your account).**

2. **Open the System Preferences application and click the Accounts icon to open the Accounts pane.**

3. **Click the Login Items tab, as shown in figure 2.10.**

4. **Add items to the list by clicking the Add (+) button at the bottom of the pane.**

5. **Use the resulting dialog box to move to and select the files you want to add to the list.** Hold the ⌘ key down to select multiple files at the same time.

6. **Click Add.**

7. **Select check boxes for any items on the list that you want to be hidden by default.** For example, if you want Mail to open but be hidden, select its check box. The next time the user logs in, the files you selected open and those whose check boxes are checked are hidden.

2.10 Any file you add to the Login Items tab opens automatically when a user logs in.

Creating Sharing Only user accounts

Typically, you create Sharing Only user accounts for groups of people who need to get to files on your MacBook. Creating a Sharing Only user account is similar to creating other types of accounts; create a new account, choose Sharing Only on the New Account pop-up menu, and complete the New Account sheet. When you are done with the creation process, you see that the only tools for the Sharing Only account are for the username, image, password reset, and MobileMe username.

You don't use a Sharing Only user account from your MacBook; its purpose is to enable people to log in to your MacBook from other computers. Provide the username and password to each person whom you want to allow access to your MacBook, and those users can log in to access files that you share.

Creating Group user accounts

Creating a Group user account is much simpler than the other types. Here's how:

1. **Open the System Preferences application.**

2. **Click the Accounts icon.**

3. **Click the Add (+) button.**

4. **On the New Account pop-up menu, choose Group.**

5. **Type the group's name in the Name field.**

6. **Click Create Group.** You move to the group's screen, on which you see all the user accounts on your MacBook (see figure 2.11).

7. **Select the check box for each user whom you want to be a member of the group.** The group is ready to be used to assign access permissions.

2.11 Select a user's check box to add him to the group.

Changing accounts

You change existing user accounts using the same set of tools that you use to create accounts. To make changes, follow these steps:

1. **Open the System Preferences application.**

2. **Click the Accounts icon.**

3. **Select the user whose account you want to change.**

4. **Use the tools in the right part of the pane to make changes to the user account, such as resetting a user's password or changing his MobileMe username.**

Note

The safest way to change an account's username is to delete the account and re-create it with a different username. However, when you delete a user account, you might delete all of its files so be careful before doing this.

Deleting accounts

If you no longer need a user account, you can delete it.

1. **Open the System Preferences application and click the Accounts icon.**

2. **Select the account that you want to delete.**

3. **Click the Remove (–) button at the bottom of the user list.** A sheet appears with three options for handling the user's Home folder:

   - **Save the Home folder in a disk image.** All the files in the user's Home folder are saved into a disk image located in the Deleted Users folder under the Users folder. You can access the files in the disk image by opening it.

   - **Don't change the Home folder.** If you choose this option, the user's Home folder remains in its current location under the user's folder in the Users folder, but its permissions are changed so that you can access it from an Administrator user account.

   - **Delete the Home folder.** If you choose this option, all traces of the user are removed from your MacBook.

4. **Click OK.** The user account is deleted and the user's Home folder is handled according to the option you selected.

Using Automatic Login

The Mac OS X Automatic Login feature does just what it says. You can choose to log in to a specific user account each time your MacBook restarts. Enable Automatic Login by following these steps:

1. **Open the System Preferences application and click the Accounts icon.**

2. **Click Login Options.** The Login Options pane appears, as shown in figure 2.12.

3. **From the Automatic Login pop-up menu, choose the name of the user that you want to be automatically logged in.**

4. **Type the user's password and click OK.** Each time your MacBook starts or restarts, the user you selected is logged in automatically.

Caution   Enabling Automatic Login makes your MacBook less secure because anyone who has access to it can use it because no additional information is needed to log in. While this feature is convenient, you should only enable Automatic Login if your MacBook is in an area that you can control and you're sure other people won't be able to use it without your knowledge.

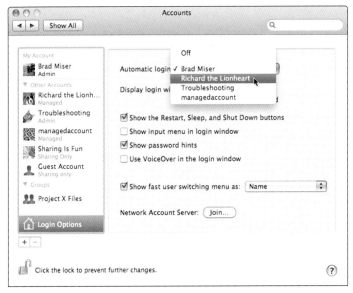

2.12 Use the Automatic Login pop-up menu to select a user account to automatically log in to your MacBook.

Configuring the Login Window

The Login window appears to prompt a user to log in. If Automatic Login is disabled, it appears when your MacBook starts up. If a user logs out of her user account, the Login window also appears. You can also make it appear by choosing Login Window in the Fast User Switching menu (this is covered in the next section). There are a number of options you can configure for the Login window. Follow these steps:

1. **Open the System Preferences application and click the Accounts icon.**

2. **Click Login Options.** The Login Options pane appears.

3. **Select a Login window option by clicking one of the following two radio buttons:**

   * **List of users.** When this option is selected, each user account's name and picture is shown in the Login window. The person logging in can click the appropriate user account to be prompted to type the password for that account. This option is more convenient because the user only has to recognize her user account and remember her password to be able to log in.

   * **Name and password.** When this option is selected, the Login window contains empty Name and Password fields. The user must type the account's name (full name or account name) and password to be able to log in.

4. **If you want to be able to restart your MacBook, put it to sleep, or shut it down from the Login window, select the Show the Restart, Sleep, and Shut Down buttons check box.**

Caution If you've enabled Automatic Login, don't select the Show the Restart, Sleep, and Shut Down buttons check box. If you do, someone can gain access to your MacBook when the Login window is displayed without having a user account by clicking the Shut Down button and then restarting the MacBook.

5. **If you want to be able to choose the language layout from the Login window, select the Show input menu in login window check box.** This is useful if people who use different languages share your MacBook.

6. **To show a hint when a user forgets his password, select the Show password hints check box.** The user can click the Forgot Password button to see the hint for his account.

7. **To have your MacBook read the text in the Login window, select the Use VoiceOver in the login window check box.**

Working with Fast User Switching

The Fast User Switching feature is great because it allows multiple users to be logged in at the same time. Instead of having to log out of your account for someone else to log in, the other user can log in by using the commands on the Fast User Switching menu. This is good because when you log out of an account, all processes are shut down, meaning that all open documents and applications are closed. If you have a lot of work ongoing, this can be a nuisance. With Fast User Switching, other users can log in while your account remains active in the background. When you log back in to your account, it is in the same state as when the other user logged in, and you can get back to what you were doing immediately.

Fast User Switching is disabled by default; to enable it, do the following:

1. **Open the System Preferences application and click the Accounts icon.**

2. **Click Login Options.**

3. **Select the Show fast user switching menu as check box.**

4. **Choose one of the following options on the pop-up menu:**

    *   **Name.** The Fast User Switching menu is indicated by the user account's full name.

    *   **Short name.** The Fast User Switching menu is indicated by the user account's user-name (short name).

    *   **Icon.** The Fast User Switching menu is indicated by a silhouette.

To use Fast User Switching, open the Fast User Switching menu on the menu bar by clicking the current user's full name, the short name, or the silhouette. The Fast User Switching menu appears (see figure 2.13).

On this menu, you see the following:

- **List of user accounts.** Each user account configured on your MacBook appears in the list.
- **Login Window.** Choose this command to cause the Login window to appear.
- **Account Preferences.** Choose this command to move to the Accounts pane of the System Preferences application.

◀   ▣▸   Fri 8:09 AM   **Brad Miser**
✓   Brad Miser
✓   Emily Miser
Marcus Aurelius   ▸
Troubleshooting Account
Login Window...
Account Preferences...

2.13 The Fast User Switching menu makes it easier to share your MacBook with others.

To switch to a different user account, select it on the menu. The password prompt appears. If the password is typed correctly, that user account becomes active. The current account remains logged in but is moved into the background.

You can have as many user accounts logged in simultaneously as you want. However, remember that each account that is logged in can have active processes, all of which use your MacBook's resources. So, you don't want to get carried away with this idea.

Genius

To quickly secure your MacBook without logging out, choose Login Window from the Fast User Switching menu. The Login window appears, but you remain logged in (you see a check mark next to your username). In order for someone to use your MacBook, he must know a valid password to be able to log in (unless you've configured a user account to not require a password).

Working with the Root User Account

Because Mac OS X is based on UNIX, it includes the Root user account. In a nutshell, the Root user account is not limited by any security permissions. If something is possible, the Root user account can do it. This is both good and bad. It's good because you can often solve problems using the Root user account that you can't solve any other way. It's bad because you can also cause problems from which it can be difficult, if not impossible, to recover. By contrast, when you use an Administrator account, you have limited access to certain system files, and so there is no way you can delete them; however, under the Root user account, anything goes, and it's possible for you to do things that cause your MacBook to be unusable.

You should only use the Root user account for troubleshooting. While you shouldn't use the Root user account often, when you need to use the Root user account, you'll really need it.

By default, the Root user account is disabled. You must enable it before you can log in to use it. You can enable the Root user account with the Directory Utility application, as described in the following steps:

1. **Open the Accounts pane of the System Preferences application, select Login Options, and click Join or Edit.**

2. **At the resulting prompt, click Open Directory Utility.**

3. **Click the Lock icon.**

Genius

If you're comfortable using UNIX commands, you can also enable and use the Root user account by opening the Terminal application and entering the appropriate commands to enable the Root user account, set its password, and log in.

4. **Type an Administrator username (if necessary) and password, and click OK.**

5. **Choose Edit ⇨ Enable Root User.** You're prompted to create a password for the Root user account.

6. **Type a password in the Password and Verify fields (see figure 2.14).** I recommend using a different password than what you use for your normal user account so that it's more secure.

7. **Click OK.** The sheet closes, but nothing else appears to happen. Don't worry, the Root user account is now enabled and you can use it.

8. **Quit the Directory Utility application.**

Because it has unlimited permissions, you can add or remove files to any directory on your MacBook while you are logged in under the Root user account, including those for other user accounts. You can also make changes to any system file, which is where the Root user account's power and danger come from.

Note

The full name of the Root user account is System Administrator. You therefore see that term instead of Root wherever the full account name is shown.

2.14 Create a secure password for the root account to prevent unintended access to it.

To log in to the Root user account, start from the Login window by choosing Login Window on the Fast User Switching menu, logging out of the current account, or restarting your MacBook (if Automatic Login is disabled). If the Login window is configured to show a list of users, scroll down and select the Other username; the Name and Password fields appear. If the Login Window is configured to show name and password, you don't need to scroll because these appear immediately. Type **root** as the name, type the password you created for the Root user account, and click Login. You log in as the Root user account (or under root, as UNIX aficionados would say). The Root user account's desktop appears, and you can get to work. (Another difference between the root and other user accounts is that the root's Home folder contains only two folders, which are Desktop and Library.)

Genius

If you want to disable the root account, open the Directory Utility application and choose Edit ➪ Disable Root User. You can change the Root user account's password by choosing Edit ➪ Change Root Password.

When you are logged in to the Root user account, you can use your MacBook as you can with other user accounts, except — and this is a big exception — you have no security limitations. You can place files into any folder, delete any files, or complete any other action you try, regardless of the potential outcome. And, if you use the System Preferences application, you see that you no longer have to authenticate because all possible actions are always enabled for the root account.

Caution

Be careful when you are working under the root account. You can cause serious damage to Mac OS X as well as to data you have stored on your MacBook. You should be logged in under the root account only for the minimum time necessary to accomplish specific tasks. Log in, do what you need to, and then log out of root again. This minimizes the chance of doing something you didn't intend to.

What Are My Internet Connection Options?

Being able to take advantage of the Internet is almost as important a skill as being able to read (of course, you have to be able to read to be able to use the Internet, and so reading still wins on the importance scale). Fortunately, your MacBook is a perfect tool for getting the most out of the Internet. In order to use the Internet, you must be able to connect to it, which is where this chapter comes in.

Setting Up a Local Network with Internet Access

There are many ways to connect your MacBook to the Internet. Fortunately, one of the great things about using a MacBook and related Apple technology is that you don't have to worry about all the technical details involved. It's quite easy to create and manage a local network that provides Internet access and other services, including file sharing, to multiple computers.

This chapter focuses on networks built around an Apple AirPort Extreme Base Station or Time Capsule because either one of these makes managing a network easy while providing all the features that most people need for a local network (a Time Capsule also provides wireless backup, ideal for your MacBook). MacBook networking technology supports wireless and wired networking standards, so you can use just about any network components designed to the same standards to accomplish the same purposes, but with a bit more effort and complexity, and who needs that?

There are two general steps to creating a local network. First, install and configure the AirPort Extreme Base Station or Time Capsule. Second, connect devices, such as computers and printers, to the wireless or wired network provided by the base station.

Installing and configuring an AirPort Extreme Base Station or Time Capsule

An Apple AirPort Extreme Base Station is a relatively simple device. It contains a transmitter that broadcasts the signal over which the wireless network is provided, and it has four Ethernet ports. One, the WAN (wide area network) port, connects to a broadband Internet connection, which is most commonly connected to a cable or DSL modem. The other three ports connect to an Ethernet network or to Ethernet-equipped devices, including computers, printers, and Ethernet hubs. Along with the power adapter port, the base station offers a USB port to which you can connect a USB printer or USB hard drive to share a printer or a hard drive with the network.

A Time Capsule is an AirPort Extreme Base Station with the addition of an internal hard drive; you can use this drive to store any kind of data, but it is ideal for backing up your MacBook using Mac OS X's Time Machine. Because this chapter focuses on the network aspects of these devices, you should consider the two devices equivalent throughout the rest of this chapter (the same steps will work for either device), and so you'll see the more generic term *base station*, which refers to either device. (Backing up with a Time Capsule and Time Machine is covered in Chapter 14.)

Got Internet?

I assume that you already have an Internet account that uses a cable modem or DSL (Digital Subscriber Line) modem to connect to the Internet. There are other ways you can connect, such as with a satellite or even with a dial-up connection, but a cable or DSL connection is ideal for most people. Fortunately, unless you live in a rural area, you probably have one or more of these options available to you. If you have cable TV service in your area, it is highly likely that cable Internet service is also available. To see whether DSL is available to you, check out dsl.theispguide.com to determine what DSL service providers are available in your area. After you obtain an Internet account and install the appropriate modem, you're ready to create a local network to provide Internet access to your MacBook, as well as any other computers that share your space.

If possible, locate the base station in a central area so that it provides the maximum amount of wireless coverage where you install it. In most houses, a base station provides adequate signal strength, even if you locate it at one end of the house and place computers that you want to network at the other end. However, the closer the computers are to the base station, the stronger the signal is. A stronger signal means a faster, more reliable connection.

After you place the base station in its location, attach its power adapter to the base station and plug it into a wall outlet. Use an Ethernet cable to connect the cable or DSL modem to the base station's WAN Ethernet port.

You can connect an Ethernet device to each of the three LAN (local area network) Ethernet ports on the base station (see figure 3.1). For example, you can connect a network printer and a computer, or to add more than three devices, you can connect one of the ports to an Ethernet hub and then connect additional Ethernet devices to that hub.

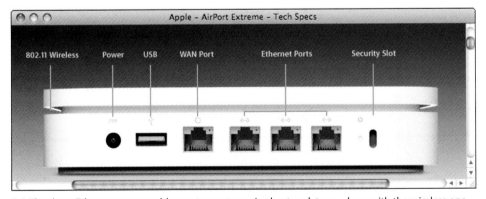

3.1 The three Ethernet ports enable you to create a wired network to go along with the wireless one.

If you want to share a USB printer with all the computers that can access the network, connect the printer's USB cable to the USB port on the base station. Likewise, you can connect a USB hard drive to the base station's USB port to share that drive on the network.

After you install the base station, you need to configure it. You can configure it manually through the AirPort Utility application, or you can use the same application with a guided approach. With either method, configure the base station from a computer with which it can communicate, either through AirPort or through an Ethernet network. To configure the base station wirelessly, make sure AirPort is enabled on your MacBook (see the section on connecting via a wireless network later in this chapter). To configure the base station through Ethernet, connect your MacBook to one of the Ethernet ports on the base station or to a port on an Ethernet hub connected to the base station.

Genius

To use the guided approach, open the AirPort Utility application located in the Utilities folder in the Applications folder. Select the base station and click Continue. Follow the on-screen instructions to complete the configuration.

You must use the manual approach to configure certain aspects of the base station (and it's often easier and faster to use this approach anyway); the following steps show you how to configure a base station manually. Note that these steps are based on configuring a base station that has been configured previously. If you're starting with a brand-new base station, the details you see might be slightly different, but the overall process is the same. For example, you'll be prompted to name a new base station, whereas a previously used base station already has a name.

To configure the base station's identification and configuration password, perform the following steps:

1. **Open the AirPort Utility located in the Utilities folder in the Applications folder.** The base stations with which your MacBook can communicate are shown in the left pane of the window. You see all the base stations currently in range of the MacBook you are using, and whether they communicate wirelessly or over an Ethernet connection. As soon as the application opens, it looks for new software. If new firmware is available for the base stations, the application prompts you to download and install it. If the base station is using the current version, you see a message saying so.

2. **Select the base station you want to configure.** If there is only one base station in range, it is selected automatically.

3. **Click Manual Setup.** You're prompted to type the base station's password.

Note

Two passwords are associated with a base station. One password is required to be able to administer the base station. The other password is required to join the wireless network provided by the base station (unless the network isn't secure). Usually, you should use different passwords because you may be providing the network password to people whom you don't want to be able to configure the base station.

4. **Type the password and click OK.** You next see a window that has the base station name as its title and that includes several tabs. The upper tabs provide access to general configuration areas, such as Internet, while the lower tabs provide the configuration tools for the selected area.

5. **Click the AirPort tab.**

6. **Click the Base Station or Time Capsule sub-tab, as shown in figure 3.2.**

7. **Type the base station name in the Time Capsule Name field.** This is the name of the base station itself, not the name of the network it provides.

Genius

To enter the contact information for the base station, its location, status light configuration, and how frequently it checks for new software, click Options.

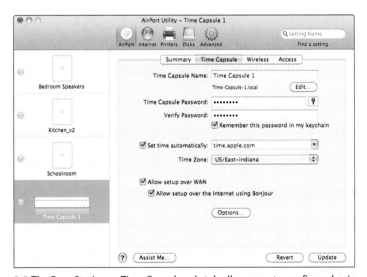

3.2 The Base Station or Time Capsule sub-tab allows you to configure basic attributes, such as the base station's name.

8. **Type the administration password in the Time Capsule Password and Verify Password fields.** Again, this is the password you use to configure the base station, not the one you use to access the network it provides.

9. **Select the Remember this password in my keychain check box.** This causes your MacBook to remember the password so that you don't have to type it each time you configure the base station from your MacBook.

10. **Select the Set time automatically check box, choose the appropriate server on the pop-up menu, and choose your time zone on the Time Zone pop-up menu.**

11. **To allow the base station to be configured over its Ethernet WAN connection, select the Allow configuration over WAN port check box.**

To configure the wireless network that the base station provides, follow these steps:

1. **Click the Wireless sub-tab.** On this tab, you configure the wireless network being provided by the base station (see figure 3.3).

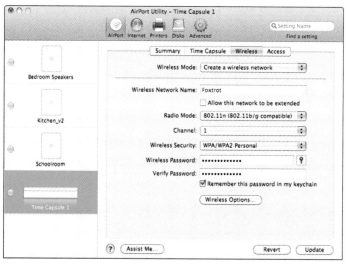

3.3 Use the Wireless sub-tab to create the wireless network provided by the base station.

2. **Use the Wireless Mode pop-up menu to choose Create a wireless network.**

3. **Type the wireless network's name in the Network Name field.** This is the name that you choose to access the network being provided by the base station.

Note WDS (Wireless Distribution System) is a way to link base stations together to create larger networks. If you choose Participate in a WDS network on the Wireless Mode pop-up menu, you can set up the base station to communicate with other base stations.

4. **Use the Radio Mode pop-up menu to determine the wireless standards supported on the network.** The more standards you allow, such as 802.11n (802.11b/g compatible), the more types of devices are able to connect to the network.

5. **Use the Channel pop-up menu to select the channel over which the base station communicates.** Generally, the default channel works fine, but if you are having trouble communicating with devices, you can try different channels to improve signal transmission and reception. If you have multiple AirPort networks in the same area, you can use the Channel pop-up menu to have each network use a different channel so that they don't interfere with one another.

6. **Use the Wireless Security pop-up menu to choose one of these security options:**

   - **WPA/WPA2 Personal.** WPA (Wi-Fi Protected Access) is the most secure encryption technique supported on an AirPort network. However, using WPA can limit the access of some devices to the network. Use this option for a network that includes only Macintosh computers unless you're sure the other devices (including Windows computers) that you want to connect can support WPA.

   - **WEP.** WEP (Wired Equivalent Privacy) is an encryption strategy that attempts to provide wireless networks with the same level of protection that wired networks have. This option provides a good level of security, while being more compatible with Windows and other devices. For networks that include older Macs or Windows computers, select this option. There are two levels of WEP security: 128 bit or 40 bit. Almost all modern hardware and software can support 128 bit, so you should select this option because it is the more secure of the two. Use 40 bit only if you need to connect older devices to the network.

   - **None.** If you select this option, your network won't be secured and anyone within range can join it without a password. You should not use this option unless you are very sure that unauthorized users cannot access your network. This option leaves your network, and all the devices connected to it, vulnerable to attack. I don't recommend that you use this option because there isn't a good reason to have an unsecured network.

Note

WEP and WPA have Enterprise options. These are designed for large networks that use authentication servers. You are very unlikely to need these options for a network located in a home or small business.

7. **Type the network password in the Wireless Password and Verify Password fields.** This is the password that people have to type to be able to connect to the secured network.

8. **Select the Remember this password in my keychain check box.** This causes your MacBook to remember the network's password so that you don't have to type it when you connect.

To connect the base station to the Internet, follow these steps:

1. **Click the Internet tab.**

2. **Click the Internet Connection sub-tab, as shown in Figure 3.4.**

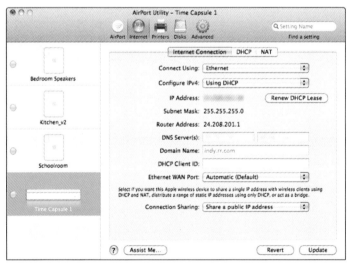

3.4 Use the Internet Connection sub-tab to configure your Internet account on the base station.

Note

There are many ways an Internet connection can be configured, and the details of each method are different. However, most cable and DSL Internet accounts are configured using details that are similar to those shown in these steps. Review the information you received from your Internet service provider to determine the details that you need to use to configure the base station to access your Internet account.

3. **Choose Ethernet on the Connect Using pop-up menu.**

4. **Choose Using DHCP on the Configure IPv4 pop-up menu.**

5. **On the Connection Sharing pop-up menu, choose Share a public IP address.**

6. **Click the NAT sub-tab.** Make sure the Enable NAT Port Mapping Protocol check box is selected. The base station uses NAT (Network Address Translation) to shield devices that are connected to it from Internet attacks. In order to hack a device, you need its address, and NAT hides the addresses of the devices connected to the base station. Make sure that NAT is enabled for your network.

After you configure all the settings you want the base station to use, click Update. The base station is configured according to the settings you entered. When the process is complete, the base station restarts and its wireless network becomes available.

Building a local network

The base station is the heart of the local network. In addition to providing an Internet connection to the other devices on the network, it makes many other services available, such as file sharing and printer sharing. To add devices to the network being provided by the base station, build the network by connecting wireless devices to the network the base provides, connecting a USB printer or hard drive to the base station's USB port, connecting a network printer to one of its Ethernet ports, or adding an Ethernet router and connecting more Ethernet devices to it.

In most cases, adding a device to your network is simple. You first make the physical or wireless connection between the network and the device, and then configure the device to connect to and use the network's resources, such as its Internet connection.

Connecting via a Wireless Network

To be able to connect to an AirPort network, you first enable AirPort on your MacBook. Once AirPort is enabled, you can find and connect to a wireless network.

To configure your MacBook to use AirPort, follow these steps:

1. **Open the System Preferences application and click the Network icon to open the Network pane.**

2. **Click the AirPort option in the list of available network options in the left part of the pane.** The AirPort tools appear in the right part of the pane.

3. **If AirPort is currently off, turn it on by clicking the Turn AirPort On button.** AirPort services start, and your MacBook begins scanning for available networks (you see radiating

waves at the top of the AirPort menu if it is enabled). If you've previously connected to an available network, you join that network automatically and its name appears on the Network Name pop-up menu.

4. **If you want to be prompted to join new networks, select the Ask to join new networks check box.** With this enabled, when you move your MacBook into an area with networks you've not connected to previously, you're prompted to connect to those networks.

5. **Select the Show AirPort status in menu bar check box to put the AirPort menu on your menu bar.** You can use this menu to quickly select and control your AirPort connection.

6. **Click the Advanced button.** You see the Advanced options sheet, which you can use to configure additional aspects of your AirPort connection.

7. **Click the AirPort tab (see figure 3.5).**

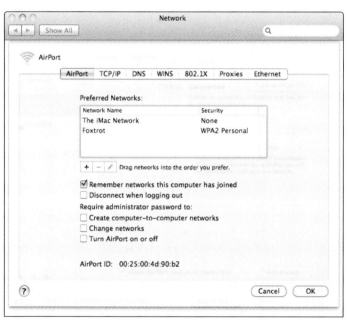

3.5 This sheet provides several useful options that you should configure to make working with AirPort networks even faster and easier.

8. **If you don't want your MacBook to automatically remember networks that you've used previously, deselect the Remember networks this computer has joined check box.** Networks that you remember become your preferred networks that you join automatically by default, but you can disable this behavior if you don't want to automatically join networks.

Genius

9. **If you want to automatically disconnect from networks when you log out of your user account, select the Disconnect when logging out check box.** You might want to select this option if there is some sort of time limitation or fee structure on the network that you connect to.

10. **Click OK.** The Advanced sheet closes. Your MacBook is ready for wireless communication.

To manage your wireless network connections, open the AirPort menu (see figure 3.6).

The AirPort menu contains the following:

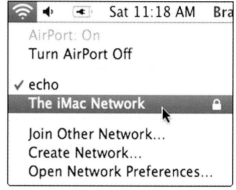

3.6 The AirPort menu is a fast and easy way to identify wireless networks in range of your MacBook.

- **Signal strength of the current network.** When you are connected to a wireless network, the number of darkened waves at the top of the menu indicates the strength of the signal.

- **AirPort status.** The first two items relate to AirPort status. If it is turned on, you see AirPort: On at the top of the menu with the command Turn AirPort Off underneath it. If your MacBook is searching for a network to which to connect, the status is Scanning. If AirPort is not enabled, the status is AirPort: Off and the command is Turn AirPort On.

- **Available networks.** The second section of the menu shows you all the networks within range of your MacBook. If you are currently connected to a network, it is marked with a check mark. If a network is marked with the Lock icon, that network is secure and you need a password to join it.

- **Join Other Network.** You use this command to join a closed network for which you must know the network name and, almost always, the password.

- **Create Network.** This command enables you to set up a wireless network between computers. Choose the command and use the resulting dialog box to create a wireless network. Other computers can use the network that you create to share files, play network games, and access other services that you want to provide.

- ● **Open Network Preferences.** This command opens the Network pane of the System Preferences application.

If a network is open, meaning that its information is broadcast publicly, then it appears on the AirPort menu. To join an open network, perform the following steps:

1. **Open the AirPort menu.**
2. **Select the network you want to join.** If no password is required, you join the network immediately, its name is checked on the list of networks, and you see the signal strength at the top of the AirPort menu; you can skip the rest of these steps and can start using the network's resources. If a password is required, you're prompted to provide it.
3. **Type the network's password.**
4. **If you want to see the password you entered, select the Show password check box.** This can be useful because sometimes network passwords are convoluted and it can be hard to tell whether you typed it correctly.
5. **Select the Remember this network check box.**
6. **Click OK (see figure 3.7).** You join the network and its resources become available to you.

3.7 If you select the Remember this network check box, you see this dialog box only the first time you connect to a network.

Genius

You can also join wireless networks from the Network pane of the System Preferences application. Choose the network you want to join on the Network Name pop-up menu and type the password at the prompt.

To control access to a network more tightly, it can be closed. This means that its name doesn't appear on the AirPort menu because its identity or existence isn't broadcast. To be able to access a closed network, you need to know it exists, what its name is, the kind of security it uses, and its password. If you have all that information, you can join it by doing the following:

1. **Open the AirPort menu.**

2. **Select Join Other Network.** A network information dialog box appears (see figure 3.8).

3. **Type the network's name in the Network Name field.**

4. **Choose the kind of security the network uses in the Security pop-up menu.**

5. **Type the network's password.**

6. **Click Join.** You join the network and its resources become available to you.

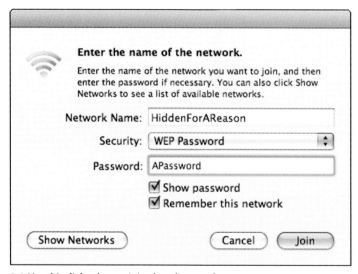

3.8 Use this dialog box to join closed networks.

Connecting via an Ethernet Connection

Ethernet connections are fast; in fact, your MacBook may perform better with an Ethernet connection than it does with a wireless connection. This might not be too noticeable for Internet activity, but transferring files within a local network is much, much faster. Ethernet connections are also more secure because their signals travel over a cable, so you have to be physically connected to the network with a wire, making it much harder for someone to intercept or interfere with the signal. Of course, the problem with Ethernet connections is that your MacBook has to be physically connected to the network to be able to use an Ethernet connection.

Caution

You can connect a cable or DSL modem directly to the Ethernet port on your MacBook to provide it with an Internet connection. I don't recommend this because it exposes the MacBook to attacks from the Internet. If you do connect it directly, make sure you enable the Mac OS X firewall by opening the Security pane of the System Preferences application, clicking the Firewall tab, and clicking Start before you connect the computer to the modem.

If you've installed an AirPort Extreme Base Station or Time Capsule and it has at least one open port, you can use that port to access the network, including its Internet connection. You can also connect your MacBook to an Ethernet hub connected to the base station.

When you travel, Ethernet ports into a network are generally available in businesses, schools, and hotels. In hotels, ports are enabled, but in businesses or schools, most open ports are disabled for security. If a port isn't enabled, you need to contact someone in the IT organization to have it enabled for you.

To connect your MacBook to an Ethernet network, follow these steps:

1. **Connect one end of an Ethernet cable to an available Ethernet port on the network.**

2. **Connect the other end to the Ethernet port on your MacBook.**

3. **Open the System Preferences application and click the Network icon.** The Network pane appears.

4. **Select Ethernet from the list of available connections.** Status information is shown at the right (see figure 3.9). If you see Connected, your MacBook is connected to an active network. If the status is something else, such as Not Connected, check the connections to make sure the cable is plugged in correctly. If the status continues to be something other than Connected, the Ethernet port to which your MacBook is connected may not be active.

5. **Select Using DHCP on the Configure pop-up menu.**

6. **Click Apply.** The MacBook begins using the network's resources, such as an Internet connection.

Genius

It's a good idea to carry an Ethernet cable with you as part of your MacBook toolkit, as some locations that offer an Ethernet connection don't provide a cable.

3.9 Select Ethernet on the list of available connections to see the status of that connection.

Connecting via a Wireless Broadband Card

Using a wireless broadband card, you can get a high-speed Internet connection from anywhere within the service area covered by the card and service plan you are using.

If you travel regularly, a wireless broadband card can be a much more convenient way to connect to the Internet while you are on the move. Because the connection is the same for you no matter where you are located, you don't have to find and sign onto networks in various locations, making a wireless broadband card much easier to use. A wireless broadband card can also be less expensive to use than purchasing temporary accounts multiple times in the same time period.

The primary downside of wireless broadband cards is that the networks they access aren't available in every location. Like cell phones, you need to be within a covered area to be able to access the service provided on the network. The other downside of a wireless broadband card is that its connection can be a bit slower than some wireless or wired connections that are available to you. Even with this usually minor limitation, you may find a wireless broadband card to be an indispensable part of your MacBook toolkit if you travel frequently.

Obtaining a wireless broadband card is a lot like buying a cell phone; you need to purchase the USB device you use to connect to the wireless network and also sign up for a service plan.

Caution

Before you sign up for an account, check the amount of data allowed per month. Some accounts are limited, which can be a problem if you transfer lots of large files or regularly watch video streamed over the Internet (such as from a Netflix account). Excess data penalty fees can be very, very expensive, especially if you are also roaming. Roaming fees alone can also be very expensive so make sure you understand what they are before using an account outside of its designated coverage area.

Most of the major cell phone providers also offer wireless broadband cards, so visit their Web sites to research the available cards. When you look for a wireless broadband card, consider the following factors:

- **Mac compatibility.** Most cards are compatible with Mac OS X version 10.4 and higher.
- **Card type.** Your MacBook is compatible with a USB broadband card.
- **Coverage areas.** Check that the network's coverage area matches up with the locations in which you use your MacBook. Make sure you focus on the coverage area for broadband connections; most maps also include coverage of the cell phone networks.
- **Connection speed.** The most important speed is the download speed because when you use the Internet, you are primarily downloading data. Of course, faster is better.
- **Contract terms.** There are a number of costs to factor into your decision, including the cost of the card itself (ranging from free to $200 or so), the cost of the account (usually about $50 per month for a one- or two-year commitment), and possible activation fees.

Caution

While research is both good and necessary, realize that trying a wireless broadband card is a bit of a gamble in terms of the coverage area and performance that you'll actually experience. For example, even if you primarily use your MacBook in covered areas, your location and objects in those areas can interfere with the performance of your connection. It's not a bad idea to ask for a trial period when you purchase a card so that you can return it if it doesn't work for you. Some providers allow this and some don't.

After you obtain a wireless broadband card, you need to install and configure it. The details depend on the specific card and the service provider that you use. The general steps to do this are as follows:

1. **Install the wireless broadband card's software.** This software includes the drivers and other software associated with the operating system and the application you use to connect to the network.

2. **Plug the card into your MacBook.**

3. **When prompted, restart your MacBook.**

Once the broadband card is installed and configured, connecting to the Internet is usually pretty simple. Again, the details depend on the specific card and service you use, but the general steps are as follows:

1. **Launch the wireless broadband card's connection application.** In the application's window, you see the types of wireless connections that are available to you, including those available through AirPort.

2. **Select the connection you want to use.**

3. **Click Connect.**

Connecting via iPhone Tethering

If you have an iPhone and a service provider that supports it, you can connect your MacBook to the Internet via your iPhone's cellular data network. This is convenient because an iPhone can connect to the Internet in many locations, and there's usually no additional charge to use tethering functionality (however, you need to check your contract's terms to ensure this is the case).

The specific steps you use to connect to the Internet via tethering depend on the particular network you use, but the general steps follow:

1. **Access the tethering settings on the iPhone by tapping Settings, General, Network.**

2. **Tap Internet Tethering OFF.** Its status becomes ON and the iPhone starts providing an Internet connection to tethered devices.

3. **Connect your MacBook to the iPhone's Internet connection with one of the following options:**

   - **Bluetooth.** Connect your MacBook to the iPhone via Bluetooth so the MacBook's Internet connection is via the Bluetooth connection. See Chapter 11 for information about connecting your MacBook with other devices via Bluetooth.

   - **USB.** Connect your MacBook to your iPhone using a USB cable, just like when you sync your iPhone. If the tethered connection isn't detected and available on your MacBook immediately, use the Network pane of the System Preferences application to choose the Ethernet Adapter option, choose Using DHCP on the Configure pop-up menu, and click Apply. The MacBook should be able to access the Internet via the iPhone's network.

Managing Multiple Network Connections

With Mac OS X, you can have multiple connections active at the same time, and you can determine which connection option your MacBook uses first. In this section, you learn how to configure the connections that you use. You can also use locations to create sets of connections so that you can easily reconfigure your MacBook for connectivity by choosing a location.

Configuring network connections

You use the Network pane of the System Preferences application to manage your MacBook's connections. Follow these steps:

1. **Open the Network pane of the System Preferences application.** Along the left side of the pane, you see all the connections configured on your MacBook (see figure 3.10). Connections marked with a green dot are active and connected. Connections marked with a red dot are not active. Connections marked with a yellow dot are active, but not connected to anything. The connection at the top of the list is the current one.

3.10 The Network pane provides you with detailed information about, and control over, your network connections.

2. **Select a connection.** Detailed information about the connection and controls you use to configure it appears in the right part of the pane. You've used some of these controls already to configure AirPort and Ethernet connections. Configuring other kinds of connections is similar.

3. **Remove a connection that you don't use by selecting it and clicking the Remove (–) button located at the bottom of the connection list.**

4. **Open the Action pop-up menu (the gear icon) and choose Set Service Order.** The Services sheet appears.

5. **Drag services up and down in the list until they are in the order that you want your MacBook to use them, starting at the top of the list and moving toward the bottom.** Typically, you want the fastest and most reliable connections at the top of the list. Each connection is tried in turn until one works. If you order them by their speed and reliability, the best available connection is always used.

6. **Click OK.** Your changes in the Services sheet are saved and the sheet closes.

7. **Click Apply.** The changes that you've made on the Network pane are saved and they take effect.

Using locations to manage network connections

In addition to having multiple connections active, you can use locations to define different sets of connections so that you can easily switch between them. For example, you may use one Ethernet configuration to connect to the Internet at home, and a different one to connect when you are at work. Creating a location for each set of connections makes switching between them simple because you have to configure them only once and can switch between them by simply choosing a different location. (Without locations, you may have to reconfigure the Ethernet connection each time you change the location of your MacBook.)

As you've seen, you can have multiple connections active at the same time. If you use only one configuration for each connection, you don't need to use locations. Rather, you want to use locations when you use different configurations of the same type of connections, such as the Ethernet connection, that you use.

Your MacBook includes one default location, which is called Automatic. You can create new locations when you need them (you can also change or delete existing locations).

To configure a new network location, follow these steps:

1. **Open the Network pane of the System Preferences application.** The current location is shown on the Location pop-up menu at the top of the pane.

2. **On the Location pop-up menu, choose Edit Locations.** The Locations sheet appears. In the top pane of the sheet, you see the current locations that are configured on your MacBook.

3. **Click the Add (+) button located at the bottom of the sheet.** A new location called Untitled appears.

4. **Type a name for the new location and press Return.**

5. **Click Done.** The new location is saved and you return to the Network pane. The location you created is shown on the Location pop-up menu (see figure 3.11).

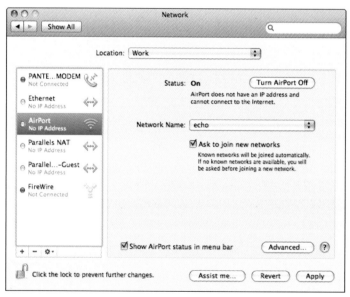

3.11 The location called Work is currently selected on the Location pop-up menu and is ready to be configured.

6. **Configure the location by doing any of the following:**

   - Select a connection and configure it.

   - Delete a connection that you don't want to include in the location.

   - Add a connection by clicking the Add (+) button located at the bottom of the list of connections. On the resulting sheet, select the interface you want to use on the

Interface pop-up menu, type a name, and click Create. The connection is added to the list and you can configure it.

- Set the order in which you want the connections in the location to be used.

7. **When you finish, click Apply.** Your changes are saved and the location becomes active.

Genius If one of the current locations is similar to the one you want to create, select it on the Locations sheet, open the Action drop-down menu, and choose Duplicate Location. Then give the copy a different name. This is faster than re-creating a location from scratch.

To change the location you are using, do one of the following:

- **Open the Network pane of the System Preferences application and choose the location you want to use on the Location pop-up menu.** If the Apply button becomes active, click it to apply the location; some configuration changes require this, while others don't.

- **Choose Apple menu ⇨ Location ⇨ *locationname*, where *locationname* is the name of the location you want to use.** After you select a location, it is marked with a check mark on the menu to show you that it is active.

You can edit or remove locations by following these steps:

1. **Open the Network pane of the System Preferences application.**

2. **Choose Edit Locations from the Location pop-up menu.** The Locations sheet appears.

Genius If you have created at least one location, you can quickly jump to the Network pane by choosing Apple menu ⇨ Location ⇨ Network Preferences.

3. **Perform any of the following tasks:**

- To rename the location, select it, open the Action drop-down menu, choose Rename Location, type the new name, and press Return.

- To delete a location that you no longer use, select it and click the Remove (–) button at the bottom of the sheet.

- To duplicate a location, select it, open the Action drop-down menu, choose Duplicate Location, type the new location's name, and press Return.

4. **Click Done.** You return to the Network pane.

Troubleshooting an Internet Connection

The time will come when you try to connect to a Web site or send email and you'll see error messages instead (see figure 3.12). While this probably won't happen very often, you need to know what to do when a good Internet connection goes bad. In general, the solutions to most connection problems are relatively straightforward.

3.12 Houston, we have a problem.

One of the difficulties in solving an Internet/network problem is that there are typically a number of links in the chain, including your MacBook, other computers, an Ethernet hub, and printers, to name a few. There are, however, three general sources of problems: computers and other devices connected to the network (clients), an AirPort Base Station or Time Capsule, and the cable or DSL modem that you use to connect to the Internet.

Because there are multiple devices, the first step in solving an Internet/network issue is to determine the source of the problem. The three sources of problems can be classified into two areas: client devices or the network. To determine which area is the source of an issue, try the same action that resulted in an error on your MacBook on a different computer that's on the same network and that uses the same connection, such as an AirPort network. If the problem also occurs with other computers, you know the problem is related to the network, which is discussed in the next section. If the problem doesn't occur on a different computer, you know it's specific to your MacBook, which is discussed later in the chapter.

Solving a network problem

Solving a network problem can be tricky because there are a number of potential sources of problems within the network and some that reside outside of the network and outside of your control. Start with basic steps to see whether you can determine which part of the network is causing you problems so that you can begin to solve them. Working from the first element in the chain, do the following:

1. **Check the status of the modem.** Most modems have activity lights that indicate whether the modem is powered up and has a working connection. Check these lights to make sure the modem appears to be powered up and connected to the Internet. If the modem appears to be working, move to Step 2. If the modem doesn't appear to be working, move to Step 7.

2. **Check the status of the AirPort Base Station.** It also has a light that uses color and flashing lights to indicate its status (see figure 3.13). If the light indicates the base station is working (in the current version, the status light is solid green when the base station is working correctly), move to Step 3. If not (for example, if the status light is flashing amber), move to Step 8.

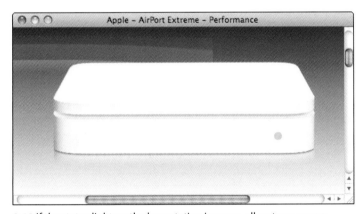

Apple – AirPort Extreme – Performance

3.13 If the status light on the base station is green, all systems are go.

3. **Disconnect power from the base station and from the modem.**

4. **Wait at least 20 seconds.**

5. **Connect power to the base station and then to the modem.** These simple steps often reset a network and restore the connection.

6. **Try what you were doing when you first encountered the problem.** If it's successful, you're finished and you can go on about your business. If not, continue with the next steps.

7. **If the modem's power light is on (which it probably is) but the connection light is not, contact your Internet service provider to make sure service is available.** Periodically check the modem status lights until the normal status lights appear; when they do, you should be good to go. If service is available, the provider can run some diagnostics from the source to determine whether your modem is connected. This can determine whether the problem lies between your modem and the provider, or is an issue with the modem and its configuration. If the source of the problem is the modem itself, the provider can help you troubleshoot and solve the issue.

Genius

If Internet connectivity is critical to you, consider adding a backup Internet connection that you can use if your primary connection goes down. One choice for this is a wireless broadband card, which is useful for other purposes as well. Another option is to be aware of available hot spots in your area so that if your primary Internet connection goes down, you can take your MacBook to a hot spot to work until your connection is restored.

8. **Remove power from the base station, wait 10 seconds, and connect it again.**

9. **Check the base station's status light.** If the light goes green, the problem is solved. If not, you need to further isolate the problem.

10. **Ensure the firewall is set on your MacBook.**

Caution

Never connect a computer directly to a cable or DSL modem without some sort of firewall protection. To enable the Mac OS X firewall, open the Security pane of the System Preferences application, click the Firewall tab, and click Start. Even with this option enabled, it's not a good idea to leave the computer directly connected for more than a minute or two.

11. **Connect the MacBook directly to the cable or DSL modem using an Ethernet cable.**

Note

To get a connection directly from the modem, your MacBook must have the Ethernet connection enabled, which is covered earlier in the chapter.

12. **Try an Internet activity.** If it works, you know the problem is with the base station, and you can continue with these steps. If you can't get an Internet connection directly from the modem, you know the problem is with the modem or the Internet connection itself; contact your provider for assistance.

13. **Troubleshoot the base station until you solve its problem.** You might need to reset it and reconfigure it. See the documentation that came with the base station or use the Apple support Web site at www.apple.com/support/airport for help.

Note

When you can't access a Web page because of a network issue, Safari presents the Network Diagnostics button. Click this button to start the diagnostics application, and follow its instructions to try to solve the problem.

Solving a MacBook problem

When you know the network is performing and other devices have connectivity, you can focus on the MacBook to solve the issue. Follow these steps:

1. **Try a different Internet application.** If one application works, but the other does not, you know the problem is related to a specific application and you can troubleshoot that application. If no Internet application works, continue with the following steps.

2. **Open the Network pane of the System Preferences application.**

3. **Check the status of the various connections.** If the status is Not Connected for a connection (see figure 3.14), you need to reconfigure that connection to get the connection working.

4. **If the status is Connected, choose Apple menu ⇨ Restart.**

5. **Click Restart at the prompt.**

6. **After the MacBook restarts, try the activity again.** Restarting when you have a problem is always a good thing to try because it's easy to do and solves a lot of different issues.

3.14 This MacBook isn't connected.

Finding help for problems

While the steps in this section help with many problems, they certainly won't solve all problems. When they don't work, you have a couple of options. First, find a computer that can connect to the Internet and move to www.apple.com/support or www.google.com. Search for the specific problem you are having and use the results you find to solve it. Second, disconnect everything from your network and connect your MacBook directly to the modem (ensuring the firewall is on first). If the connection works, you know the problem is related to the network; add other devices one-by-one, starting with the base station, until you find the source of the problem. If the connection doesn't work, you need help from your Internet provider to be able to solve the problem.

What Can I Do on a Local Network?

If you connect your MacBook to the Internet with an AirPort Extreme Base Station or Time Capsule, as described in Chapter 3, you create a local network at the same time. Any devices connected to your local network, whether through a wired Ethernet connection or a wireless one, can communicate with the other devices on your network. This is a good thing because Mac OS X includes a lot of network features that you'll find to be very useful. Perhaps the most useful of these features is the ability to share files, but there are plenty of other powerful network features to explore and use.

Sharing Files

If you have more than one computer on your local network, the ability to share files among those computers is really useful because you can easily move files between them. You can also store files on one computer and work on them while using any other computer on the network. The three general sharing skills you'll learn in this section are:

- Configuring your MacBook to share files with other computers
- Accessing files that are being shared with you
- Sharing files with Windows computers

Sharing your files with others

To enable other computers to access files stored on your MacBook, you need to accomplish the first two of the following tasks, while the third task is optional:

- Configure user accounts to access your MacBook from other computers.
- Configure file sharing services on your MacBook.
- Set specific security privileges on the files and folders you share.

Configuring Sharing user accounts

To be able to access files on your MacBook, a user must have a valid user account on your MacBook that he uses to log in to your computer to access the files that you are sharing. Group is the only type of user account you can't use to share your files. Any Administrator, Standard, Managed with Parental Controls, or Sharing user accounts can access your MacBook; the Sharing type of user account is especially intended to provide only sharing access to your MacBook, while the access that the other types have depend on the type. For example, an Administrator user account has administrator access to your MacBook when logged in across the network.

If sharing files is all you want the user to be able to do while logged in to your MacBook, create a Sharing user account (see figure 4.1). If you want to provide broader access to your computer, use a Standard or Administrator account instead. (See Chapter 2 for help creating and managing the user accounts on your MacBook.)

Note

By default, a user account called Guest Account exists on your MacBook (and every Mac, for that matter). This is a Sharing Only account that doesn't require a password to use. Initially, it provides access only to the Public folders in each user's Home folder. However, when you provide permissions to Everyone (more on this later), those permissions apply to the Guest Account.

4.1 A Sharing account, like the Maximus account highlighted here, is ideal for enabling people to access the files on your MacBook.

Configuring file sharing

The second part of enabling file sharing is to configure your MacBook to share its files, choose the folders you want to share, and determine the user accounts and permissions with which you want to share those folders. Here's how to perform these tasks:

1. **Open the System Preferences application.**

2. **Click the Sharing icon.** The Sharing pane opens.

3. **To set the name by which your computer is recognized on the network, type a name for the computer in the Computer Name field.** The default name is *yourname*'s MacBook, where *yourname* is the name you entered when you configured your MacBook for the first time during the startup process. You can leave this name as is or create a different name.

Note

The name you see in the Computer Name field is a bit of a nickname. The real name for your computer is shown in the text below "Computer Name." This name is created based on the name you typed, but it is translated into acceptable syntax, and the extension ".local" is appended to it. For example, any spaces in the name you create are replaced with "-" and other special characters that aren't allowed are transformed. If you click Edit, you can edit the "true" name of your computer on the network.

4. **Select the On check box next to the File Sharing service in the left pane of the window.** File sharing starts up, you see its status change to On, and you see your computer's address and name just below the Status text. Below this, you see the Sharing Folders section; this list shows the folders currently being shared. By default, the Public folder with each user account's Home folder is shared (which is why it is called a Public folder). In the Users section, you see the user accounts with which the selected folder is shared and the permission each user account has to that folder.

5. **To share a folder, click the Add (+) button at the bottom of the Shared Folders list.** The Select sheet appears.

6. **Move to and choose the folder you want to share.** You can only share folders for which you have Read & Write access.

7. **Click Add.** You return to the Sharing pane, and the folder you selected is added to the Shared Folders list; you see the current user accounts and associated permissions in the Users section. Initially, you see that your user account has Read & Write permissions, while Everyone has No Access (meaning that you are the only one who can use the folder).

Note

Everyone does actually mean what it says. It represents absolutely everyone that uses your MacBook or that can access it over the network. When you set a permission for Everyone, that permission is applied to all user accounts, except those for which you set specific access permissions.

8. **To allow a user account to access the folder, click the Add (+) button at the bottom of the Users list.** The User Account sheet appears, showing all of the user accounts configured on your MacBook (see figure 4.2).

9. **Select the user accounts with which you want to share the folder.**

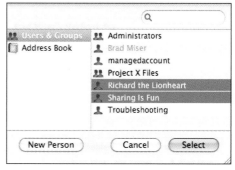

4.2 Choose the users with whom you want to share the selected folder on this sheet.

Genius If you click the Address Book option in the User Account sheet, you can access any person in your Address Book. If you select a contact in your Address Book, you're prompted to create a user account for that person to allow him to share files on your MacBook.

10. **Click Select.** You return to the Sharing pane and see the users on the Users list. After you add a user to the list, you set the permissions that this user has to the folder.

Genius If you'll be accessing files on your MacBook from other Macs, it's a good idea to create a user account with the same name and password on each computer to make it easier for you to log in.

11. **Select a user on the Users list on the Sharing pane.**

12. **On the pop-up menu at the right edge of the Users list, choose the permissions for the folder that the selected user account has from the following options:**

    - **Read & Write.** The user account can open and change the contents of the folder.

    - **Read Only.** The user can see and open the items in the folder, but she can't change them.

    - **Write Only (Drop Box).** The user can't see the contents of the folder or change them. All he can do is place files within the folder.

    - **No Access.** This option, available only for Everyone, prevents any access to the folder by anyone except the users shown on the Users list.

13. **Repeat Steps 11 and 12 for each user on the Users list (see figure 4.3).**

14. **To remove a user's access to the folder, choose the user, click the Remove (–) button at the bottom of the Users list, and click OK in the warning sheet.**

15. **To unshare a folder, choose it on the Shared Folders list, click the Remove (–) button at the bottom of the Shared Folders list, and click OK in the warning sheet.**

After you complete these steps, all that remains is to provide the user account information to the people with whom you'll be sharing your files.

4.3 Richard the Lionheart and Brad Miser can see and change items in the Pictures folder while all other accounts can't do anything with it.

Say Hello to Bonjour

Bonjour is the name of the Apple technology introduced way back in Mac OS X version 10.2 that makes it possible for devices on a network to automatically find each other. This means you don't have to bother with addresses or browsing though various paths to find the device you want to work with. Bonjour enables you to automatically find all the Macs on your network. Many other devices, such as printers, are also easily found with Bonjour. Even Windows computers can use Bonjour as long as they have the Apple Bonjour for Windows software installed.

Setting sharing permissions for folders and files from the Finder

As you saw in the previous section, you can share folders from the Sharing pane of the System Preferences application. You can also view and set sharing information for files and folders from within Finder windows. Check it out:

1. **Open a Finder window and move to the folder or file for which you want to get or set sharing information.**

2. **Select the file or folder.**

3. **Choose File ⇨ Get Info.** The Info window appears.

4. **Expand the Sharing & Permissions section.** You see each user account as well as the permissions that each account has to the file or folder you selected in Step 2 (see figure 4.4).

5. **To set permissions for the folder, authenticate yourself under an Administrator account.**

6. **Click the Add (+) button to add users for the folder, or select users and click the Remove (–) button at the bottom of the window to remove users for the folder.**

7. **Use the Privilege pop-up menus to set the access permission for each user.**

Accessing files shared with you

While it is better to give than receive, there's also the expression share and share alike. You can access files being shared with you in a couple of ways:

4.4 In the Sharing & Permissions section, you see and can set the access that users have to a folder or file.

- Browsing using the sidebar

- Moving directly to a shared source by its address

Both of these methods work, but the browsing option is the easiest and fastest. If you are accessing a device that supports Bonjour, browsing is definitely the way to go.

Using the sidebar to access shared files

Thanks to Bonjour, as soon as your MacBook is connected to a network, any computers that are sharing files are immediately recognized and mounted on your desktop, making it easy to access the files they are sharing. When you want to access shared files, perform the following steps:

1. **Open a Finder window in the Columns view.** Use this view for consistency with these steps and easier access to the shared files.

2. **In the Shared section of the sidebar, select the computer with the files that you want to access.** In the first pane, you see the computer's name, its icon, your current connected status (as Guest, which happens automatically), and the Public folders for each user account on that computer.

Genius

You don't need to log in to access Public files and folders because you are automatically logged in under the Guest account as soon as your MacBook detects another computer on the network that has file sharing enabled.

3. **Click the Connect As button.** The Login dialog box appears. The Registered User option is selected automatically.

4. **In the Name field, type the name of the user account you want to use to log in.** This should be the name of the user account that has been created for you to access the files you are allowed to share.

5. **Type the account's password in the Password field.**

6. **Select the Remember this password in my keychain check box.** This enables you to log in automatically in the future.

7. **Click Connect.** Your MacBook connects to the computer and mounts all the folders being shared with you in the Finder window; the resources you see are those for which the user account you are using has Read, Write Only (Drop Box), or Read & Write permissions (see figure 4.5).

8. **Select the folder containing the files with which you want to work.** The files in that folder become available to you under the following conditions:

   - If you have Read Only permission to a folder, you can view the files it contains (you can't save any changes you make to the files) or drag them to a different location to copy them there. You can't move any files into the folder, delete files from it, or save any files there.

   - If you have Read & Write permission to a folder, you can do anything you want with the files it contains, including making changes, copying, and deleting them.

- If you have Write Only (Drop Box) permission to a folder, you can't see its contents. All you can do is drag files into the folder to copy them there.

Genius

If you copy a file from a folder for which you have Read Only permissions to a new location on your MacBook, it is copied in the Locked state. If you try to make changes to the file in its new location, you are warned that it is a Locked file, and the Overwrite and Don't Overwrite buttons appear. If you choose Overwrite, a new version of the file is created that contains the changes you made and that is unlocked; from that point forward, it behaves just like a file you created on your MacBook.

4.5 I've logged in to the computer called BradsiMac under the Brad Miser account.

Accessing shared files using a URL

For those computers that are not using Bonjour, you can move directly to a computer that is sharing its files using its address on the network. Try this:

1. **If the computer you want to access is a Mac, open the Sharing pane of the System Preferences application and select File Sharing.** You see the computer's address (starting with afp://) under the File Sharing status information. Use the address to log in to the computer.

2. **From your MacBook's desktop, choose Go ➪ Connect to Server.** The Connect to Server dialog box appears (see figure 4.6).

3. **Type the address of the computer you want to access in the Server Address field.**

4. **Click Connect.** The Login dialog box appears.

4.6 Using the Connect to Server command, you can log in to a file-sharing computer through its network address.

Caution

If your network uses Dynamic Host Control Protocol (most do), the address of computers can change over time. If you try to connect to a computer that you've successfully connected to before, check its address again to see if it has changed. If you use Bonjour to connect to a computer, you don't have to worry about this, because the address changes are managed automatically.

5. **In the Name field, type the name of the user account you want to use to log in.**

6. **Type that account's password in the Password field.**

7. **Select the Remember this password in my keychain check box.** This enables you to log in automatically in the future.

8. **Click Connect.** The Volume Selection dialog box appears. In this dialog box, you see the folders and volumes that are available to your user account on the computer to which you are logging in.

9. **Select the volumes you want to use.**

10. **Click OK.** Your MacBook connects to the other computer, and each volume you selected is mounted on your desktop. You can then use the contents of the volume according to the permissions the user account has for each item.

Genius

If you regularly use an address to connect to a computer, add it as a favorite by clicking the Add (+) button in the Connect to Server dialog box; the address is added to the list of favorites shown under the Server Address field. You can move back to an address by selecting it and clicking Connect. You can also return to a recent server by opening the Recent pop-up menu (clock) located at the right edge of the Connect to Server dialog box.

Sharing files with Windows PCs

If your network includes both Macs and Windows PCs, you can share files between them. The process is similar to sharing files between Macintosh computers, but there are some differences (which you could have probably guessed).

Sharing files on a MacBook with Windows PCs

Configuring files to share with Windows PCs is accomplished very similarly to sharing files with Macs, but you need to enable Windows file sharing by also doing the following:

1. **On the Sharing pane of the System Preferences application, click the Options button.** The Options sheet appears (see figure 4.7).

2. **Select the Share files and folders using SMB (Windows) check box.**

3. **Select the On check box for a user account that you want to be able to access files on your MacBook from a Windows PC.** The Password dialog box appears.

4.7 Activate Windows file sharing on the Options sheet.

Note

You can't enable Windows sharing for a user account that is a Sharing Only account.

4. **At the prompt, type the user account's password in the Password field.** This is the same password you created when you set up the user account.

5. **Click OK.** The dialog box closes and you return to the Options sheet.

6. **Click Done.** The selected files are available from Windows PCs on the network.

Genius

You configure Windows sharing by user account; you control the folders that are shared using the tools on the Sharing tab. You can't share some folders with only Windows or only Macs. You can only enable file sharing for Windows by user account and control access to those files using the Shared Folders and Users tools. If you want to configure a folder to limit sharing only to Windows PCs, create a unique user account for Windows PC users.

Accessing files from a Windows PC

After you configure your MacBook to share files with Windows computers, you can access them from a Windows PC. There are a lot of versions of Windows out there, and many variations and details related to networking for each. This section describes a fairly common configuration of a Windows XP SP2 computer accessing a wireless network provided through a Time Capsule. If you have a different configuration, the details might be a bit different for you, but the overall process should be similar. Also, these steps assume that the Windows computer is already connected to the local network through a wireless or wired connection.

You can access shared files from a Windows PC by performing the following steps:

1. **On the PC, open the My Computer folder in a Windows Explorer window.**

2. **Click the My Network Places link in the Other Places section.**

3. **Click the Add a network place link in the Network Tasks section.** The Add Network Place Wizard opens.

4. **Click Next.**

5. **Select the Choose another network location option.**

6. **Click Next.**

7. **Type the path to and name of the shared folder you want to access on the Windows PC in the Internet or network address field (see figure 4.8).** The path starts with \\ followed by the computer's name and the specific folder you want to access. The computer's name is based on the "real" computer name, which is shown on the Sharing pane of the System Preferences application. For example, if your computer's name is *mymacbookpro.local* and the folder you have shared is called *sharedfiles*, the information you type in the box is *mymacbookpro.local**sharedfiles*.

8. **Click Next.** You're prompted to log in to the MacBook.

9. **In the User name field, type the username for an account on the MacBook that has Windows sharing permissions enabled.**

10. **Type the account's password in the Password field.**

11. **Click OK.** You see the Name screen.

12. **Type a name for the shared folder.** This can be any name you want and is how you recognize the shared folders on the PC. The default name is a combination of the folder's name, the computer's name, and its location. This tends to be very long, and so you might want to go with something simpler and shorter.

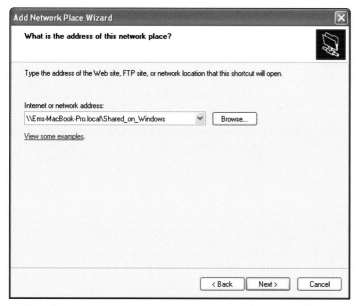

Add Network Place Wizard

What is the address of this network place?

Type the address of the Web site, FTP site, or network location that this shortcut will open.

Internet or network address:

`\\Ems-MacBook-Pro.local\Shared_on_Windows`   Browse...

View some examples.

< Back   Next >   Cancel

4.8 Type the path to the folder you want to share with Windows PCs.

13. **Click Next.** You see the Complete screen. This confirms that you have successfully accessed the shared folder.

14. **Click Finish.** The shared folder opens on the Windows desktop, and you can access its contents based on your user security.

After you access a shared folder on the Windows PC, it remains in the My Network Places folder on the PC; you can return to the shared folder at any time by opening the My Network Places folder. If you log out of the Windows PC, you're prompted to log in to the MacBook the next time you access the shared folder.

Caution If the Windows PC is connected to a Virtual Private Network (VPN), disconnect from that network before setting up sharing on the local network. Some VPN software can block Macs from being able to access a Windows computer.

Sharing files on a Windows PC

To share a folder and its files that are stored on a Windows PC, perform the following steps:

1. **Right-click the folder on the Windows PC that you want to share.**

2. **Choose Properties.** The Properties dialog box appears.

3. **Click the Sharing tab.**

4. **Click the Share this folder radio button.**

5. **Click Permissions.** The Permissions dialog box appears.

6. **Choose a user or group at the top of the dialog box.**

7. **Select the Allow check box to allow, or the Deny check box to deny, each of the following permissions:**

   * **Change.** The user account can open and change the contents of the folder.

   * **Full Control.** The user can perform any action.

   * **Read.** The user can only see the contents of the folder.

8. **Click OK.** You return to the Sharing tab (see figure 4.9).

9. **Click OK.** You're ready to access the shared folder from another computer on the network.

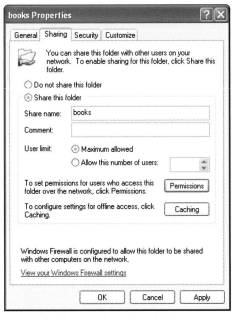

4.9 Use the Sharing tab to share folders on a Windows PC.

Accessing files shared on a Windows PC using a Mac

To be able to access shared files on a Windows PC, you need to know its address on the network and have a username and password. To log in, perform the following steps:

1. **From the desktop, choose Go ⇨ Connect to Server.** The Connect to Server dialog box appears.

2. **Type the address of the computer you want to access in the Server Address field.** The address should start with smb:// followed by the computer's IP address and the name of the shared folder. So, if the computer's IP address is *1.2.3.4* and the folder you are accessing is called *books*, the address you type would be *smb://1.2.3.4/books* (see figure 4.10).

4.10 Logging in to a Windows PC is very similar to logging in to a Mac.

3. **Click Connect.** The Login dialog box appears.

4. **In the Name field, type the name of the user account you want to use to log in.** If your user account is part of a domain on the Windows PC, you must add the domain and \ as a prefix to the user account, as in *xyz\useraccount*, where *xyz* is the domain with which *useraccount* is associated.

5. **Type that account's password in the Password field.**

6. **Select the Remember this password in my keychain check box.** This enables you to log in automatically.

7. **Click Connect.** The shared folder is mounted on your desktop and you can access it according to your permissions.

Genius

To determine the address of a Windows PC, choose Start menu ➪ All Programs ➪ Accessories ➪ Command Prompt. At the command prompt, type **ipconfig** and press Enter. The IP address appears in the resulting information.

Sharing Screens

With screen sharing, you can control a Mac over the local network just as if you were sitting in front of it. This is very useful for helping other users on your network. Instead of moving to their locations, you can simply log in to their computers to provide help.

Like file sharing, you can configure screen-sharing permissions on your MacBook. You can also share the screens of other Macs that have screen-sharing permissions configured.

Sharing your MacBook with other Macs

To share your MacBook screen with other Macs on your network, configure screen-sharing permissions. Follow these steps:

1. **Open the Sharing pane of the System Preferences application.**

2. **Choose the Screen Sharing service on the service list.** The controls for screen sharing appear.

3. **Click Computer Settings.** The Computer Settings sheet appears.

4. **Select the Anyone may request permission to control screen check box if you want to allow anyone who can access your MacBook to request to share your screen.** If you leave this unchecked, only user accounts for whom you provide screen-sharing permissions are able to control your MacBook.

5. **Select the VNC viewers may control screen with password check box, and type a password if you want people using Virtual Network Computing connections to be able to control your MacBook.** For a local network, you don't really need to allow this, and so in most cases, leave this unchecked.

6. **Click OK.** The sheet closes.

7. **In the Allow access for section, choose one of the following options:**

   ○ Click All users to allow anyone who can access your MacBook over the network to share its screen.

   ○ Click Only these users to create a list of user accounts that can share your screen. To create the list, click the Add (+) button at the bottom of the user list. The User Account sheet appears. Select the user accounts you want to share your screen and click Select. You return to the Sharing pane and the user accounts you selected are shown on the user list.

8. **Select the On check box for Screen Sharing.** Screen sharing services start and your MacBook is available to users on your local network according to the access permissions you set. The Screen Sharing status becomes On, and under that status you see the screen-sharing address of your MacBook on the network (see figure 4.11).

4.11 This MacBook can share its screen with three user accounts.

If you allow anyone to request to share your screen, then when someone wants to share your MacBook, you see a permission dialog box on your screen. To allow your screen to be shared, click Share Screen.

Sharing another Mac on a local network

You can access other Macs being shared with you by browsing the network for available computers or by moving to a specific address.

To connect to another Mac to share its screen, perform the following steps:

1. **Open a Finder window in Columns view.** You can share screens starting from any Finder window view, but using the Columns view makes your steps consistent with these.

2. **In the SHARED section of the sidebar, select and log in to the Mac whose screen you want to share.**

3. **Click Share Screen (this command appears only if the user account you used in Step 2 has screen-sharing permission).** The Share Screen Permission dialog box appears (see figure 4.12).

4. **Use one of the following options to share the other Mac's screen:**

   - To request permission to share the screen, click the By asking for permission radio button, click Connect, and wait for the person using the Mac whose screen you want to share to grant permission.

4.12 Use the Share Screen Permission dialog box to access another Mac on your network.

   - To log in using a user account with screen-sharing permissions, click the As a registered user radio button, type the username in the Name field, type the password in the Password field, select the Remember this password in my keychain check box, and click Connect.

   Once the other person's desktop appears within the Screen Sharing window on your MacBook desktop, you can work with the shared Mac as you would your own.

You can also connect to a Mac to share its screen by typing its address on the network. To determine the address of a Mac whose screen you want to share, open its Sharing pane, select the Screen Sharing service, and note the address just under the Screen Sharing status information. The Mac's screen-sharing address starts with vnc://.

Once you have the other Mac's address, you can share its screen using the following steps:

1. **From the desktop, choose Go ⇨ Connect to Server.** The Connect to Server dialog box appears.

2. **Type the address of the computer whose screen you want to share in the Server Address field.** This address is something like *vnc://1.2.3.4.*

3. **Click Connect.** The Share Screen Permission dialog box appears.

4. **Use one of the following options to share the other Mac's screen:**

   - To request permission to share the screen, click the By asking for permission radio button and click Connect and wait for the person using the Mac whose screen you want to share to grant permission.

   - To log in using a user account with screen-sharing permissions, click the As a registered user radio button, type the username in the Name field, type the password in the Password field, select the Remember this password in my keychain check box, and click Connect.

   Once the other person's desktop appears within the Screen Sharing window on your MacBook desktop, you can work with the shared Mac as you would your own.

When you share a Mac's screen, you use the Screen Sharing application. Its window, which has the name of the Mac whose screen you are sharing as its title, contains the desktop of the Mac whose screen you are sharing, including open Finder windows, applications, and documents (see figure 4.13). When your cursor is inside the Screen Sharing application window, any action you take is done on the Mac whose screen you are sharing. When you move outside the window, the cursor for your MacBook separates from the shared Mac's cursor and the shared Mac's cursor freezes (unless, of course, the user at that Mac is doing something, in which case you see the results of his actions).

When you access a shared Mac, its screen is automatically scaled to fit into the Screen Sharing application window. The desktop you see in the Screen Sharing window depends on the resolution of the Mac's desktop you are sharing. If it is very large, such as a 24-inch iMac that also has an external display connected to it, the information in the shared window is quite small so that it all fits on your MacBook screen. You can access the Display pane of the System Preferences application on the shared Mac to decrease its resolution so that the image appears larger on your desktop. Or, you can choose View ⇨ Turn Scaling Off to make the screen its actual size; if the shared Mac's screen is larger than yours, you have to scroll to see all of it.

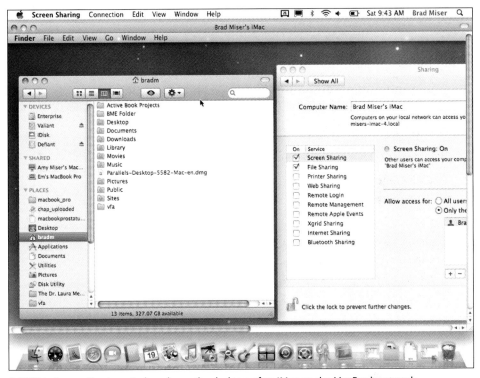

4.13 This Screen Sharing window shows the desktop of an iMac on the MacBook network.

Caution

When you use screen sharing, you have the permissions granted by the user account you use. Be careful about what you are doing on the shared computer so that you don't accidentally do something. For example, don't use the shortcut ⌘+Q to quit applications when you are using the Screen Sharing application because that closes the active application on the shared Mac, not the Screen Sharing application itself. Use the Quit command on the Screen Sharing menu instead.

To move information from the shared computer to yours, copy that information on the shared computer and choose Edit ➪ Get Clipboard. This copies what you pasted to the Clipboard on your MacBook, where you can paste it into your applications. To move information in the other direction, copy it on your MacBook and choose Edit ➪ Send Clipboard. This moves the data from your Clipboard to the Clipboard on the shared Mac, where it can be pasted into documents that are open there.

Genius If you have a MobileMe account, you can also share screens across the Internet. So, you could access a Mac at home while you are traveling with your MacBook. To do this, you set screen-sharing permissions. Type your MobileMe username and password on each computer (in the MobileMe pane of the System Preferences application) among which you want to share screens. Then use the Back To My Mac tab to configure screen sharing across the Internet. You can also share screens over the Internet through iChat, as you see in Chapter 9.

Sharing Printers

Printers are a great resource to share on a network because you seldom need one printer for each computer. More typically, one or two printers on the network are more than sufficient for everyone's printing needs. There are two basic ways to use printer sharing to make printers available on a network. You can connect a USB printer to an AirPort Extreme Base Station or Time Capsule and share it from there, or you can connect a USB or Ethernet printer directly to your MacBook and share it with the network.

Note If a printer is networkable, you don't need to share it. Instead, connect the printer to the network through an Ethernet or wireless connection. This is better than printer sharing because no computer or base station resources are required for the networked printers.

Sharing USB printers connected to a base station

To share a USB printer from a base station, perform the following steps:

1. **Connect the printer to the USB port on the AirPort Extreme Base Station or Time Capsule.**

2. **Open the AirPort Utility located in the Utilities folder in the Applications folder.** The base stations with which your MacBook can communicate are shown in the left pane of the window.

3. **Select the base station to which the printer is attached.**

4. **Click Manual Setup.** You're prompted to type the base station's password (if its password is saved on your keychain, it is entered automatically). The Manual Setup screen appears.

5. **Click the Printers tab.** The connected printer is shown under the USB Printers field.

6. **Type the name of the printer in the Name field.** This is the name that users select to configure the printer on their Macs.

7. **Click Update.** The base station is updated and restarts. Any computers on its network can use the printer connected to it.

Note To be able to access a shared printer, each computer must have the printer's software installed; fortunately, Mac OS X includes the software for most printers by default.

Sharing printers connected to a Mac

If a Mac has a printer connected to it directly through Ethernet or USB, you can share that printer with the network. However, in order for other computers to use that printer, the Mac to which it is connected must be active (it can't be asleep) and currently connected to the same network. Because you'll probably move your MacBook around a lot, this isn't convenient. However, if your network includes a desktop Mac to which a printer is connected, you can share it using the following steps:

1. **Connect and configure the printer to the Mac from which it is being shared.**

2. **Open the Sharing pane of the System Preferences application.**

3. **Select the On check box for the Printer Sharing service.** The service starts up.

4. **Select the check box for the printer you want to share.** Other computers can use the printer by adding it; the printer's name is the current printer name with *@yourmacbook*, where *yourmacbook* is the name of the computer to which the printer is attached.

Sharing an Internet Connection

Any Mac can share its Internet connection with other computers, similar to a base station. While I don't recommend this for a permanent network (one reason is because the Mac has to be active all the time for the network to be available), it can be very useful when you are traveling with your MacBook. You can share an Internet connection that you are getting through Ethernet with other computers using AirPort, or you can share an Internet connection that you are getting through AirPort over your MacBook's Ethernet port. Here's how:

1. **Connect and configure your MacBook to access the Internet.**

2. **Open the Sharing pane of the System Preferences application.**

3. **Select the Internet Sharing service.** Its controls appear in the right part of the pane.

4. **On the Share your connection from pop-up menu, choose Ethernet if you get your connection through Ethernet, or AirPort if you get your connection through AirPort.**

5. **Select the On check box for the connection that other computers use to get their Internet connection from your MacBook.** For example, if your MacBook is using Ethernet for Internet access, select the On check box for AirPort.

6. **If you selected AirPort in Step 5, click AirPort Options; if not, skip to Step 13.** The AirPort Options sheet appears (see figure 4.14).

7. **Type a name for the network you are creating in the Name field.** This is how others identify the network you provide.

8. **Choose the channel for the network on the Channel pop-up menu.** Automatic is usually the best choice, but you can choose a specific channel if your network has problems.

9. **Select the Enable encryption (using WEP) check box.** I recommend that you always create a secure network.

4.14 Use the AirPort Options sheet to create an AirPort network over which you can share an Internet connection.

10. **Type a password for the network in the Password and Confirm Password fields.** If you're sharing your connection with Windows computers, make the password exactly 13 characters long.

11. **On the WEP Key Length pop-up menu, choose 128-bit.**

12. **Click OK.** The sheet closes, and you return to the Sharing pane.

13. **Select the On check box for the Internet Sharing service.**

14. **Click Start in the resulting confirmation sheet.** Your MacBook starts sharing its Internet connection. Other computers can connect to the Internet by joining the MacBook's wireless network if you are sharing via AirPort or by being connected to your MacBook's Ethernet or FireWire ports directly or through a hub (see figure 4.15).

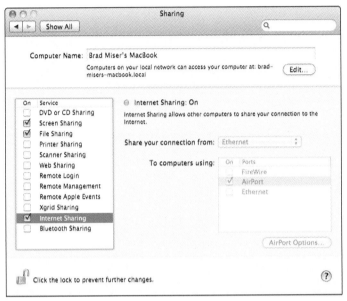

4.15 This MacBook is sharing its Ethernet Internet connection through an AirPort wireless network.

Sharing with Applications

A number of applications also provide sharing on a local network. Using iTunes, you can share your library with the network so that other people can listen to and view its contents. You can also share your iPhoto libraries on the network so that people can access the photos in your database. Of course, you can access iTunes and iPhoto libraries that are being shared by others on the network, as well.

To set up sharing in those applications, open the Sharing tabs of their Preferences dialog boxes. Select the Look for shared libraries/photos check boxes to access resources that are being shared with you. Select the Share my library/photos check boxes to share your libraries on the network. Use the controls on the tab to define what you share, its share name, and whether a password is required.

How Do I Take Advantage of MobileMe?

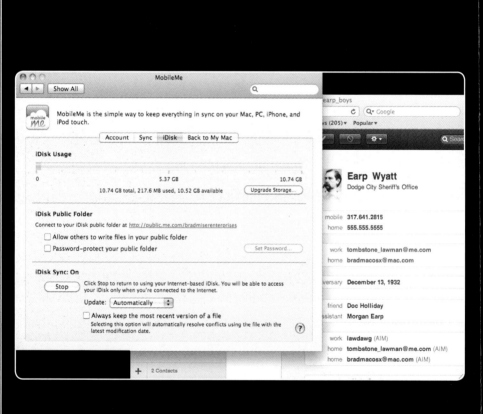

To become a genius, take advantage of the Apple MobileMe services to expand your MacBook to encompass (literally) the Internet. With MobileMe, you aren't just an Internet consumer; the Internet becomes an extension of your MacBook's desktop. A MobileMe account provides a number of great features that I think you'll find indispensable: iDisk, data synchronization, and email, for example. In order to access these features, you need to have a MobileMe account, which you can easily and inexpensively obtain and configure on your MacBook in just a few minutes.

Obtaining a MobileMe Account

To use MobileMe, you must have a MobileMe account. A MobileMe account includes, by default, 20GB of storage space on Apple servers, an email account, space for online galleries of your photos, and more. You can also purchase a family account that provides several user accounts under a single MobileMe account (for distinct email addresses and iDisks). At the time of this writing, the cost of an individual MobileMe account is $99 per year, while the cost of a family account is $149 per year. You can also upgrade accounts by adding disk space.

Note The disk space included with a MobileMe account is used for two purposes: iDisk and email storage space. The total space included with a MobileMe account is the total space for both kinds of data; you can choose how this space is allocated.

To get your MobileMe account, perform the following steps:

1. **Open the System Preferences application.**

2. **Click the MobileMe icon.** The MobileMe pane appears (see figure 5.1).

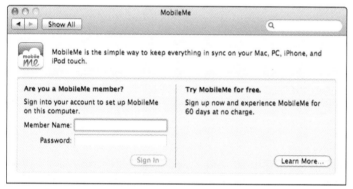

5.1 Use the MobileMe pane to obtain a MobileMe account and to configure it on your MacBook.

3. **Click Learn More.** Your Web browser opens and moves to the MobileMe Web site.

4. **Click Free Trial.** The first page of a two-step form appears.

5. **Fill out the information on this page.**

Caution Be thoughtful about what you choose as your member name; in addition to using this to log in to MobileMe, it becomes part of your email address. You can't change this name after you create a MobileMe account.

6. **Click Continue.**

7. **In a similar way, complete the second page of the form.** The information you must provide includes a credit or debit card, but your card is not charged until the trial period ends or you choose to convert the free trial account into a full (paid) account. When your account is created, the Welcome to MobileMe screen appears and provides information that you need to use your MobileMe account, namely your member name and password.

Note All free trial accounts are individual accounts. To create a family account, you must convert your trial account into a paid account (this happens automatically when the trial period ends unless you cancel your account) and then upgrade from the individual account to a family account.

Configuring a MobileMe account

After you have a MobileMe account, configure its information in the System Preferences application so that you can automatically access your iDisk from the desktop and so the MobileMe email account is configured in the Mail application for you.

1. **Open the System Preferences application.**

2. **Click the MobileMe icon.**

3. **Type your member name.**

4. **Type your password.**

5. **Click Sign In.** Your account information is configured on your MacBook and you can access MobileMe services from your desktop (see figure 5.2).

Genius You can use the same MobileMe account on multiple computers at the same time, which makes sense because one of the service's main benefits is synchronization among multiple devices. If you have more than one Mac, log in to your MobileMe account on each of them.

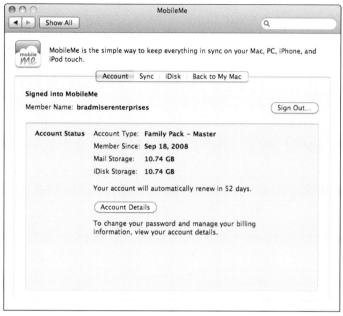

5.2 After you enter your MobileMe account information, the MobileMe pane changes to provide the tools you use to configure your MobileMe services on your MacBook.

Logging in to your MobileMe Web site

In addition to working with MobileMe on your MacBook, you have access to your own MobileMe Web site that provides Web applications for email, contacts, calendars, iDisk access and file sharing, and photo and video sharing that you can use through a Web browser on any computer; the supported browsers are Safari, Firefox, and Internet Explorer (Windows PCs only).

You also manage your MobileMe account from your Web site. For example, you might want to convert a trial account to be a full account or you might upgrade your disk space. To log in to your Web site and manage your account or use one of the MobileMe Web applications, follow these steps:

1. **Open a supported Web browser and move to www.me.com.**

2. **Type your member name and password.**

3. **If you are using a secure computer, select the Keep me logged in for two weeks check box.** This keeps you logged in to your MobileMe Web site for a period of up to two weeks, even if you move away from the Web site or stop and then restart your Web browser.

4. **Click Log In.** Your Web site opens. In the toolbar at the top of the window, you see the buttons you click to access the various applications, which are (from left to right) Mail,

Contacts, Calendar, Gallery, iDisk, and Account Settings (see figure 5.3). The active application is marked with an upward-facing triangle and you see its tools in the lower part of the browser window.

5. **Click the Account Settings button.**

6. **Type your MobileMe password and click Continue.** You are prompted to provide your password any time you access your account settings. (Also,

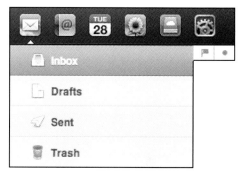

5.3 Click one of the application buttons on your MobileMe Web site to use that application.

unlike the other MobileMe Web applications, you are logged out of MobileMe when the Application Settings application is open but there is no activity for a period of 15 minutes.) You move to the Account Settings Web page. The Summary page shows information about your account, such as its type, your email address, and how much disk space you have. Along the left side of the window are tabs you use to configure different aspects of your account (see figure 5.4).

5.4 To change various aspects of your MobileMe account, click the related Account Settings tabs along the left side of the window.

7. **To make changes in any of these areas, click the appropriate tab, make the changes on the resulting Web form, and click Save.** The changes you make take effect immediately.

Working with iDisks

An iDisk provides you with disk space on the MobileMe servers that you access over the Internet. An iDisk is a great way to store files because you can easily access the same files from multiple computers, such as from your MacBook and from an iMac. You can also easily share files on your iDisk and even provide a place for people to store files they want to share with you. Finally, because your iDisk is stored remotely, it's a great way to protect critical files because even if something really bad happens to your MacBook, the files continue to be available on your iDisk. Your iDisk is remote so it works a bit differently than the hard drive in your MacBook or an external hard drive to which the MacBook is connected, but the tools you need to work with it are built in to Mac OS X. You can also access your iDisk through the iDisk application in your MobileMe Web site.

Genius If you have an iPhone or iPod touch, you can install the iDisk application on it. Using this application, you can access your iDisk from your iPhone to view files, share them, and so on.

Configuring and managing your iDisk

There are two basic modes for an iDisk: unsynced or synced.

In the unsynced mode, you access the iDisk online, meaning that any files you move to or from the iDisk move across the Internet immediately. The benefit of this approach is that the iDisk doesn't take up any space on your MacBook's hard drive. The downside is that you have to be connected to the Internet to be able to access the iDisk, so if you are someplace where net access isn't available, you can't get to the files on your iDisk. If you want to store files there, you have to wait until you can connect and then manually move the files to the iDisk.

In the synced mode, a local copy of the iDisk resides on your MacBook's desktop. You move files to and from this local copy of the iDisk; the files aren't actually moved onto the online iDisk until it is synced with the local version (this can be done manually or automatically). This approach has a couple of benefits. One is that you can access the iDisk at any time because the local copy is always available. Another is that the speed of the iDisk is much faster because you are really just using your MacBook's hard drive instead of working over the Internet (the sync process takes place in the background so it doesn't interfere with your other tasks). The downside of this approach is that you also have to store all the files on the iDisk on your MacBook's hard drive. If you have plenty of hard drive space, this isn't a problem, but if you have a lot of large files on your iDisk and the space on your MacBook's hard drive is limited, you might not have enough space to have a local copy.

Your iDisk includes a Public folder, which is great for sharing files with other people. In addition to choosing the mode for your iDisk, you need to configure how the Public folder on your iDisk can be accessed. You can determine if other people can only read (copy) files from your Public folder or if they can read files from and write files to the Public folder. You can also determine if a password is needed to be able to access your Public folder.

You configure and manage your iDisk from the MobileMe pane of the System Preferences application as the following steps demonstrate:

1. **Open the MobileMe pane of the System Preferences application.**

2. **Click the iDisk tab.** At the top of the pane, you see a gauge showing how much of your iDisk space you are currently using; the green part of the bar represents the space being used. Immediately under the gauge, you see the total size of the iDisk, how much is being used, and how much is available (see figure 5.5).

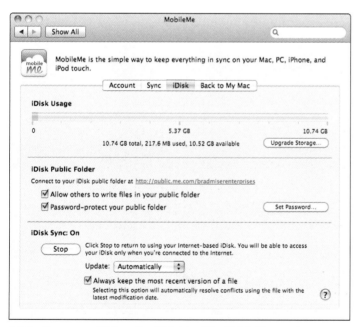

5.5 Configure your iDisk on the iDisk tab of the MobileMe pane.

3. **If you want people who access your iDisk to be able to store files in your Public folder, select the Allow others to write files in your public folder check box.**

Caution You should protect your Public folder with a password, especially if you allow others to write files to the disk. If you don't require a password and allow others to store files there, anyone who stumbles across your iDisk can store files there. That's not a good idea for a number of reasons, the most obvious of which is that you are paying for the space and want to keep control of the files posted there.

4. **To put a password on your Public folder, select the Password-protect your public folder check box.** The Password sheet appears.

5. **Type a password for the folder in the Password and Confirm fields.** Passwords must be between six and eight characters long and can't be the same as the password for your MobileMe account.

6. **Click OK.**

7. **To use your iDisk in the synced mode, click Start in the iDisk Sync section of the pane; if you don't want to sync your iDisk, skip the rest of these steps.** When you start the sync, a copy of your iDisk is made on your MacBook's hard drive.

8. **If you want the sync process to happen automatically, choose Automatically on the Update pop-up menu; if you want to manually sync the iDisk, choose Manually.**

9. **To always have the most recent version of a file synced, select the Always keep the most recent version of a file check box.** When your online and local iDisks are synced, selecting this option ensures that the newest version of a file is the one that is synced. If you don't select this option and the same file has more than one version, you're prompted to choose the version to keep. Your iDisk is ready to use.

Genius If the usage gauge shows that your iDisk is full or getting close to being full, move to the iDisk and delete files from it to free up more space. However, make sure you don't delete files that you use on your Web sites because removing files might have consequences you didn't intend. If you can't find files to remove and the disk is full, click Upgrade Storage on the Account Settings page to add more space to your iDisk.

Using your iDisk

Working with an iDisk is similar to using the hard drive in your MacBook. You can open it in any of the following ways:

- **Open a Finder window and click iDisk in the DEVICES section of the sidebar.**
- **On the Finder's menu bar, choose Go ⇨ iDisk ⇨ My iDisk.**
- **Press Shift+⌘+I.**

When you open your iDisk, you see its contents in the resulting Finder window, as shown in figure 5.6. These include a set of default folders similar to those in your Home folder, such as Documents, Movies, and Music. Like your Home folder, you can create new folders, move files around, create new files, and so on. In this respect, using an iDisk is just like using your MacBook's hard drive.

Sync button

Last sync

5.6 Using an iDisk is just like using your MacBook's hard drive — almost.

If you use the iDisk in the unsynced mode, files you copy to or from the iDisk move across the Internet. This can take some time, so don't expect the kind of response you get from your hard drive. If files are large, you see the Copy progress window on the screen when the file is moving to or from the iDisk; copying works in the background so you can just ignore the window. When the process is complete, the Copy window closes.

Note

The first time you sync an iDisk can take a long time, especially when large amounts of data are on the disk. Subsequent syncs are much faster because only files that have changed are involved. During the sync process, the Sync button rotates, and if the iDisk is selected, you see progress information in the status bar at the bottom of the Finder window.

If you use the iDisk in the synced mode, you see the Sync button next to its icon on the sidebar; you also see the time and date of the last synchronization at the bottom of the Finder window. To manually sync the disk, click the Sync button. Files on the local version are copied to the online version and vice versa until the two versions are duplicates of each other. If you selected the Automatic option, Mac OS X takes care of this for you, but you can manually sync the disks at any time by clicking the Sync button. Because with either option the files you work with are actually stored on your MacBook's hard drive, the speed when using your iDisk is the same as using your hard drive. The sync process happens in the background so you won't even notice it.

Sharing files on your iDisk

One of the best things about an iDisk is that you can use it to share files with people over the Internet. There are three ways to do this: using the iDisk Web application, using your Public folder, and sharing your entire iDisk.

When you share files with someone with the iDisk Web application, the application emails a link to the person with whom you are sharing the file. When the person receives the email, she can click the link to download the file you are sharing. So you can take care of notifying the recipient at the same time that you share the file.

Note

Most email systems have a file attachment size limit, usually 5 or 10MB. Using your iDisk to share files avoids this limitation because the emails people receive contain only a link to the files instead of the files themselves (as an attachment to email would).

To share files with someone via the iDisk Web application, perform the following steps:

1. **Place the file you want to share in the Public folder on your iDisk via either of the following options:**

Genius

To share more than one file at a time, compress them on the desktop by selecting the files, opening the contextual menu, and choosing the Compress X Items command, where X is the number of files you selected. Then move the resulting ZIP file to your Public folder to share it.

- **Open your iDisk's Public folder on your desktop and place the file you want to share in it.** If your iDisk is set to manually sync, sync the iDisk (which moves the file from your MacBook's hard drive onto your iDisk on your MobileMe Web site).

● **Log in to your MobileMe Web site and click the iDisk application button (the iDisk icon) to the left of the Account Settings button (see figure 5.7).** Select the Public folder on the left pane of the window. Click the Upload button (the upward-facing arrow on the left side of the iDisk toolbar in the top center of the window). Using the resulting Uploads dialog box, click Choose, move to and select the file you want to store in your Public folder, and click Select. The file is uploaded. When the process is complete, click Done.

Public folder   iDisk application   Upload button

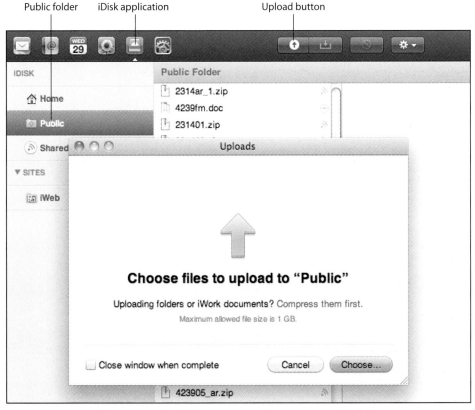

5.7 Use the iDisk application to upload files you want to share to your Public folder.

2. **Log in to your MobileMe Web site and click the iDisk application button.**

3. **Select the Public folder.**

4. **Select the file you want to share.**

5. **Click the Share File button.**

6. **In the resulting dialog box, type the email address in the top box; type multiple addresses separated by commas to share the file with more than one person at a time.**

129

Genius If the person with whom you are sharing the file has contact information stored in your MobileMe Web site's Contacts application (more on this later), the application tries to fill in the email address as you type it.

7. **Type a message that is sent along with the file in the lower box.**

8. **To set an expiration date on the file (after which the link you send no longer works), select the Link expires after check box, type a number, and choose days, weeks, or months on the pop-up menu.** (By default, sharing expires automatically after 30 days.)

9. **If you want to require the recipient to provide a password to download the file, select the Password-protect file check box and type the required password in the box.**

10. **Click Share (see figure 5.8).** An email containing a link to the shared file and your message is sent to the recipient.

11. **If you protected the file with a password in Step 9, provide the required password to the recipient.**

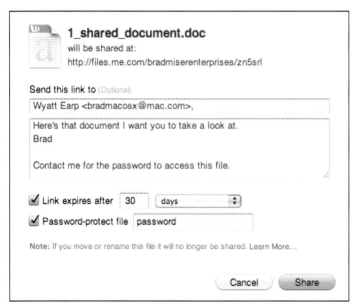

5.8 Sharing a file is as easy as completing this form.

As you learned earlier, the Public folder on your iDisk is also available on the Web; it can also be accessed directly from another Mac's desktop so someone can move files from or to your iDisk to share them. This method of file sharing has the benefit of not requiring a person to click a link for each file because he can open the Public folder and work with the files it contains. It is easier to work with and share multiple files because you are sharing a folder of files instead of sharing files individually.

To get started, place the files you want to share in the Public folder on your iDisk via either of the options described in Step 1 of the previous task.

People with whom you want to share the files can access them in either of the following ways:

 Using a Web browser to access the files. The person moves to public.me.com/ *membername*, where *membername* is your MobileMe member name. Your Public folder's Web page appears; if you set your Public folder to require a password, the visitor must provide "public" as the username and the password you created for your Public folder and then click OK to access the folder. The contents of the Public folder are shown (see figure 5.9). The visitor can download files by clicking their download buttons. If you configured your Public folder to allow visitors to upload files, the user can click the Upload button and then upload files to your folder. This is a great way to share files with others because anyone with a Web browser using any kind of computer can access the files you share.

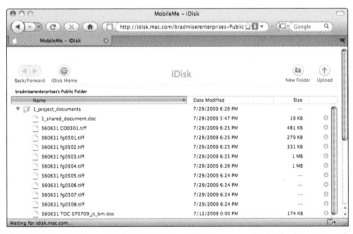

5.9 Working with your Public folder in a Web browser is similar to using a folder on your desktop.

Genius

If you allow visitors to your Public folder to have Write permission, they can create folders by clicking the New Folder button. Visitors can work with folders in the browser as you can in a Finder window in List view, such as collapsing or expanding their contents.

131

● **The person with whom you are sharing files uses a Mac.** He can mount your Public folder on his desktop and then access it from there as he would a folder stored on his computer. To so do, he chooses Go ➪ iDisk ➪ Other User's Public Folder. At the prompt, he types your MobileMe member name and clicks Connect. If you've protected your Public folder with a password, he types it and clicks Connect. Your Public folder appears on his sidebar, where he can open it and move files from the folder onto his desktop (see figure 5.10). Or if you have allowed Write permission, he can add files to the folder as well.

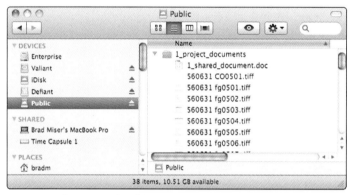

5.10 Here's the same Public folder as in figure 5.9, but now it is mounted on a Mac's desktop.

You can also share your entire iDisk with someone who uses a Mac. This enables that person to work with your iDisk as easily as you can.

Caution

When you provide access to your iDisk through this method, you must provide the person with whom you are sharing it your member name and password. This means the person has access to your iDisk *and* all the other resources your MobileMe account provides, including email, calendars, and so on. You should not share your MobileMe account with anyone unless you are positive that person can be trusted with your information.

The person to whom you want to grant access to your iDisk chooses Go ➪ iDisk ➪ Other User's iDisk. At the prompt, she types your member name and password and clicks Connect. Your iDisk is mounted on her desktop just as it is on yours and can be used in exactly the same ways (see figure 5.11).

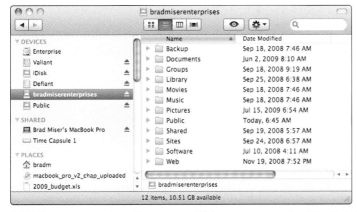

5.11 When you mount another person's iDisk on your computer, it is labeled with the person's member name.

Genius

A better way to share an entire iDisk is to upgrade your MobileMe account to a Family Pack. Then create a Family Member account and share that account's iDisk with the group of people you want to be able to access the same iDisk. This shields your primary MobileMe account while allowing you to share all the functionality an iDisk offers for sharing files. See my book *MobileMe for Small Business Portable Genius* (Wiley, 2009) for the details of using MobileMe with groups of people.

Synchronizing Data

One of the biggest benefits of MobileMe is that it provides you with a central, accessible location to store information known as the MobileMe cloud. When you store information in this cloud, it is accessible from anywhere via the Internet. This means you can keep various kinds of information synchronized between your MacBook and other devices, such as Macs, Windows PCs, iPhones, and iPod touches, which is very useful. For example, when you add a contact on your iPhone, that contact is automatically copied to the MobileMe cloud. Through the synchronization process, it is also copied to your Address Book on your MacBook.

The basic idea is that the MobileMe cloud becomes the single source where you store data, which can be accessed by multiple devices at the same time. You can also access the information stored in the MobileMe cloud directly through the applications on your MobileMe Web site (more on these later). The synchronization process ensures that each device has access to the same information.

The information you can keep in sync includes the following:

- Bookmarks
- Calendars
- Contacts
- Dashboard widgets
- Dock items
- Keychains
- Mail accounts
- Mail rules, signatures, and Smart Mailboxes
- Notes
- Preferences

In addition to selecting the kind of information you want to sync, you can also choose the direction in which information is synced, such as from MobileMe to a computer, from a computer to MobileMe, or in both directions. To configure synchronization, perform the following steps:

1. **Open the MobileMe pane of the System Preferences application and click the Sync tab (see figure 5.12).**

2. **Select the Synchronize with MobileMe check box.**

3. **On the pop-up menu, choose how you want syncs to occur.** Choose Manually to sync manually or choose a time, such as Every Hour, to sync at those times, or Automatically to have syncs performed automatically when data in either location changes.

4. **Select the check box next to each kind of data you want to include in the sync.**

5. **Click Sync Now.** The information you selected is copied onto MobileMe. If some of the information already exists, you see an alert.

6. **On the resulting dialog box's pop-up menu, choose how you want data to be synced.** For example, if you want the data on MobileMe to be merged with the information on your MacBook, choose Merge Information. Or you can choose to replace data on MobileMe with the computer's data or replace the data on the computer with MobileMe's data.

7. **Click Sync.** The sync process begins. As changes are made to data, you're notified about what's being done.

5.12 Use the Sync tab to choose the kind of information you want to synchronize.

8. **Click the Sync button to allow the sync to continue.**

9. **Repeat Step 8 at each prompt; you may have to do this several times.** When the process is complete, you see the time and date of the last sync at the bottom of the Sync tab.

You can repeat these steps on multiple Macs to synchronize all of them to the same set of data. You can also synchronize data with Windows PCs using the MobileMe control panel and iPhone/iPod touches. (Note that not all the data you can include in a MobileMe sync on a Mac can be synced with Windows PCs or iPhone/iPod touches.)

Genius

Using the MobileMe synchronization works great for data, but doesn't do anything for documents. However, your iDisk enables you to keep documents on different computers in sync. On each computer, set up your iDisk so that it is synced automatically and so it keeps the latest version of your documents. Store the documents you want to keep in sync on your iDisk. As you make changes to a document, those changes are saved to the iDisk. Because you access the same iDisk and its documents from any Mac, you can easily make sure you are using the same version of the document no matter which computer you use.

Using MobileMe Web Applications

Along with the MobileMe cloud, you've seen that your MobileMe account includes a Web site that provides applications you can use to access the information stored in your cloud. You also learned how you can use the iDisk Web application to store, organize, and share files. In this section, you find an overview of the other Web applications, along with some specific tasks to show you how useful these applications can be.

Using the MobileMe email application

Your MobileMe account includes a full-featured email account that you can use with Mac OS X's Mail or other email application. Your MobileMe email address is *membername*@me.com, where *membername* is your MobileMe member name. Using your MobileMe email with an email application is great, and you'll learn some tricks for the Mail application in Chapter 8. However, your MobileMe email is also easily accessible through the Mail application on your MobileMe Web site, which is great because that means you can work with your email from any computer with Internet access and a supported Web browser (including Windows computers).

Using the MobileMe Mail application is similar to using an email application, especially Mac OS X's Mail application, on a computer. Log in to your MobileMe Web site and click the Mail button. If you have used other email applications, you'll have no problem using the MobileMe Mail application (see figure 5.13).

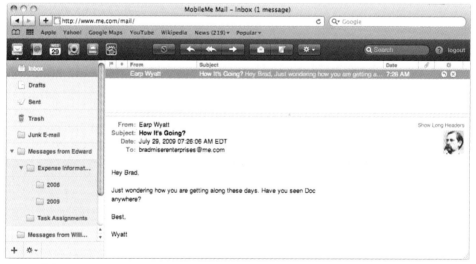

5.13 MobileMe's Mail application is similar to Mail on the Mac except you can access it through a Web browser.

While the basics of using MobileMe Web email are pretty straightforward, there are a lot of ways to customize how it works for you using the not-so-obvious preferences. Check them out:

1. **Open the Action pop-up menu (the gear icon) and choose Preferences.** The Preferences window opens (see figure 5.14).

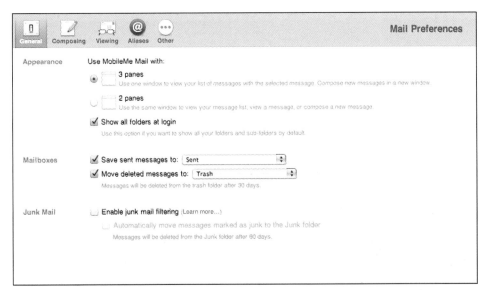

5.14 If you use MobileMe's Mail application regularly, take some time to configure its preferences to suit yours.

2. **Configure the following settings on the General tab:**

   • **Appearance.** These options enable you to determine the appearance of the Mail page, including the number of panes used and whether all folders are shown when you log in.

   • **Mailboxes.** Use these check boxes and pop-up menus to determine how sent and deleted messages are stored. If you want to conserve the space used to store email, deselect the Move deleted messages to check box; when you delete messages, they are removed from your account immediately so that they don't consume disk space.

   • **Junk Mail.** You can use the junk mail filter to try to cut back on the amount of spam you have to deal with.

3. **Configure the following settings on the Composing tab:**

   • **Composing.** If you want the original message to be quoted when you reply, which is always a good idea, select the Quote original message when replying check box. The other important option is to enable spell-checking by selecting the Check spelling before message is sent check box and then choosing the default dictionary you want to use.

❋ **Identity.** Here you can type the name you want to be shown in the From field on email you send; the default is the name you typed for your MobileMe account. To use a signature, select the Add signature to your mail check box and type the signature you want to use in the text box.

4. **Configure the following settings on the Viewing tab:**

❋ **Inbox and Folders.** Choose how many messages you want to be shown per page and what kind of previews you want to see for each message in the Inbox (Short, Long, or No); if you choose No, you only see the message subjects.

❋ **Message Contents.** Determine how HTML email is handled and whether long or short headers are shown at the top of messages.

5. **Skip over the Aliases tab for now; you'll learn about that shortly.**

6. **Configure the following settings on the Other tab:**

❋ **External Account.** If you have another email account that uses POP (Post Office Protocol, and no, I didn't make that up) and you want to be able to check email from that account using the MobileMe Mail application, select the Check mail from an external POP account check box and type the account's information in the resulting boxes. You can only add one account to the Mail application.

❋ **Forwarding.** Use these options to forward your MobileMe email. Select the Forward my email to another email account check box and type the address to which you want email forwarded. Select the middle check box if you want to keep forwarded messages in your MobileMe email Inbox. Use the bottom check box and text box to set up an automated reply to an email you receive.

7. **Click Save.** The changes take effect immediately.

Note

The Preferences dialog box is sized based on the size of the Web browser window; the Save button is at the very bottom of the dialog box. If you don't see the Save button, make the browser window larger until you do see it.

Email aliases are a great tool in the fight against spam or as a way to create custom email addresses. You can create aliases that point to your real MobileMe email address. When you shop, participate in forums, or do other activity, provide one of your alias addresses. If that address gets spammed, you can simply delete it and create another one. Or, you might want to create an email address for a specific purpose (such as being able to receive email from long-dead historical figures for a book you are writing). For example, if you are writing a book called *MacBook Portable Genius*, you can create an alias I_Love_MacBook@me.com to show your preference in computers.

Creating email aliases is easy:

Note   You have to be using a full (paid-for) MobileMe account to be able to create aliases.

1. **Click the Aliases tab of the Mail Preferences window.**
2. **Click Add New Alias.** The alias creation tools appear.
3. **Type the alias, which is everything before the "@" in the email address.** The alias must be between 3 and 20 characters and can't have unusual symbols. If you try to use something you can't, you see an error message explaining the problem.
4. **Type the name you want to appear in the From field when you send email using this alias.**
5. **Choose the color used to indicate email sent to this alias.**
6. **Click Create.** The email alias is checked. If it meets the requirements and is not being used already, it is created (see figure 5.15). If not, you have to change it until it does meet the rules and is not being used.
7. **Repeat Steps 1 through 6 until you've created all your aliases.** You can have up to five aliases.
8. **Click Save.**

Genius   Use the Active check box to turn aliases off or on. When active, email sent to the alias is delivered to it. When inactive, email sent to the alias bounces. If you receive some spam at an alias that you don't want to delete, disable it to stop the spam. When you want to use it, make it active and then disable it again when you're done with it.

5.15 Your aliases can be just about anything you want them to be.

You can provide an email alias just like you provided your real email address, such as when you are making a purchase or registering on a forum.

You can also send email using the alias:

1. **Create a new email message as usual.**

2. **On the Account pop-up menu, choose the alias that you want the message to be from (see figure 5.16).**

3. **Complete and send the message.** The alias is associated with the message so if the recipient replies to it, the reply is sent to the alias.

5.16 Pick an alias, any alias.

Using the MobileMe Contacts application

The MobileMe Contacts application enables you to access your contacts via a Web browser. This application is similar to using Mac OS X's Address Book application. Contacts appear in groups in the far-left pane (All shows all the contacts you have). When you select a group, you see the contacts it contains in the center pane. You can search for contacts using the Search bar at the top of the window or browse your contacts using the groups. When you select a contact in the center pane, its details appear in the right pane of the window (see figure 5.17).

5.17 Using the MobileMe Contacts application enables you to access your contact information via the Web.

When a contact's details are in blue, you can click them to take the related action. When you click an email address, a new message is created and addressed to that contact. If you click a URL, a new browser window opens and takes you to that address.

Genius

In any of the MobileMe applications, if you can't see all the information on the screen, click the browser window's Maximize button. Scroll bars appear so you can scroll the entire window's contents.

Using the MobileMe Calendar application

Use the Calendar application to view your own calendars along with those to which you've sub-scribed in iCal (see Chapter 16). Like other calendar applications, you can view your information by day, week, or month. If you open the Action pop-up menu and choose Show To Dos, you can also track your tasks.

Using the MobileMe Gallery application

The Gallery enables you to post photos and movies online where they can be viewed via a Web browser. The Gallery application enables you to post photos and create albums for them and to manage the albums you post. You can access your Gallery Web site by clicking its URL, which is shown at the top of the window when you select the Gallery application.

The Gallery is designed to work with iPhoto so that you can easily post your iPhoto photos and albums with a couple of mouse-clicks. In most cases, you won't need to use the Gallery application directly via your MobileMe Web site because iPhoto's tools are more powerful and you have direct access to your photos there. Still, you can use the MobileMe Gallery application to make tweaks to your posted photo sites when you don't have access to your iPhoto application.

Note

For detailed information about using iPhoto with MobileMe, see *iPhoto '09 Portable Genius* (Wiley, 2009).

Using MobileMe to host a Web site

While it isn't a specific application, you can use MobileMe to host a Web site that you create with iWeb or other applications. iWeb is designed to work seamlessly with MobileMe so that you can publish and maintain your Web sites easily and quickly.

The URL for your default Web site is: http://web.me.com/*membername*, where *membername* is your MobileMe member name. This is pretty good, but if you register your own domain name, you can publish your Web site under your personal domain instead. Here's how:

1. **Move to the Accounts Settings application by logging in to your MobileMe account, clicking the Accounts button, and typing your password.**

2. **Click the Personal Domain option.**

3. **Click Add Domain.**

4. **Type your personal domain in both fields.**

5. **Click Continue.** Your account is updated to use your personal domain.

6. **Click Done.** In the personal domain window, you see the domain you typed.

After you configure your personal domain, it can take a few hours before it becomes active. When it does, visitors can move to your MobileMe Web site by typing your personal domain URL instead of the default MobileMe domain.

Genius

To host a Web site you've created with another application (not iWeb), create the site on your desktop and upload its files to the Sites folder of your iDisk.

Using MobileMe with an iPhone or iPod Touch

You can configure an iPhone or iPod touch to access your MobileMe account. This enables you to wirelessly sync your email, contacts, calendars, and bookmarks with an iPhone via a Wi-Fi or cellular data connection or an iPod touch via a Wi-Fi network. This enables you to access the same information on your iPhone as on your MacBook.

To configure your MobileMe account, tap Settings, then tap Mail, Contacts, Calendars. Tap Add Account and then tap MobileMe. Enter your MobileMe account information and tap Save. The account is created on your iPhone or iPod touch. Then choose which information you want to sync on the iPhone. The options are: Mail, Calendars, Contacts, or Bookmarks. Finally, configure Push by tapping Fetch New Data on the Mail, Calendars, Contacts screen if you want any updates to your synced information to be pushed onto your iPhone automatically.

How Can I Manage Contact Information?

The Mac OS X Address Book enables you to store contact information for people and organizations. While that's useful in itself, it's just the beginning. You can access and use your contact information in other applications, such as Mail, Safari, and iChat, to make what you want to do easier and faster. You can also act on information stored in Address Book directly, such as opening a Web page that shows a map of an address. Naturally, you'll also want to be able to access your contacts from your iPhone; synchronizing contacts between Address Book and an iPhone is a snap.

Adding Contact Information to Address Book

Address Book uses an address card model, which I suppose originated with the Rolodex way back in the analog era. Each contact, be it a person or an organization, is represented by a card containing contact information. Address Book cards are virtual (vCards), making them flexible because you can store a variety of information on each card; you can also store different information for various contacts.

In fact, each card in Address Book can hold an unlimited number of physical addresses, phone numbers, email addresses, dates, notes, and URL addresses. Because vCards are flexible, you don't have to include each kind of information for every contact; you include only the information that you have. Address Book only displays fields that have data in them so your cards aren't cluttered with a lot of empty spaces.

Configuring the card template

When you create a new card, it is based on Address Book's card template, which determines the data fields that are on the card. You can change the information included on the template and, thus, on cards you create. You should configure the template before you start creating cards so your cards have the specific information you want them to include.

1. **Open the Address Book Preferences dialog box.**

2. **Click Template (see figure 6.1).**

3. **Modify the template by doing any of the following:**

   - Remove fields you don't want on the template by clicking the Delete button.

   - Add more fields of an existing type by clicking the Add (+) button next to that type. Choose the label for the new field on the pop-up menu to the left of the new field.

6.1 Configure the Address Book template so it contains the fields you want on cards you create.

○ Add types of fields that don't appear on the template by opening the Add Field pop-up menu at the top of the dialog box and choosing the type you want to add to the template. Fields that are already on the template are marked with a check mark and are grayed out.

4. **Close the Preferences dialog box.** New cards you create will have fields on the template.

Genius

You can override the template fields on any card by adding new fields. The new field is added to only the current card. To add a new field to cards you create in the future, add it to the template instead.

Creating a contact manually

You can create address cards for contacts you want to add to Address Book manually. Use the following steps to guide you.

1. **Open the Address Book application (see figure 6.2).** The Group pane shows the groups that have been created in the application: All contains all your cards, Directories is used with contact information servers, and Last Import shows the information you most recently imported. The Name pane shows the cards in the selected group, and the Card pane shows the details for the card selected in the Name pane.

2. **Click the Add (+) button at the bottom of the Name column.** A new, empty card based on the template appears in the Card pane.

3. **Type the contact's first name, last name, and company (if applicable).**

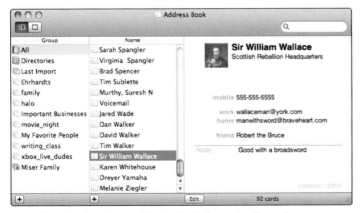

6.2 Address Book cards provide detailed information for each contact.

Note

If the card is for a company, select the Company check box and type the company name; first and last name information is optional for companies.

4. **Click the pop-up menu next to a field (such as work), select the type of contact information you want to enter, and type the information for that field.** For example, select mobile on the pop-up menu next to a Phone field and type a mobile phone number.

5. **To remove a field from the card, click its Delete button.**

Genius

If the information you want to enter isn't available on the pop-up menu, open it and choose Custom. Type the label for the field you want to add and click OK. You return to the card and the custom label appears on the card. Type the information for that field to add the custom field to the card.

6. **To add another field of the same type to a card, click the Add (+) button next to a field of the type you want to add (this appears when you've filled in all the empty fields of a specific type, such as email addresses).** A new field appears, and you can select its type and enter the appropriate information.

Note

When you select a data type, Address Book automatically creates a field in the appropriate format, such as for phone numbers when you select mobile.

7. **To add an image to the card, use one of the following options:**

    ○ Drag an image file from the desktop and drop it onto the Image well located immediately to the left of the name fields.

Genius

To apply special effects to a contact's image, click the Effects button located to the right of the Camera button on the Image sheet. The Effects dialog box appears. Page through the dialog box to preview effects and click the effect you want to apply to the image.

- Double-click the Image well, and the Image sheet appears, allowing you to browse for an image file.

- Double-click the Image well, and the Image sheet appears. Take a picture with the MacBook's camera.

8. **Drag the slider to the left to make the image smaller or drag it to the right to make it larger.**

9. **Drag the image around within the image box until the part of the image you want to be displayed is contained in the box (see figure 6.3).**

10. **Click Set.** You return to the card and the image is stored on the card.

11. **Click Edit.** The card is saved (see figure 6.4).

6.3 You can configure images for contacts; these images appear when you receive email as well as calls from the contact on an iPhone.

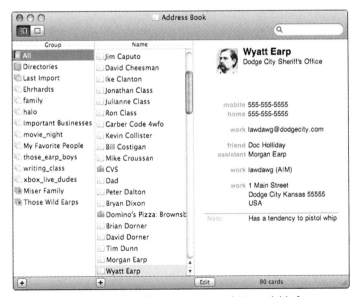

6.4 After you complete the information on a card, it's available for you to refer to or use (such as to send an email).

Importing vCards

Creating vCards manually is a lot of fun and all, but it's a lot easier to import a vCard that you receive from someone else. One of the most common ways to receive vCards is through email as attachments; vCard files have .vcf as their filename extension. Just drag the vCard from the email onto your desktop.

To add a vCard to Address Book, drag the vCard file from the desktop and drop it onto the Address Book window. Click Add in the resulting sheet, and the card is added to your Address Book. You can edit and use cards created from vCards just like cards you create manually.

Genius

If you have a MobileMe account, it's easy to keep your Address Book in sync on all your devices so that current contact information is available for you, regardless of the devices on which you created the card. See Chapter 5 for details.

Adding contact information from email

Many applications that involve contact information allow you to add that information to your Address Book. When you receive email in Mail, you can add the sender's name and email address to Address Book using the following steps:

1. **Move the pointer over the address shown next to From, Cc, or Bcc.**
2. **When the address becomes highlighted, click the trackpad button to open the action menu.**
3. **Choose Add to Address Book.** A new card is created with as much information as Address Book can extract, usually the first and last name along with the email address.
4. **Use Address Book to edit the card such as to add other information to it.**

Editing cards

As time passes, contact information changes, and you might want to edit or add more information to existing cards. With Address Book, editing your cards is very similar to creating them in the first place.

1. **Select the card you want to edit in the Name pane.**
2. **Click Edit.** All the current fields become editable, and the empty fields that were on the template when the card was created appear.
3. **Use the edit tools to make changes to the card.**
4. **Click Edit.** Your changes are saved.

Your Address Card

One of the most important cards in Address Book is your own. When you first started your MacBook and worked through the registration process, the information you entered was added to a card in Address Book. This card identifies your contact information in various places, including the Safari AutoFill feature that enables you to quickly complete Web forms. You should review and update your card as needed so that its information is current.

To jump to your card, choose Card ⇨ Go To My Card. Your card is selected in the Name pane and appears in the Card pane; notice that your card is the only one in the Name pane with the Silhouette icon and the text label "me." Review the information on your card and make any changes necessary using the previous steps.

You can make any card your card by selecting it and then choosing Card ⇨ Make This My Card. And you can send your card to others as a vCard by dragging it from the Name list onto your desktop. A vCard is created, with your name as its filename. You can attach that file to email.

Working with Cards

After your Address Book is full of cards, you start to get a lot of benefits from the work you've done. You can browse your contact information or search for specific information. You can also change the way you see contact information.

Browsing for cards

Unless you have many, many cards in Address Book, browsing can often be the fastest way to find cards that you want to use. When you browse for contact information, you can usually get to specific cards without typing any information, making the process fast and easy.

Setting format and sort preferences

Make sure Address Book displays names and sorts cards according to your preferences. Follow these steps:

1. **Choose Address Book ⇨ Preferences.**

2. **Click the General tab (see figure 6.5).**

3. **In the Show first name section, click Before last name if you want names to be shown as first name then last name, or click Following last name if you prefer the last name-first name format.**

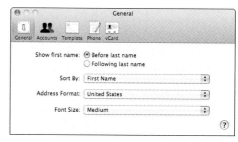

4. **On the Sort By pop-up menu, choose Last Name to have cards sorted by last name, or First Name to sort the Name pane by first name.**

6.5 Configure Address Book to display the first name first (or second).

5. **On the Address Format menu, choose the country whose formatting you want to be used for physical addresses.**

6. **On the Font Size menu, choose the relative size of the font used for card information.**

7. **Click the Phone tab.**

8. **Use the check box and menus to configure if and how Address Book automatically formats phone numbers you enter.**

9. **Close the Preferences dialog box.**

Genius

You can copy the URL to a map for an address so that you can email it to someone else or add it to a document. Find the card containing the address you want to map out. Perform a secondary click on the address. Choose Copy URL of map. The URL for the map is created and copied to the Clipboard. Move to a document, such as an email message, and paste the URL.

Browsing for cards with three panes

When Address Book is displaying its three panes, you can browse for cards by doing the following:

1. **In the Group pane, select the group that you want to browse; to browse all your contacts, click All.**

2. **Use the scroll bar in the Name pane to browse up and down the list of cards.**

3. **Select the card that you want to use.** The card you selected displays in the Card pane.

Browsing for cards with one pane

Address Book has a one-pane mode that shows only the Card pane. You can browse your contacts using the one-pane view, as you can see in the following steps:

1. **Choose View ⇨ Card Only.** The Group and Name panes are hidden, and you see only cards (see figure 6.6).

2. **Click the right-facing arrow at the bottom of the window or press the down-arrow key to browse down one card, or click the left-facing arrow or press the up-facing arrow to browse up one card, until you see the card you want to work with.**

Searching for cards

When you search for cards in Address Book, it searches all the fields on all your cards simultaneously. To search for cards, perform these steps:

1. **Select the group that you want to search; to search all your contacts, click All.** All the cards in the selected group appear in the Name pane.

6.6 You can make the Address Book window more compact by choosing the Card Only view.

2. **Type search text in the Search box.** As you type, Address Book starts searching all the fields in the cards; as it finds matches, it shows you the matching cards in the Name pane.

3. **Continue typing in the Search box until the card in which you are interested appears in the Name pane.**

4. **Select the card that you want to use (see figure 6.7).**

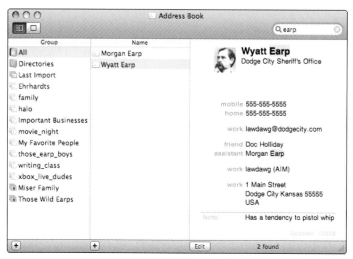

6.7 When you search, Address Book highlights the search term on each card that it finds.

To end a search, click the Clear button, which is the x within the gray circle in the Search bar. All the cards in the selected group appear again.

Genius

To see multiple cards at the same time, move to the first card you want to see and choose Card ➪ Open in Separate Window (or press ⌘+I). The card opens in its own window. Move to the next card and do the same thing. You can open as many cards as you want, with each being in an independent window.

Organizing Cards with Groups

Groups are useful because you can do one action and it will affect all the cards in that group. For example, you can create a group containing family members whom you regularly email. Then you can address a message to the one group, instead of addressing each person individually.

There are two kinds of groups in Address Book. Manual groups are those you create and then manually place cards in. Smart Groups are a collection of criteria; Address Book places cards into Smart Groups automatically, based on their criteria.

Creating groups manually

To create a group, follow these steps:

1. **Click the Add (+) button located at the bottom of the Group pane.** A new group appears in the Group pane with its name ready to be edited.

2. **Type the name of the group and press Return.** You can name a group anything you want.

3. **Browse or search for the first card you want to add to the group.**

4. **Drag the card from the Name pane and drop it onto the group to which you want to add it (see figure 6.8).**

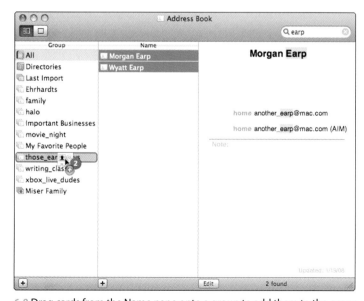

6.8 Drag cards from the Name pane onto a group to add them to the group.

Creating Smart Groups

Smart Groups are also collections of cards, but unlike regular groups, you don't have to manually add each card to the group. Instead, you define criteria for the cards you want to be included in the Smart Group, and Address Book automatically adds the appropriate cards. For example, suppose you want a group for everyone with the same last name; you can simply create a Smart Group with that criterion, and Address Book adds all the people with that last name to the group automatically.

Creating a Smart Group is quite different from creating a regular group, as you can see in the following steps:

1. **Choose File ⇨ New Smart Group.** The New Smart Group sheet appears (see figure 6.9).

2. **Type the name of the group.**

3. **Choose the first field you want to include in the criteria on the first pop-up menu, which is Card by default.** For example, to base a criterion on name, choose Name.

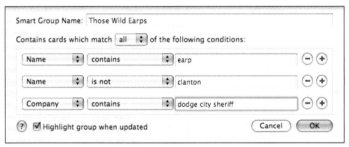

6.9 This Smart Group includes all my contacts named "earp" whose company contains "dodge city sheriff" and whose name is not "clanton."

4. **Choose how you want the information you enter to be included on the center pop-up menu.** Going back to the Name example, the options on the center menu include the following: contains, does not contain, is, is not, and so on.

5. **Type the information that you want to be part of the criterion in the empty fields.** If you selected Name and contains on the pop-up menus, type the name you want the criterion to find.

6. **Click the Add (+) button at the end of the criterion to add another criterion to the group.**

7. **If the group has at least two criteria, choose all on the top pop-up menu if all of the criteria must be met for a card to be included in the group, or choose any if only one of them does.**

8. **If you want the group to be highlighted when it changes, select the Highlight group when updated check box.** Smart Groups are dynamic, meaning that when a new card is added that meets the group's conditions or a current card changes so that it does, the card is automatically added to the group. Likewise, if a card's information changes so that it no longer fits into the group, it is removed automatically. If you select this check box, the group is highlighted any time the cards that it contains change.

9. **Click OK.** The Smart Group is created and all the cards that meet the criteria you defined are added to it automatically.

Genius

Another way to create a group is to select the cards you want to place in the group. Choose File ➪ New Group From Selection. A new group is created and the cards you selected are placed in it; type its name and press Return to complete the group.

Changing groups

You'll probably want to change your groups over time. The following might be helpful:

- To add cards to a manual group, drag them onto it.

- To remove cards from a manual group, select the group, select the card you want to remove from it, and press the Delete key. Click Remove from Group. The card is removed from the group, but continues to be in Address Book.

- To change a Smart Group, select it and choose Edit ➪ Edit Smart Group. Then change the criteria it uses, and the cards contained in the group are changed automatically.

- To delete a group, select it, press the Delete key, and confirm it at the prompt.

Genius

You can easily search for information related to any card on your MacBook. Select the card for which you want to search on your MacBook. Hold the Ctrl key down and click the card. Choose Spotlight "*cardname*," where *cardname* is the name of the card you selected. A search is performed and a Finder window appears showing the results. Double-click any of the results to see the details of the found item.

Synchronizing Contact Information with an iPhone or iPod Touch

If you have an iPhone or iPod touch, you'll want to keep your contact information on your device in sync with your Address Book on your computer. You can do this using iTunes or MobileMe. The advantage to using iTunes is that you don't need to spend any money to get a MobileMe account and you can synchronize your contact information when you sync your audio, video, applications, and other content. The benefit of using MobileMe is that your contact information can be synced wirelessly and automatically.

Synchronizing via iTunes

You can easily move your contact information from Address Book onto your iPhone or iPod touch by synchronizing it. Here's how:

1. **Connect the iPhone or iPod touch to your MacBook.** iTunes opens if it's not open already.

2. **Select the iPhone or iPod touch on the iTunes source list (see figure 6.10).**

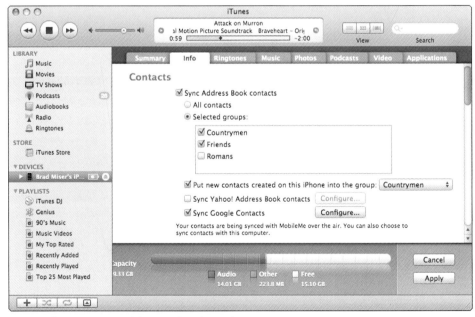

6.10 Synchronizing your Address Book with an iPhone is a great way to ensure that your contact information is always available to you.

3. **Click the Info tab.**

4. **Select the Sync Address Book contacts check box.**

5. **Select either All contacts or Selected groups to determine which contacts are synced.**

6. **If you choose Selected groups, select the check box for each group whose information you want to include in the sync.**

7. **If you want contacts you create on the iPhone or iPod touch to be placed within a specific group in Address Book, select the Put new contacts created on this iPhone into the group check box and choose the group on the pop-up menu.**

8. **If you use Yahoo! Address Book or Google Contacts and want to sync those contacts, select the related Sync check box and log in to your account at the prompt.**

9. **Scroll down the screen until you see the Advanced section.**

10. **If you want the contact information on the iPhone or iPod touch to be replaced by your contacts in Address Book the next time it is synced, select the Contacts check box.** If you don't select this check box, the contact information on the iPhone is merged with your Address Book information.

11. **Click Apply.** The changes you made are saved and the contact information on the iPhone or iPod touch is synced.

Synchronizing via MobileMe

Syncing your contact information with MobileMe is wireless and you can set how frequently information is updated. Changes you make on the iPhone or iPod touch are moved back to the MobileMe cloud; if your MacBook is set to synchronize through MobileMe, too, it receives those changes during the next sync (see Chapter 5 for more information).

To configure an iPhone or iPod touch for MobileMe syncing, perform the following steps:

1. **On the iPhone or iPod touch, tap Settings to open the Settings application.**

2. **Tap Mail, Contacts, Calendars.**

3. **Tap Add Account and then tap MobileMe.**

4. **Enter your name, your MobileMe member email address, your MobileMe password, a description of the account, and then tap Save (see figure 6.11).**

5. **Tap OFF next to Contacts and, if required, indicate if you want the current contact information to be deleted or kept and if you want the existing contacts on your iPhone or iPod touch to be merged with the contacts in your MobileMe cloud.** Contact syncing starts and the Contacts status becomes ON.

6. **Configure Calendar and Bookmark syncing in the same way.**

7. **Tap Done.**

8. **Tap Fetch New Data.**

9. **If you want changes to data on the MobileMe cloud or on the iPhone or iPod touch to be transferred immediately, enable Push by setting its status to ON.**

10. **Set the time interval at which the iPhone or iPod touch should check for new data or transfer its changed data**

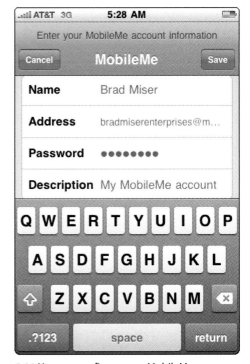

6.11 You can configure your MobileMe on an iPhone to have access to your contacts.

by fetching; tap Manually if you only want to get information on your command.

Genius

You can configure different MobileMe sync options for email, calendars, and contacts by moving to the Fetch New Data screen and tapping Advanced. Then tap the Mail part of your account and tap Push, Fetch, or Manual. Do the same for the Contacts, Calendars part of your account. For example, you might want to set Push for your email because it changes more quickly, and have calendar and contact updates moved through Fetch.

Printing from Address Book

Address Book includes powerful printing functions that you can use to print mailing labels, envelopes, lists, and a pocket address book. You can print each of these using similar steps. Because printing envelopes is the feature I find the most useful, I've used printing an envelope using a color laser printer as an example in the following steps:

Genius

You can use Address Book information to create a mailing label in another application. Find a card containing the address for which you want a mailing label. Hold the Ctrl key down and click the address you want to use. Choose Copy mailing label. Open the application you use to print envelopes or labels. If the address isn't inserted automatically, choose Edit ⇨ Paste. When the address is in the application, use its printing feature to print the envelope or label.

1. **Select the cards for which you want to print envelopes.**

2. **Choose File ⇨ Print.** The Print dialog box appears, as shown in figure 6.12.

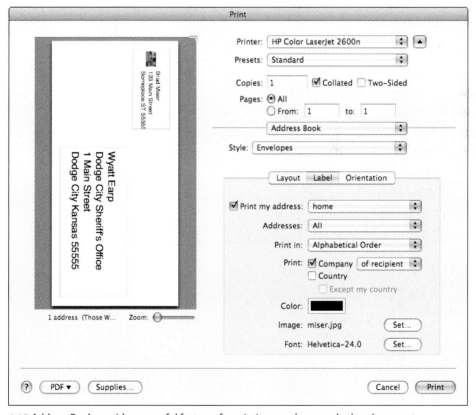

6.12 Address Book provides powerful features for printing envelopes and other documents.

3. **Expand the dialog box so that you can see all its options by clicking the downward-facing triangle next to the Printer pop-up menu.** The top half of the dialog box contains printer controls, while everything underneath the Address Book pop-up menu is used to configure what and how you are going to print.

4. **On the Style pop-up menu, choose Envelopes.**

5. **Click the Label tab if it isn't selected already.**

6. **If you want to include your return address, select the Print my address check box.**

7. **On the Addresses pop-up menu, choose All if you want to have an envelope for each of the addresses for each contact, or choose the specific address that you want to be used if you want to print only one envelope per contact.**

8. **Use the Print in pop-up menu to choose the order in which the envelopes are printed.** You can choose alphabetical order or order them by postal code. This is important if you've created a form letter so that the envelopes and letters are printed in the same order.

9. **To set the color of the text, click the Color button and use the Color Selector to choose the text color.**

10. **To include an image in your return address, click the upper Set button and use the resulting dialog box to move to and select an image.**

11. **To set the font used, click the lower Set button.** The return and delivery addresses use the same font, but the size you set is only for the delivery address. The return address is scaled according to the size of the delivery address font.

12. **Configure the printer settings as needed and click Print.**

Genius

You can use the Layout tab to change the layout for different kinds of envelopes. Use the Orientation tab to change how the envelope feeds into the printer.

Sharing Your Address Book

You can share your Address Book with people who use MobileMe. Open the Address Book Preferences. Click the Sharing tab. Select the Share your address book check box. Click the Add button, and select the other MobileMe users with whom you want to share your Address Book. Click the Send Invitation button to let people know they can access your contact information.

How Can I Go Beyond Email Basics with Mail?

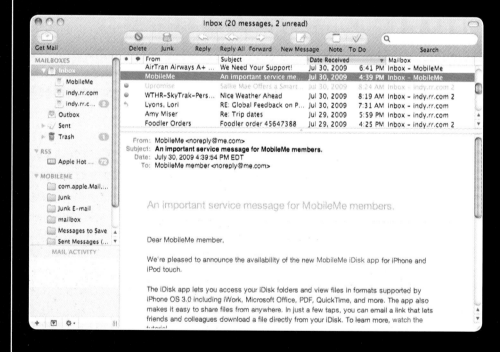

Email just might be one of the most powerful and convenient forms of communication ever. Okay, that might be a bit dramatic, but email is definitely convenient for both sender and receiver because it can be sent and read according to their schedules. And email doesn't interrupt people; it waits patiently in their Inboxes until they have a chance to get to it. The Mac OS X Mail application is quite powerful, and you've probably already used it to send and receive email. This chapter builds on those basic skills to show you how to go farther with your email in Mail.

Configuring Email Accounts

One of Mail's benefits is that you can configure many email accounts in it and easily work with all or just one of those accounts at any point in time. There are many kinds of email accounts with which Mail can work, including the following:

● **MobileMe.** If you have a MobileMe account, you also have a MobileMe email account. This is convenient because you can use Mail to access your email, or you can use the MobileMe Web site to work with it almost as easily (see figure 7.1).

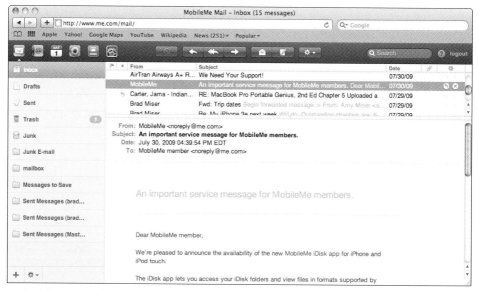

7.1 A MobileMe email account has a lot of benefits, including being able to access your email within Mail or on the Web.

● **POP.** Post Office Protocol accounts are one of the most common types provided by many Internet service providers and other organizations that provide email services. POP is a client-based protocol, meaning that email is typically downloaded to the computer on which it is read and removed from the email server (most include an option to leave email on the server). Under POP, the client is the authoritative source of email for an account.

● **IMAP.** Internet Message Access Protocol is a newer email protocol. It is primarily a server-based protocol, meaning that email is usually left on the server while it is read, and the server itself is the authoritative source of email for an account.

● **Exchange.** Microsoft Exchange Server technology is dominant in the business world for managing email.

While there are technical differences among these kinds of accounts, those are seldom important in the email activities that you perform. The differences show up primarily in how you configure Mail to work with the various types of accounts.

There are a number of attributes that you need to know about in order to configure an email account in Mail. These vary from account type to account type, but the following attributes are common:

- **Email address.** You often can create the initial part of the address, but the domain (everything after the @) comes from the provider.

- **Incoming mail server address.** Mail that you receive is delivered through an incoming mail server.

- **Username.** This is usually everything before the @ in your email address.

- **Password.** Sometimes you will have two: one for the incoming mail server and one for the outgoing mail server.

- **Outgoing mail server address.** To send email, you need to configure the outgoing mail server through which it will be sent.

- **User authentication.** To configure an authenticated account, you need a username and password for the authentication. Accounts use different kinds of authentication; you don't need to understand the technical details, you just need to know which specific kinds of authentication your accounts use so you can configure them correctly.

When you obtain an email account, you receive information for each of the attributes that you need to configure to be able to work with that account.

Configuring a MobileMe email account

One of the benefits of MobileMe email is that a MobileMe email account is configured automatically when you register your account in the MobileMe pane of the System Preferences application. However, just in case you ever need to reconfigure it for some reason, perform the following steps to set up MobileMe email:

1. **Launch Mail and open Preferences.**

2. **Click the Accounts tab.** In the list on the left side of the Accounts pane are currently configured accounts. When you select an account on this list, the tools you use to work with the account are shown in the right part of the pane.

3. **Click the Add (+) button located at the bottom of the list.** The Add Account sheet appears.

4. **Type your name in the Full Name field.** This is the name that is shown as the From name on email that you send. It defaults to be the name you entered when you first started your MacBook, but you can change it to something else if you want.

5. **Type the email address for the account in the Email Address field.**

6. **Type the password for the account in the Password field.**

7. **Click Create.** Mail logs in to your MobileMe account. If successful, the sheet closes and you see the account on the Accounts list. It is selected and you see its configuration information in the right pane of the window (see figure 7.2). You can use the account as is, or you can configure more fully by continuing with these steps.

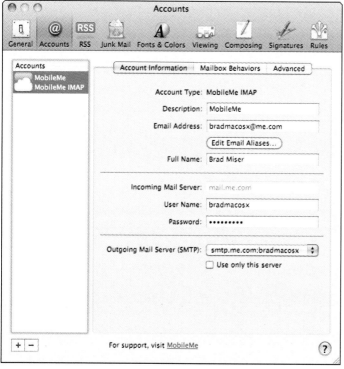

7.2 Doing the basic configuration of a MobileMe account requires you to only type your name, member name, and password.

Note

One of the best features of a MobileMe account is that you can configure and use aliases. If you click the Edit Email Aliases button, you move to your MobileMe Web site where you can configure your aliases. See Chapter 5 for more information about aliases.

8. **Change the default description, which is MobileMe, to something more meaningful, such as your email address.** This is especially useful if you have multiple accounts of the same type because the description identifies the account in several places within Mail.

9. **Click the Mailbox Behaviors tab (see figure 7.3).**

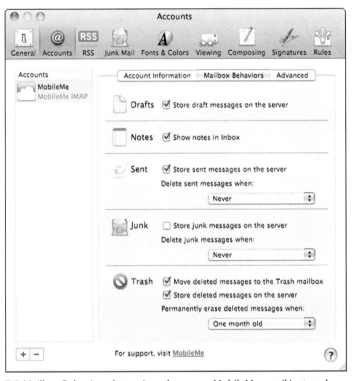

7.3 Mailbox Behaviors determine where your MobileMe email is stored.

10. **Select the Store check boxes to store email on the MobileMe server or deselect them to store email on your MacBook.** For example, if you select the Store draft messages on the server check box, messages saved in the Draft state are stored online where you can access them from any device using the email account; if this is unchecked, these messages are only stored on your MacBook. The reason this is significant is that you are allotted a specific amount of online space so you want to make sure you use it most efficiently.

11. **Use the pop-up menus to determine when Mail deletes or permanently erases sent, junk, or trash messages.** The longer the time set is, the longer the messages are available to you, but the more storage space they require.

12. Use the Trash check boxes to determine what Mail does with messages you delete.

13. Click the Advanced tab (see figure 7.4).

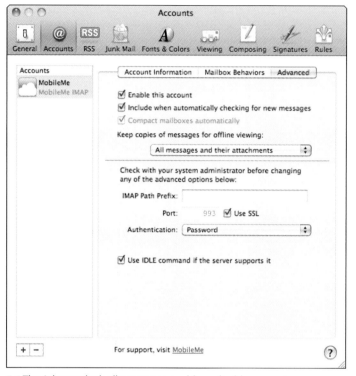

7.4 The Advanced tab allows you to enable or disable accounts.

14. **To temporarily stop working with the account, deselect the Enable this account check box; select it to resume using the account.**

15. **Use the Keep copies of messages for offline viewing pop-up menu to determine where messages and attachments are stored.** The default is to keep copies of all messages and attachments on your MacBook, but you can choose other actions, such as storing messages only while ignoring attachments to save some hard drive space.

16. **Close the Preferences window and save your changes.**

Genius

If you use MobileMe email aliases, you only need to configure your primary MobileMe email address in Mail. That's because email sent to one of your aliases is actually delivered to the primary address. However, it can be helpful to set the colors associated with each alias so you can easily tell to which alias a message was sent (see Chapter 5).

Configuring a POP email account

Many email accounts use POP. You can add and configure a POP account in Mail with the following steps:

1. **Launch Mail and open Preferences.**

2. **Click the Accounts tab.**

3. **Click the Add (+) button located at the bottom of the list.** The Add Account sheet appears.

4. **Type your name in the Full Name field.** This is the name that is shown as the From name on email that you send.

5. **Type the email address for the account in the Email Address field.**

6. **Type the password for the account in the Password field.**

7. **Click Continue.**

8. **At the prompt, click Setup Manually.** You see the Incoming Mail Server window.

9. **On the Account Type pop-up menu, choose POP.**

10. **Type a description of the account in the Description field.**

11. **Type *popserveraddress*, where *popserveraddress* is the name of your incoming mail server, in the Incoming Mail Server field.** This is usually something like pop-server.*provider*.com, where *provider* is the domain name of your email account provider, but this address can take other forms, as well. The important point is to use the address included in the account information provided to you.

Genius

Mail tries to configure information, such as server addresses, based on information you enter. Sometimes it's right, and sometimes it's not. Make sure you carefully review this information and change it as needed before you move on to the next step.

12. **Type your account's username and password.** Make sure this is for the incoming server, which can sometimes be different than the outgoing server.

13. **Click Continue.** You see the Incoming Mail Security window.

14. **If the account uses Secure Sockets Layer (SSL) security, select that check box.**

15. **Choose the type of authentication the account uses for incoming email on the Authentication pop-up menu.** Again, make sure this is for incoming email as the security settings may be different than for outgoing email. You see the Outgoing Mail Server window.

16. **Type a description of the outgoing server in the Description field.**

17. **Type *smtp-server.provider.com*, where *provider* is the name of the account's provider, in the Outgoing Mail Server field.** Make sure this matches the information you received from your provider.

18. **If the provider uses authentication, select the Use Authentication check box and type your account's authentication username and password.** This can be the same as for incoming mail, or it may be different.

19. **Click Continue.**

20. **At the prompt, click Setup Manually.** You see the Outgoing Mail Server window.

21. **If the account uses Secure Sockets Layer (SSL) security, select that check box.**

22. **Choose the type of authentication the account uses for outgoing email on the Authentication pop-up menu.** You see the Outgoing Mail Server window.

23. **Click Continue.** You see the Account Summary window.

24. **Click Create.** The account is created, and its mailboxes are added to the Accounts window.

25. **Select the account on the Accounts list and use the Account Information, Mailbox Behaviors, and Advanced tabs to more fully configure it.** This is similar to using these tabs for a MobileMe account, though the options you see are different because the account types are different.

26. **Close the Preferences window and save your changes.**

Configuring an IMAP account

If you've configured a MobileMe account (the details are covered earlier in the chapter), you've already learned how to configure an IMAP account because MobileMe accounts are IMAP accounts. In most cases, you only have to type your name, account username, and account password for Mail to be able to access your account. Once created, you can configure specific actions for the account, such as where certain kinds of mail are stored.

Configuring an Exchange account

How or if you can configure Mail to access an Exchange email account depends on how the organization providing the account allows it to be accessed. The only way to know which path you need to take is to contact your IT organization to find out what version of Exchange is being used and if IMAP access to your Exchange account is allowed.

If IMAP access to your Exchange email is provided, you can configure your Exchange account in Mail similar to other IMAP accounts, with some differences.

When you reach the Incoming Mail Server screen, you need to select either Exchange 2007 or Exchange IMAP. Each of these presents slightly different configuration details for you to provide to be able to configure the account.

If your account is provided through Exchange 2007, all you need is your incoming mail server account information. You can also add your Address Book contacts and iCal calendars to your Exchange account by selecting the related check boxes (see figure 7.5). This is the ideal situation because Mail automatically discovers all the required elements to access your Exchange account for you, similar to how it works with a MobileMe account. And you can have access to your Address and iCal information within any application you use to access Exchange, such as Outlook on a Windows PC.

7.5 Configuring an Exchange account with Exchange 2007 is quite simple.

If your account is provided through an older version of Exchange, things get a bit more compli-cated. If the account is provided via IMAP, you can configure it using an incoming mail server simi-lar to other IMAP accounts.

1. **Move to the Add Account sheet and configure it with your name, email address, and password.**

2. **Click Continue.**

3. **On the Account Type pop-up menu, choose Exchange IMAP.**

4. **Type a description of the account.**

5. **Type the incoming mail server address.**

6. **Type your username as *domain\username*.** You need to get your domain from your IT organization.

7. **In the Outlook Web Access field, type the address of your OWA server without any prefix, as in owa.company.com.** Like the domain, there's no way to figure out this address; you must get it from your IT organization. In some cases, the address will have / exchange at the end; just type the server address you get from your IT group. When you configure this address, Mail filters out all non-email items from your account before downloading them to Mail.

8. **Complete the account setup as with other kinds of accounts.**

In many cases, organizations don't allow IMAP access to an Exchange account, in which case you won't be able to access the account in Mail.

If you can access your Exchange account via an Outlook Web Access (OWA) server, you can get to your email, contacts, and other Exchange information via a Web browser (see figure 7.6). Move to your organization's OWA server, type your username and password, and log in. In most cases, you have to include a domain in front of your username, such as in xyz\username.

If the organization doesn't provide IMAP or OWA access to your Exchange email, you have to run Windows on your MacBook so that you can use Outlook to access it (see Chapter 15 for more infor-mation). You can do this using Boot Camp or one of the virtualization applications that are avail-able, such as Parallels Desktop for Mac.

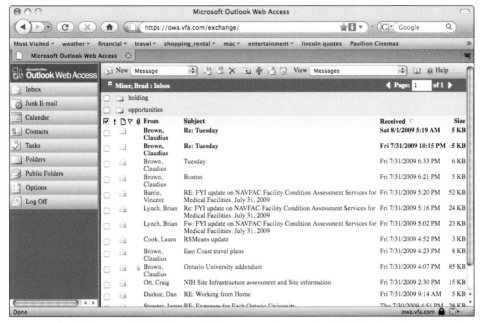

7.6 Accessing Exchange via a Web browser isn't as convenient as using Mail, but it works pretty well.

Testing email accounts

After you configure your email accounts, expand the Inbox by clicking the right-facing triangle next to it. Under the Inbox, you see an Inbox for each email account that you configured (see figure 7.7). If you don't see an icon containing an exclamation point, the accounts are properly configured and are ready to use. If you do see this icon, you need to correct the account configuration.

As a final test, send email to and from each address to make sure that they are all configured as you want them to be. If you find any problems or want to make any changes, open the Accounts pane of the Preferences dialog box, select the account you want to change, and use the three tabs to make needed changes.

7.7 No caution icon means that these three email accounts have been successfully configured in Mail.

Working with File Attachments

Email is one of the easiest and fastest ways to exchange files with other people. Using Mail, you can attach files of any type to emails that you send.

Genius

One limitation of sending files through email is that most email gateways have a limit on the size of file attachments; this limit is typically 5MB or 10MB. Another issue can be sharing files with people who use a different email client, especially on Windows computers. If you have large files or if you aren't sure which email application the recipient uses, it's better to use MobileMe to share files because you don't have to think about these issues. See Chapter 5 for details.

Sending compressed files through email

I'm going to recommend something here that many people don't do as standard practice, which is that you compress files before attaching them to email messages, even if you are sending only one file with a message. There are three reasons why I recommend this. One is that sending a compressed file requires less bandwidth to manage. Second, compressing files before you send them also reduces the chances that your message is screened out by spam or virus filters on the recipient's email. Third, when you send a compressed file, it gives the user a single file to deal with, instead of an attachment for each file.

So, before moving into Mail, compress the files you want to send using the following steps:

1. **Move to a Finder window showing the files you want to send.**

2. **Select the files you want to send (remember that you can hold the ⌘ key down while clicking files to select multiple files at the same time).**

3. **Choose File ⇨ Compress # items, where # is the number of files you selected.** The files you selected are compressed into a ZIP file. Mac OS X uses ZIP as its default compression scheme; this is a very good thing because it is also the dominant compression standard on Windows computers.

4. **Rename the ZIP file.** The default name for ZIP files is always Archive.zip, when you compress more than one file (if you compress one file, the compressed file's name is the same except for the change in filename extension).

After you prepare the compressed file, you can attach it to an email message with any of the following techniques:

- **Drag the file onto the New Message window.**

- **While the message to which you want to attach files is active, choose File ⇨ Attach File.** Then use the Choose File sheet to select the file you want to attach.

- **While the message to which you want to attach files is active, press Shift+⌘+A.** Then use the Choose File sheet to select the file you want to attach.

- **Click the Attach button on the New Message window's toolbar.** The Choose File sheet appears; use it to select the file you want to attach to a message.

Caution

The way Mail embeds file attachments into messages can cause problems for some email applications. In that case, you need to find another way to transfer the file, such as using your iDisk or via an FTP site.

Of course, I realize that many times people attach noncompressed files to email (and I do that more than occasionally myself). When you place a file that hasn't been compressed in a new message window, you see a thumbnail preview of the file with its icon, the filename, and its size in parentheses. If the file type is one that can be displayed in the message, such as a TIFF image or a PDF file, you actually see the contents of the file embedded in the body of the message (see figure 7.8).

Preparing attachments for Windows users

Because Mac and Windows operating systems use different file format structures, Windows users sometimes end up with two files when

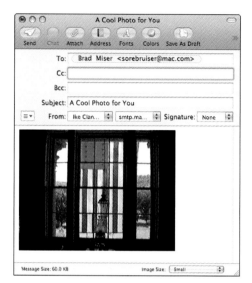

7.8 When you attach a single file, Mail displays a preview if it can.

you email them attachments. One is the usable file and the other is unusable to them (the names of the files are filename and _filename). Recipients can use the first one and safely ignore the second one. However, it is still confusing.

You can choose to attach individual attachments as Windows-friendly by selecting the Send Windows-Friendly Attachments check box in the Attach File dialog box. If you always want to send files in the Windows-friendly format, choose Edit ➪ Attachments ➪ Always Send Windows-Friendly Attachments.

Genius

You can use the Photo Browser in the New Message toolbar to easily find photos in your iPhoto library and drag them into a new message window to attach them to an email that you create.

Working with files you receive

When you receive a message that has files attached to it, you see the files in the body of the message. As when you send files in a message, you see the file's icon, name, and size. If Mail can display the content of the attached files, you see that content in the message body. You can use file attachments in the following ways:

- **Click Quick Look.** The Quick Look window opens and you can preview the contents of the files using the Quick Look window controls (see figure 7.9).

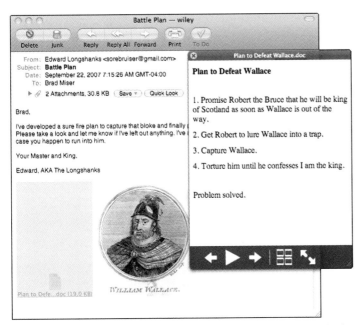

7.9 Here I am using the Quick Look function to preview the files attached to this message.

- ⊚ **Choose File ⇨ Save Attachments.**

- ⊚ **Click the Save button next to the attachment information at the top of the message.** The file is saved to your Downloads folder.

- ⊚ **If multiple files are attached, open the Save pop-up menu and choose Save All to save the files to your Downloads folder or choose the specific file you want to save.**

- ⊚ **If multiple files are attached, click the expansion triangle next to the attachment line in the message's header and work with each file individually.**

- ⊚ **Double-click a file's icon to open it.**

- ⊚ **Drag a file's icon from the message onto a folder on your Mac's desktop to save it there.**

- ⊚ **Open the attachment's contextual menu and select one of the listed actions, such as Open Attachment, which opens it in its native application; Open With, which enables you to select the application in which you want the file to open; Save Attachment, which prompts you to choose a location in which to save the file; or Save to Downloads folder, which saves the attachment in your designated Downloads folder.**

If the contents of the file are being displayed and you would rather see just an icon, open the file's contextual menu and select View as icon. To view the file's content again, open the menu and select View in Place.

Organizing Email

As you send and receive email, you'll end up with a lot of messages that you need to manage. Fortunately, Mail provides you with a number of ways to organize your email, including mailboxes, Smart Mailboxes, and Smart Mailbox folders.

Using mailboxes

You can create your own mailboxes to organize your messages; these are much like folders on your desktop. The mailboxes you create are shown in the Mailbox pane, below the Inbox and other special mailboxes. You can also create nested mailboxes to create a hierarchy of mailboxes in which you store your messages. Here's how:

1. **Click the Add (+) button at the bottom of the Mailbox pane.**

2. **On the resulting pop-up menu, select New Mailbox.** The New Mailbox sheet appears (see figure 7.10).

3. **On the Location pop-up menu, select the location where the mailbox you are creating will be stored.** If you select On My Mac, the folder is created on your computer. If you use an IMAP or MobileMe account, you can select that account to create a folder on that account's server.

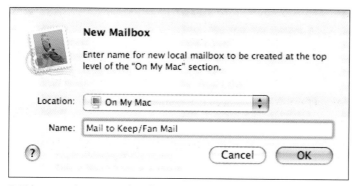

New Mailbox

Enter name for new local mailbox to be created at the top level of the "On My Mac" section.

Location: [🖥 On My Mac ▲▼]

Name: [Mail to Keep/Fan Mail]

(?)   (Cancel)   (OK)

7.10 I am creating a nested mailbox.

4. **Type the name of the mailbox you want to create in the Name field.** To create a nested mailbox, type the name of each mailbox, separated by a slash (/). For example, to create a mailbox called Fan Mail within a mailbox called Mail to Keep, you would type Mail to Keep/Fan Mail. To create a separate mailbox, just type the mailbox's name.

5. **Click OK.** The mailbox is created and appears in the Mailbox pane in the location you selected.

Genius

After you create folders, you can place them within one another to create nested folders, by dragging a folder onto the folder in which you want to place it.

To use the mailboxes you create, you move messages between them, just like you move folders and files between folders on your desktop. You can move messages from one mailbox to another in many ways:

- **Drag and drop a message from the Message List pane onto a mailbox.** This moves the message from the Inbox into the folder. If the Inbox is stored on a server (an IMAP account), the messages that you move to folders stored on your MacBook no longer count against your storage space allocation.

- **Drag messages from the Message List pane in one Viewer to the Message List pane in another Viewer.** This copies the messages to the mailbox shown in the second Viewer window.

- **Select messages and then choose Message ⇨ Move To.** On the menu, select the mailbox to which you want to transfer the messages.

- **Select messages and then choose Message ⇨ Copy To.** On the menu, select the mailbox to which you want to create a copy of the selected messages.

- **Select messages and then choose Message ⇨ Move Again to move the selected messages into the same mailbox into which you most recently transferred mail.**

- **Select messages and press Option+⌘+T to move the selected messages into the same mailbox into which you most recently transferred mail.**

- **Open a message's contextual menu and select the Move To, Copy To, Move Again, or Apply Rules command (you'll learn how to work with rules later in this chapter).**

- **Select messages and then choose Message ⇨ Apply Rules.** Select a rule that transfers the messages.

Using Smart Mailboxes

You can use Smart Mailboxes to organize your email automatically, based on criteria you define. For example, you might want to collect all the email you receive from a group of people with whom you are working on a project in a specific folder. Rather than having to place these messages in the folder by dragging them out of your Inbox individually, you can create a Smart Mailbox so that mail you receive from these people is automatically placed in the appropriate folder.

However, when mail is shown under a Smart Mailbox, it isn't actually stored there. Because a Smart Mailbox is a set of conditions rather than a place, it shows messages stored in other locations, rather than being a place where those messages are stored. So, if a message in an IMAP Inbox matches a Smart Mailbox's conditions, it is shown under that mailbox, but it also appears in the Inbox for the IMAP account. You should use mailboxes to store and organize email on your MacBook; use Smart Mailboxes to show messages stored in various folders in one place.

To create a Smart Mailbox, complete the following steps:

1. **Click the Add (+) button at the bottom of the Mailbox pane.**

2. **On the resulting pop-up menu, select New Smart Mailbox.** The Smart Mailbox sheet appears (see figure 7.11).

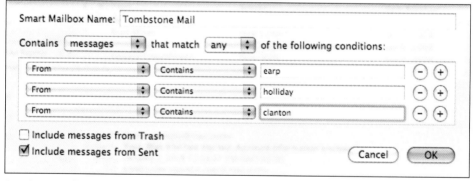

7.11 Smart Mailboxes organize your email for you automatically; this Smart Mailbox collects all my email from my pals in Tombstone.

3. **Name the Smart Mailbox by typing its name in the Smart Mailbox Name box.**

4. **Select the first condition for the mailbox on the first pop-up menu in the conditions box.** By default, this menu shows From, which bases the condition on the name or email address in the From field.

5. **Select the operand for the condition on the second pop-up menu.** What you see on this menu depends on the condition you selected. For example, to create a Smart Mailbox for mail from a specific person, you would select Contains or Is equal to.

6. **Type the condition text or date in the box.** For example, type a person's name if you are creating a Smart Mailbox to collect mail from that specific person.

7. **To add another condition, click the Add (+) button on the right side of the sheet and configure it with Steps 4 through 6.**

8. **If you have configured more than one condition, select all on the matching pop-up menu above the condition list if all the conditions must be true for mail to be stored in the Smart Mailbox, or select any if only one of the conditions must be true.**

9. **If you want messages that are in the Trash folders to be included in the Smart Mailbox, select the Include messages from Trash check box.**

10. **If you want messages that are in the Sent folders to be included in the Smart Mailbox, select the Include messages from Sent check box.**

11. **To remove a condition you no longer want to use, click the Remove (–) button located on the condition's row.**

12. **Click OK.** The Smart Mailbox is created in the SMART MAILBOXES section of the Mailbox pane. Any email that meets its conditions is organized under that mailbox.

Genius

To change the conditions for an existing Smart Mailbox, open its contextual menu and select Edit Smart Mailbox or just double-click the Smart Folder's icon. Use the resulting Smart Mailbox sheet to make changes to it. When you click OK, email that meets the new conditions is shown when you select the Smart Mailbox.

Using Smart Mailbox folders

If you want to organize your Smart Mailboxes, you can create a Smart Mailbox folder and then place your Smart Mailboxes within it. Follow these steps:

1. **Choose a folder in the ON MY MAC section.**

2. **Choose Mailbox ⇨ New Smart Mailbox Folder.** The Smart Mailbox Folder sheet appears.

3. **Name the new Smart Mailbox folder.**

4. **Click OK.** The Smart Mailbox folder appears in the SMART MAILBOXES section.

5. **Drag Smart Mailboxes into the Smart Mailbox folder that you created to place them there.** When you do this, an expansion triangle appears so that you can expand the Smart Mailbox folder to see its contents.

Using the Junk Mail Tool in Mail

Email is great, but it isn't perfect; its major imperfection is junk mail or spam. Spam refers to any email message you receive that you don't want to receive. You've no doubt seen messages for various products that are of little to no interest to you, such as fabulous money-making opportunities and other messages that require your time to manage.

Caution Never click a link in any email message unless you are absolutely sure of the sender. When you click a link, your email address can be identified as being active and in use, which guarantees that the flow of spam to it will increase exponentially if the original message is spam. This includes links that claim to unsubscribe you from future messages. Unfortunately, spammers are quite good at making their messages look like they are from legitimate sources.

To configure the Junk Mail tool, perform the following steps:

1. **Open the Mail Preferences dialog box.**

2. **Click the Junk Mail tab.** The Junk Mail tools appear (see figure 7.12).

3. **Turn the tool on by selecting the Enable junk mail filtering check box.**

4. **Select one of the following options to determine what Mail does with junk mail:**

   - **Mark as junk mail, but leave it in my Inbox.** This option causes Mail to change the color of junk mail to an ugly brown, but leaves it in your Inbox.

   - **Move it to the Junk mailbox.** When you choose this option, a Junk mailbox is created and any messages that are identified as junk are moved into it automatically.

   - **Perform custom actions.** When you select this option, you can click Advanced to create a rule to deal with junk mail. You learn how to work with rules later in this chapter. When a message is identified as junk, the junk rule is implemented.

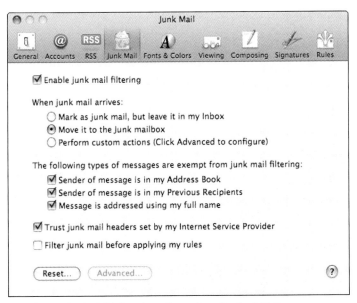

7.12 To use the Junk Mail tool, configure it on the Junk Mail pane.

5. **Select the following check boxes to exempt mail from being identified as junk if it meets the related condition:**

   - **Sender of message is in my Address Book**

   - **Sender of message is in my Previous Recipients**

   - **Message is addressed using my full name**

6. **Select the Trust junk mail headers set by my Internet Service Provider check box if you want to allow this option.** Many ISPs have filters in their email systems that flag email as junk. If you want Mail to treat messages with these flags as junk, select the check box. If this option is unchecked, Mail ignores these flags.

7. **If you want the junk mail filter to act before any rules you've created do, select the Filter junk mail before applying my rules check box.**

8. **Close the Mail Preferences dialog box.** The Junk Mail tool starts working; any junk in your Inbox is marked or moved accordingly.

Caution

Never click a link in any message that asks you to update your account information; these are always attempts to steal your identity.

As the Junk Mail tool works, here's what happens and how you can use it:

- When you receive email that the tool identifies as junk, it is either marked as junk in your Inbox or moved to the Junk folder, depending on your preferences.

- As the junk accumulates, review it; then delete it if it's really junk from the Inbox or from the Junk mailbox.

- If a message should have been marked as junk, but wasn't, select the message and choose Message ⇨ Mark ⇨ As Junk Mail or press Shift+⌘+J. The message is marked as junk and moved to the Junk folder if that preference is set. Mail also tries to learn from this, and will mark similar messages (such as those from the sender) as junk in the future.

- If a message shouldn't have been marked as junk, but was, select the message and choose Message ⇨ Mark ⇨ As Not Junk Mail or press Shift+⌘+J. The junk tag is removed from the message, and Mail learns from this so that it won't identify similar messages in the future as junk. If the junk message is in the Junk folder, you have to manually move it back into the Inbox or other mailbox.

- You can also use the Junk or Not Junk buttons that appear at the top of messages in the Reading pane to change the junk status of individual messages.

Automatically Managing Email with Rules

You can automate your email by configuring and using rules. For example, you might want to create a mailbox for the mail from a certain person and have that mail automatically transferred to and stored in that mailbox. Or you might have the messages from a mailing list to which you are subscribed placed in a specific mailbox for later reading. There are a large number of actions you can perform with Mail Rules.

Like other Mail tools, you can start by configuring rules using the Mail Preferences dialog box:

1. **Open the Mail Preferences dialog box.**

2. **Click the Rules tab.** The Rules tools appear. In the pane, you see a list of all the current rules that are configured; those marked with a check mark are active.

3. **Click the Add Rule button.** The New Rule sheet appears (see figure 7.13).

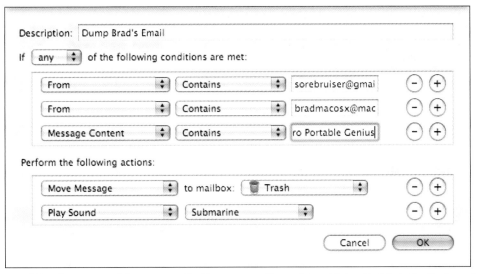

Description: Dump Brad's Email

If [any ▲▼] of the following conditions are met:

From ▲▼	Contains ▲▼	sorebruiser@gmai	⊖ ⊕
From ▲▼	Contains ▲▼	bradmacosx@mac	⊖ ⊕
Message Content ▲▼	Contains ▲▼	ro Portable Genius	⊖ ⊕

Perform the following actions:

| Move Message ▲▼ | to mailbox: 🗑 Trash ▲▼ | ⊖ ⊕ |
| Play Sound ▲▼ | Submarine ▲▼ | ⊖ ⊕ |

(Cancel) (OK)

7.13 This rule moves mail from my email addresses or mail containing this book's title to the Trash, and it plays the Submarine sound.

4. **Name the rule by typing a description.**

5. **Use the If pop-up menu to determine whether at least one criterion (select any) or all the criteria (select all) in the rule must be met for the actions in the rule to be taken.**

6. **Use the first condition pop-up menu to select the first criterion on which the rule acts.** You can select any of the fields in a message, and you can also select from various criteria, such as whether the sender is in your Address Book.

7. **Use the Contains pop-up menu to select how the criterion relates to the value you type (for example, Contains and Is equal to).**

8. **Type the value for which the rule will be implemented, if applicable, or use a pop-up menu to select a value.**

9. **To add another condition for the rule, click the Add (+) button at the right side of the sheet.**

10. **Use the menus in the Perform the following actions area to select the actions that will be performed by the rule.** For example, if you choose the Move Message action, you would then choose the location to which the message is moved to on the mailbox pop-up menu.

11. **To add another action, click the Add (+) button on the right side of the sheet.**

12. **Click OK.** The rule is created and you are prompted to apply the rule to the messages that are currently in selected mailboxes.

13. **Click Apply if you want the actions in the rule to be applied to the messages that are currently in your Inbox, or click Don't Apply if you want the rule to be ignored for your current messages.** You return to the Rules pane and see the rule you created.

14. **Close the Mail Preferences dialog box.** The rules you created take effect for all the messages you receive in the future.

On the Rules pane, you can also perform the following actions:

- **Deselect a rule's check box to temporarily disable it.**

- **Select a rule and click Edit to change its conditions or actions.**

- **Select a rule and click Duplicate to make a copy of it.** This is a good way to test changes to a rule; make changes to the copy and keep the original as is until you're sure you want to keep the changes.

- **Select a rule and click Remove to delete it.**

It's a good idea to test your rules to make sure they do what you intend and that they don't do what you don't intend. You can create messages on which to test your rules, or you can use existing messages and apply the rules to them manually to see whether the rules do what you intended. Select a message to which the rule should apply, hold the Ctrl key down, click, and choose Apply Rules on the menu.

Now select a message to which the rules shouldn't apply and choose the Apply Rules command again. If the rules don't have any effect, you can be confident that they aren't acting on messages they shouldn't (you'll have to try this a number of times to be sure).

Working with RSS Feeds

RSS feeds are streams of information that change as time passes. Many Web sites, especially news sites, offer RSS feeds to which you can subscribe. You can use Mail to read RSS feeds, which is convenient because they are delivered to your Inbox automatically.

Note

Adding RSS feeds to Mail

Before you can read RSS feeds in Mail, you need to subscribe to the feed. You can do this by choosing a Safari bookmark to the feed or by typing a feed's URL directly. Because it's the more flexible option, the following steps show you how to subscribe to a feed using its URL:

1. **Choose File ⇨ Add RSS Feeds.** The RSS Feeds sheet appears.

2. **Click the Specify a custom feed URL radio button.**

3. **Type the feed's URL in the field.** The URL for RSS feeds starts with feed://.

4. **If you want the feed's messages to appear in your Inbox, select the Show in Inbox check box.** In most cases, it's better not to select this option so that your Inbox doesn't get cluttered with feed messages.

5. **Click Add (see figure 7.14).** You are subscribed to the feed and it is added to the RSS section of your Inbox.

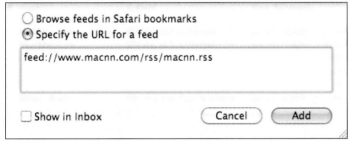

7.14 This feed provides a steady stream of Mac news.

Reading RSS feeds

To read a feed, expand the RSS section. You see each feed to which you are subscribed. Select the feed you want to read; its messages appear on the Messages list (see figure 7.15). To read a message, select it; its contents appear in the Reading pane. Click the Read more link to open the full story in your Web browser.

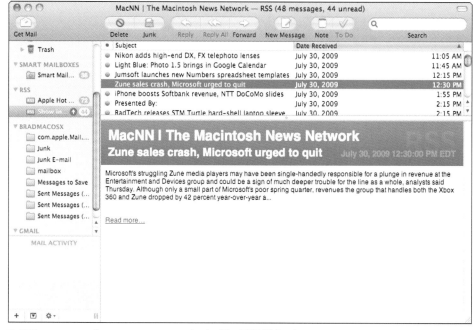

7.15 Here you see the current messages in the MacNN RSS feed.

Configuring RSS preferences

To complete your RSS experience, configure RSS preferences as follows:

1. **Open the Mail Preferences dialog box.**

2. **Click the RSS tab.**

3. **Choose a selection on the Default RSS Reader menu to choose the application that you want to use by default to read feeds.**

4. **On the Check for Updates pop-up menu, choose how frequently Mail checks for updates to your feeds.**

5. **Use the Remove articles pop-up menu to determine when Mail removes articles in your feeds.**

6. **Close the Mail Preferences dialog box.**

Communicate with iChat?

There's something extremely compelling about having a high-quality video chat with someone who is far away; did I mention that it's free if you have a MobileMe account? Of course, you can also use iChat for text (you can use an AIM, Jabber, or Google Talk account for text chatting with iChat) and audio chats. Among its many useful features is that iChat allows users to share their desktops, which is great for helping someone, being helped yourself, or collaborating.

Configuring iChat

Before you start chatting, you need to do some basic configuration to prepare iChat, the most important of which is configuring the accounts you're going to use to chat. There are two basic paths to this end. One is when you first start iChat and the Assistant walks you through the account setup steps. The other is manual configuration, which you can use to set up accounts at any time. You'll want to use various iChat Preferences to tweak iChat to make it work as well as possible for you.

Creating and configuring accounts

To be able to chat, you need to configure iChat with at least one chat account. To get started, launch iChat and use the following steps to configure it through the Assistant, which starts with the Welcome screen:

1. **Review the information in the Welcome screen.**

2. **Click Continue.** The Set up a new iChat Account window appears. If you have a MobileMe account configured for the current user account, the account information is configured automatically to use that account.

Note

If you see a reference to a .Mac account, you can safely ignore it; just select MobileMe on the pop-up menu and type your MobileMe account information.

3. **On the Account Type pop-up menu, choose AIM, MobileMe, Jabber, or Google Talk.** The rest of these steps assume you are using a MobileMe or AIM account. The details of using a Jabber or Google Talk account are a bit different.

4. **Type the account username and password information and click Continue.** If you are configuring a MobileMe account, the Encrypted iChat window appears. If you selected an AIM account, the Conclusion screen appears and you can skip to Step 7.

5. **If you want to use encrypted chats with other MobileMe users who have enabled it, select the Enabled iChat Encryption check box and click Continue.**

6. **Read the information about encrypted iChats and click Continue.** The Conclusion screen appears.

7. **Click Done.** The basic configuration of iChat is complete and you move into the chatting windows. You can start setting up buddies for chatting or continue on to learn how to configure iChat manually.

iChat offers a number of preferences that you can use to configure the way it works. You don't have to set all of these preferences at once; you should plan on adjusting them over time to tweak the way iChat works. To access iChat preferences, choose iChat⇨Preferences. The Preferences window has a number of tabs that are summarized in the following sections. As you explore all the preferences iChat offers, watch for others not mentioned here that might be useful to you.

You can use the Accounts tab to add new chat accounts and to make changes to your existing accounts (see figure 8.1). You can create and use multiple kinds of accounts within iChat, including any of the following: MobileMe, .Mac (precursor to MobileMe), AIM (AOL Instant Messenger), Jabber, and Google Talk.

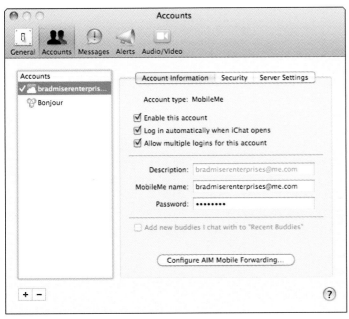

8.1 Use the Accounts tab to add accounts or configure your existing iChat accounts.

To configure a new iChat account of any of these types, open the Accounts tab and click the Add (+) button at the bottom of the Accounts list. The Account Setup sheet appears. Use this to create a new account just as when you first launched iChat and the Assistant led you through the process (see the steps earlier in this section).

You can configure as many accounts within iChat as you want. For example, you might want one account for work-related chats and another for social chatting.

To configure existing iChat user accounts, open the Accounts tab of the Preferences window and select the chat account you want to configure from the list in the left side of the window. Then use the tools and settings in the right side of the window to configure the account's details. Because some of the configuration options are different for certain types of accounts, you might or might not see all of the useful options summarized in the following lists.

Note

You have to be logged out of an account before you can make some changes on the Account Information or Server Settings subtabs. To log out, move to a buddy list for the account and choose Offline on the status pop-up menu. You have to be logged in to make changes on the Security subtab. To log in, choose Available on the status pop-up menu.

On the Account Information subtab, some of the more useful settings are:

- **Enable this account.** Deselect this check box to temporarily disable an account. You won't be able to open the account's buddy list or use it to chat until you select the check box again.

- **Log in automatically when iChat opens.** Select this check box if you want to log in to the account as soon as you open iChat. If you don't select this, you need to manually change the account's status to log in.

- **Description.** This is the name of the account shown on the accounts list, and more importantly, at the top of buddy lists. For some accounts, it defaults to the email address, which can be kind of long. Consider creating a shorter, more easily identifiable description.

- **Add new buddies I chat with to "Recent Buddies."** When you select this check box, anyone with whom you chat is added to your recent list, making it easier to chat with him again.

Note

To delete an account, select it and click the Remove (–) button. (In most cases, you can just disable an account using the Enable this account check box instead.)

The Security subtab enables you to configure some security-related aspects to your chats. Options include:

- **Block others from seeing my status as idle.** If you select this check box, your status never appears as Idle (which usually indicates you are logged in, but nothing is happening on your computer). If you're concerned that people might interpret this status inappropriately, you might want to hide it.

- **Privacy levels.** The radio button determines the people who can see your status when your account is available for chatting. For example, if you select Allow people in my Buddy List, only people who you have configured as chat buddies can see your status. You also choose to allow or block specific people from accessing your status. The tighter you set your privacy, the fewer people will be able to try to chat with you.

You only need to use the Server settings subtab if you are having trouble chatting with the standard configuration. This isn't likely unless you are using your MacBook behind a firewall of some kind, in which case you'll need help from the system administrator to be able to chat (some organizations frown on chatting and will block attempts to do so).

Genius

You can use Bonjour to chat on a local network. Select Bonjour on the Accounts list. Because it doesn't cross outside of your local network, you see only the Account Preferences subtab. Select the Enable Bonjour instant messaging check box and use the other options to configure the way it works. This is particularly useful if you want to enable chatting within your network, but not over the Internet (such as if you have young children).

Setting General preferences

The aptly named General tab of the iChat Preferences dialog box enables you to configure some general behaviors. Here are some of the more useful settings (see figure 8.2):

- **Show status in menu bar.** This places an iChat menu on your menu bar. From there, you can easily change your chat status, see which of your buddies is available, and move to your buddy lists. If you enable this, you can also automatically set your account status to Available when you log in and to Offline when you quit iChat.

- **Confirm before sending files.** You can exchange files with others through chats. It's a good idea to enable this setting so that you don't send any files that you don't intend to.

● **Set my status to Away after the computer is inactive.** This is useful because it auto-matically lets people know you aren't actively using your computer so they shouldn't expect a response from you.

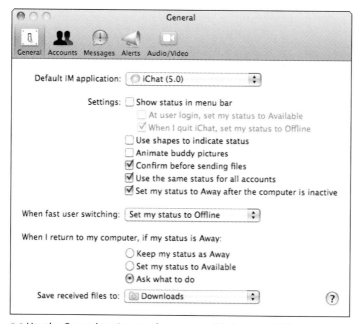

8.2 Use the General settings to change overall behaviors of iChat.

● **When fast user switching.** Use this pop-up menu to automatically set your status when someone else logs in to your MacBook.

● **When I return to my computer, if my status is Away.** Use these radio buttons to set an iChat status when you return to your user account.

● **Save received files to.** Use this pop-up menu to select the folder into which files are stored when you receive them through iChat.

Setting Messages preferences

The Messages pane enables you to set various formatting options for your messages (see figure 8.3). Following are some useful controls:

● **Pop-up menus.** Use these menus to set the colors for your text balloons and the text that appears within them. If you leave the Reformat incoming messages option unselected, then messages are formatted according to the sender's preferences. If you select this check box, you can set the format for other participant's messages.

- **Set Font buttons.** Use these buttons to select the font for your chats (sending and receiving).

8.3 Use the Messages preferences to format how your text chats appear and to set options, such as saving transcripts.

- **Use a keyboard shortcut to bring iChat to the front.** Select this check box and choose the keyboard shortcut on the pop-up menu to bring iChat quickly to the front.

- **Collect chats in a single window.** When you select this check box, iChat places all of your chats in one window instead of having a separate window for each chat.

Setting Alerts preferences

Use the Alerts pane to set the alerts and notifications that iChat uses to get your attention. Select the event for which you want to configure an alert on the Event pop-up menu, and then select the specific alert on the check boxes and pop-up menus to configure it. You can choose a sound, bouncing the iChat icon on the Dock, running an AppleScript, or an announcement. There are many different events about which you can be alerted, including when you log in and log out. You want to strike a balance between being notified appropriately and being annoyed, so I recommend you set alerts for just a couple of key events, especially if you use iChat frequently.

Setting Audio/Video preferences

You can use these preferences to prepare for audio and video chats. Following are the important settings:

- **Image preview.** At the top of the pane, you see the current image that is being received from your MacBook's iSight camera. If you can see yourself well, then people with whom you chat will also be able to.

- **Audio meter.** Just under the image preview is an audio meter that provides a graphic representation of the volume level being received. You can use the built-in microphone or another audio input device, such as a Bluetooth headset.

- **Microphone and Sound output.** Use these pop-up menus to determine where the audio input comes from, such as Internal microphone to use your MacBook's built-in mic, and where sound from chats is played, such as external speakers.

- **Repeated ring sound when invited to an audio or video chat.** When this check box is selected and you are invited to an audio or video conference, you hear a ring until you respond to the request.

Working with Buddies

The people with whom you chat are called buddies, and in order to chat with others, you must configure them as buddies. There are two kinds of buddy lists. One type is for the people whom your MacBook can see on a local network through Bonjour. The other type, and the one you are likely to deal with more often, is for people who are configured in your Address Book and have a MobileMe email address, a Jabber account, or an AIM screen name.

By default, when you open iChat, you see two windows: One is titled Bonjour List, and the other is labeled with the name/description of the account with which it is associated. An example of a Buddy List is shown in figure 8.4. The people shown on the Bonjour List are found automatically when your Mac searches your local network for Bonjour users. You add people with whom you want to chat on the Buddy List. You can chat with people on either list in the same way.

Genius

To change your status, open the pop-up menu immediately below your name at the top of the Buddy List window, and choose the status you want to set.

Because using the Buddy List is the more common way, I will focus on it for the rest of this chapter, but you can do anything with the Bonjour List that you can with the Buddy List.

At the top of the Buddy List window, you see your information, including your name, status, video icon, and the photo associated with your name. The most important of these is status, which applies to you and all of your buddies.

The dot next to a buddy's name indicates her status. A green dot means the buddy is available (those who have permission to see your status know that you are available for an iChat when your status is Available). Text is also associated with each status, and you can have multiple text labels for your Available status; the default is Available when you are online, but you can make it anything you want. A red dot means the buddy is online, but unavailable. Like the Available status, you can associate different text messages with your Unavailable status; the default is Away. When no dot is shown, the buddy is Offline, meaning

8.4 The Buddy List shows the people with whom you can chat, along with their current status.

he isn't signed in to chatting services. When a gray dot appears, it means that the buddy's messages are being forwarded to his phone. When the dot is yellow, the buddy is idle.

In the Buddy List window, buddies are organized, based on whether their status is Online or Offline. In the Buddies section, you see your buddies who are currently online. Someone who is online may or may not be available. If you see a green dot, the buddy is online and available for chatting; you also see a status message below her name. If you see a red dot, the buddy is online, but not available for chatting (you also see the current Away status message under the name).

The Offline category contains all your buddies who are currently offline. These buddies are disabled and you can't even try to chat with any of them.

Note

As buddies change status, you hear alerts as you have configured them on the Alerts tab of the iChat Preferences dialog box.

Adding chat buddies

There are several ways to add people to your Buddy List so that you can chat with one. You can create a buddy in iChat, or you can add someone who is in your Address Book as a buddy.

Creating a buddy in iChat

To create a new buddy in iChat, do the following:

1. **Click the Add (+) button located in the lower-left corner of the Buddy List window.**

2. **Select Add Buddy.** The Add Buddy sheet appears.

3. **Type the buddy's account name.** This will be whatever the person has provided to you.

4. **Associate the buddy with a group by selecting it on the Add to group pop-up menu.**

5. **Type the buddy's first name in the First Name field and the last name in the Last Name field (see figure 8.5).**

6. **Click Add.** The buddy is added to your Buddy List. If the buddy is online, he appears in the Buddies section. If not, he appears in the Offline section.

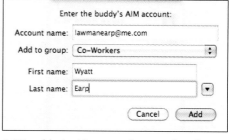

8.5 To add a buddy to your list, complete the information on this sheet.

Caution

iChat doesn't check the account information that you enter to make sure it's correct. If the account information for a buddy is wrong, his status is always Offline.

Genius

Create groups in which you can place buddies by clicking the Add (+) button in a Buddy List window and choosing Add Group. If you don't want to have your buddies organized by group, choose View ▷ Use Groups.

Adding someone from your Address Book as a buddy

To add someone who is already in your Address Book as a buddy, use the following steps:

1. **Click the Add (+) button located in the lower-left corner of the Buddy List window.**

2. **Select Add Buddy.** The Add Buddy sheet appears.

3. **Click the Expand button (downward-pointing triangle next to the Last Name field).** The lower pane of the sheet expands, and you see a mini-Address Book viewer.

4. **Search or browse for the person you want to add as a buddy.**

5. **Select the name and email address or AIM account of the person you want to add (see figure 8.6).**

6. **Associate the buddy with a group by selecting it on the Add to group pop-up menu.**

7. **Click Add.** The buddy is added to your Buddy List. If the buddy is online, she appears in the Buddies section. If not, she appears in the Offline section.

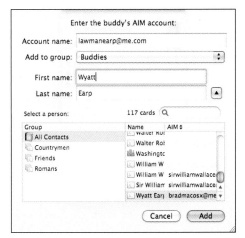

8.6 You can also add a buddy by selecting a contact from your Address Book.

Genius

You can change the information for a buddy, including name, image, and lots of other information, by selecting the buddy you want to change, opening the contextual menu, and selecting Show Info.

Chatting with Text

Instant or text messaging is a preferred way of communicating for many people. Text chats are easy to do, fast, and convenient. Using iChat, start your own text chats or answer someone's request to text chat with you. You can also chat with more than one person at the same time.

You can text chat with others by using the following steps:

1. **Select the buddy with whom you want to chat (see figure 8.7).** If the person is on the Offline list, he isn't available for chatting. Even if the person is online, make sure the status indicator shows that he is available for chatting before you initiate a chat session (look for the green dot).

2. **Click the Text Chat button, which is the A located at the bottom of the window.** An empty Instant Message window appears.

3. **Type your message in the text bar at the bottom of the window.**

4. **When you are ready to send what you typed, press Return.** Your message appears in a text bubble in that user's iChat or other text messaging application. When you receive a reply to your message, you see the person's picture along with the text he sent.

5. **Continue chatting (see figure 8.8).**

8.8 As your buddy chats, you see his response formatted as you configured using the Messages pane of the Preferences tool.

8.7 When a buddy shows green you can request a chat.

6. **When you finish chatting, close the chat window and confirm that's what you want to do.**

You can respond to invitations that you receive to start a text conversation. When a person wants to chat with you, a box appears on your screen with the name of the person who sent it as its title and the text she sent. Respond to the request by following these steps:

1. **Click the initial text chat window (see figure 8.9).** It expands to a chat window that includes the text bar and the following buttons:

   - **Block.** Click this button to decline the chat and block future requests from the sender.

   - **Decline.** Click this button to decline the chat. Nothing is sent back to the person who is trying to chat with you.

   - **Accept.** Click this button to accept the chat.

8.9 When you click in a text chat invitation, you can choose how to respond.

2. **Type your response in the text bar.**

3. **Press Return.** Your text is sent.

4. **Continue the chat.**

When someone leaves the chat, you'll see a status message saying so at the bottom of the window.

You can include more than two people in a chat by performing the following steps:

1. **Select the buddies with whom you want to chat by holding the ⌘ key down while you click their icons.**

2. **Click the Text Chat button.** You see the text chat window, with each buddy that is included in the chat shown at the top of the window.

3. **Type your message.**

4. **Press Return.** The message is sent to each buddy.

As a buddy responds, his message appears in your window. Everyone who joins the chat sees the messages from each participant as they come in (see figure 8.10).

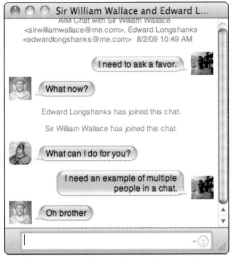

8.10 You can text chat with multiple people at the same time.

Chatting with Audio

An iChat audio chat is pretty much like talking on the telephone. Starting an audio chat isn't any harder than starting a text chat, either, as you can see in the following steps:

1. **Select the buddy with whom you want to chat.**

2. **Click the Audio Chat button (the telephone receiver) at the bottom of the Buddy List window.** If the button is disabled, the buddy isn't available for audio chats, and you have to use a text chat instead. The Audio Chat window appears.

3. **When the buddy accepts the request, start chatting.**

4. **As you chat, use the following controls to manage your chat session (see figure 8.11):**

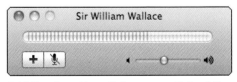

8.11 Chatting with audio is as easy as it should be.

- **Audio meter.** Use the Audio meter to gauge your own volume. As you speak, the green part of the bar should move to at least the halfway point. If not, you can use the Input level control on the Sound pane of the System Preferences application.

- **Add buddies.** Click the Add (+) button located in the lower-left corner of the window to add more people to the audio chat. Just like text chats, you can add multiple people to an audio chat. You can have up to ten people in the same audio chat.

- **Mute.** Click the Mute button (the microphone with a slash through it) to mute your end of the conversation. Click it again to unmute your sound so that people can hear you again.

- **Volume slider.** Drag to the right to increase the volume or to the left to decrease it.

When someone wants to audio chat with you, you see a window with the person's name as its title and the Audio icon. Click the window and then click one of the following buttons:

- **Text Reply.** Declines the audio invitation and starts a text chat.

- **Decline.** Declines the audio invitation. The person who sent it to you sees a status message stating that you declined.

- **Accept.** Accepts the invitation and starts the chat.

Note

If you are listening to iTunes when you start an audio or video chat, it automatically pauses. It starts playing again when the chat ends.

Chatting with Video

Using iChat to videoconference is amazingly cool, and it is as simple to use as the other types of chatting. However, a video chat requires a lot of bandwidth, so it is more sensitive to the Internet connection of each person who is involved in the chat. Note that you can only video chat with someone who is using iChat or the most current version of Instant Messenger for Windows (assuming the other person has a working camera for the Windows computer, of course).

To video chat, do the following:

1. **Select the buddy with whom you want to chat.**
2. **Click the Video Chat button (the video camera) at the bottom of the Buddy List window.** If the Video Chat button doesn't become active when you select a buddy, the

buddy is not capable of video chatting with you. The video chat window opens, and you see the green "on" light next to the iSight camera. You see a preview of the view that others see of yourself, and a message that iChat is waiting for a response.

When the buddy accepts your chat invitation, you see her image in the larger part of the chat window. The smaller, inset preview window shows you what the other person is seeing in her chat window (see figure 8.12).

8.12 During a video chat, the image of you that other people see is shown in the small preview window.

3. **Talk to and see the other person.**

4. **As you chat, you can manage your chat session in the following ways:**

   - **Add buddies.** Click the Add (+) button to add more people to the video chat. You can have up to three other people involved.

   - **Mute.** To mute your end of the conversation, click the Mute button; click it again to unmute it.

   - **Fill Screen.** To make the chat window fill the desktop, click the Fill Screen button (the arrows pointing away from each other). To see the toolbar while in full screen mode, move the pointer.

   - **Effects.** When you click the Effects button, you see the Video Effects palette. You can browse the available effects and click one to apply it to your image. The preview updates, and other participants will see you as the effect changes you.

Note

If the audio or video is sporadic or you can't hear or see the other participants, in most cases, the cause is that one or more of the participants don't have sufficient bandwidth to do video chats.

Applying Backgrounds During a Video Chat

You can apply backgrounds to video chats that make it appear as if you are someplace you aren't. A background can be a static image or a video. iChat includes some backgrounds by default, and you can also use your own images as backgrounds.

To add a default background, do the following:

1. **Start a video chat.** While you are waiting for the chat to start, you can use the following steps to set the background.

2. **Click the Effects button.**

3. **Scroll to the right in the Video Effects palette until you see the images and video that are provided by default.**

4. **Click the image or video that you want to apply as a background.**

5. **Move out of the camera view at the prompt.**

6. **When the prompt disappears, move back into the picture. It will look as if you are actually in front of the background. The effect isn't perfect, but it is pretty amazing.**

To add your own images or video as backgrounds, do the following:

1. **Choose Video ⇨ Show Video Effects.** The Video Effects palette appears.

2. **Scroll in the palette until you see the User Backdrop categories.**

3. **Drag an image file or video clip into one of the User Backdrop wells.**

4. **Click the image or video that you want to apply as a background.**

5. **Start a video chat and apply the background you added.**

Sharing Desktops During a Chat

You can share your desktop with people you chat with. When you do this, the person with whom you share it can control your computer. The other person sees your desktop on his screen and can manipulate your computer using his keyboard and mouse (or trackpad). Using a similar process, you can share someone else's desktop to control that person's computer from afar.

Accessing a desktop being shared with you

You can share someone else's desktop to take control of her computer. Here's how:

1. **Start the sharing session in one of the following two ways:**

   - **Select the buddy whose desktop you want to share.** Click the Share Desktop button (the two boxes to the right of the camera button). Select Ask to Share *buddy*'s screen, where *buddy* is the name of the buddy you selected. When your request is accepted, you see a message that the sharing feature is starting, and two windows appear on your screen (see figure 8.13).

   - **When you receive a request to share your screen, click Accept.** You see a starting sharing message, and two windows appear on your screen (see figure 8.13). One window is the buddy's desktop, which is the larger window by default. The other, smaller window is a preview of your desktop, which is labeled with *My Computer*.

8.13 When you share someone else's desktop, you can control her computer.

2. **You can work with the buddy's computer just as if you were sitting in front of it.** For example, you can make changes to documents or use commands on menus. An audio chat is started automatically so you can communicate with the other person.

3. **To move back to your desktop, click the My Computer window.** The two windows flip-flop so that your desktop is now the larger window so you can control your MacBook.

4. **Control your MacBook again.**

5. **Click back in the other computer's window to control it again.**

6. **When you finish sharing, click the Close button on the My Computer window.**

Note
Like video chats, screen sharing is very dependent on a high-bandwidth Internet connection for the participants. If you try to use an insufficient connection, there may be a large time lag between when one person performs an action and its effect on the computer being shared.

Sharing your desktop with someone else

To share your desktop with someone else, perform the following steps:

1. **Select the buddy with whom you want to share your desktop.**

2. **Click the Share Desktop button (the two boxes to the right of the camera button).** If the Share Desktop button doesn't become active when you select a buddy, the buddy is not capable of sharing your desktop.

3. **Select Share My Screen with** *buddy*, **where** *buddy* **is the name of the buddy you selected.** iChat sends a screen-sharing request to the buddy you selected, and you see the Screen Sharing window.

   When the buddy accepts your invitation, the buddy with whom you are sharing your screen can now use your MacBook. He can also talk to you because, when you share the desktop, you also have an audio chat session going. Expect to see your MacBook do things without any help from you.

Caution
When you share your screen, you are sharing control of your MacBook. Someone who shares your screen can do anything remotely that you can do directly.

Sharing a Document During a Chat

In some cases, you might want to just share a document with someone else. You can do this with iChat Theater. This is ideal for making remote presentations. You can show the presentation and provide narration. Here's how to do your own remote presentations:

1. **Choose File ⇨ Share a File With iChat Theater.** You see the Share with iChat Theater dialog box.

2. **Move to and select the document (such as a presentation) that you want to share.**

3. **Click Share.** You see a message stating that iChat Theater is ready to begin.

4. **Select the buddy with whom you want to share the document.**

5. **Start a video chat.** When the buddy accepts your invitation, you see the Video Chat window. You also see a window showing the document you are sharing. In the lower-left corner of the window, you see a preview window showing the buddy with whom you're chatting (see figure 8.14).

6. **Move through the document and speak to your chat buddy.** If you share a Keynote presentation, you can use the Keynote controls to present the document.

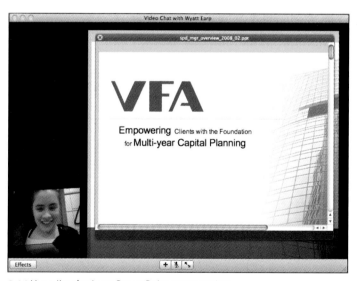

8.14 Here, I'm sharing a PowerPoint presentation.

Chatting On

iChat is a powerful application that includes a lot of features and capabilities that I don't have space to cover here. Here is a brief description of some of them:

- **By default, when your MacBook goes to sleep or when the screen saver activates, your status is automatically changed to Away.**

- **You can have multiple chats of various types going on with different people at the same time.** Each chat appears in its own independent chat window, unless you select the Collect chats into a single window check box on the Messages pane of the iChat Preferences dialog box.

- **Use your status settings to prevent unwanted interruptions.** For example, if you are online but busy with something, open your status menu and choose Away or one of the other unavailable statuses. You can also select the Offline status to prevent any invitations.

- **If you have trouble with a video chat, choose Video ⇨ Connection Doctor.** The Connection Doctor opens and shows you statistics about the conference (see figure 8.15).

- **Use the Video menu to configure and control various video and audio settings.** For example, choose Video ⇨ Record Chat to record a chat session.

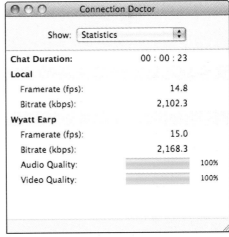

8.15 The Connection Doctor can help you understand problems you are having with chats.

How Can I Manage My Calendars?

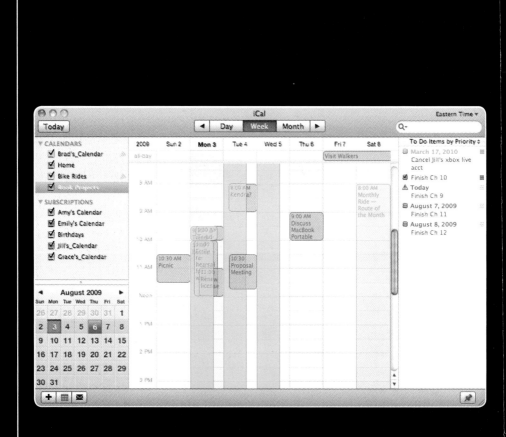

With iCal, you can manage your own time by creating calendars that help you to be where you're supposed to be when you're supposed to be there. You can also use to-do items to ensure that you accomplish important, or even not-so-important, tasks. As a personal calendar tool, iCal is very useful, and if that's all it did it would be worth using. However, iCal is also designed for calendar collaboration. You can publish calendars so that others can view your calendars in iCal running on their Macs. Likewise, you can subscribe to other people's calendars so that you see all calendar events of interest to you in one place.

Setting Up iCal

iCal is a complete calendar tool that enables you to take control over your busy life and helps you coordinate with other people. In this section, you learn how to get started with iCal, from setting important preferences to configuring your calendars, events, and to-do items.

Configuring iCal preferences

Before you jump into managing your calendars with iCal, take a few moments to configure some of its preferences so that it works the way you want. iCal's Preferences window has three tabs: General, Accounts, and Advanced.

On the General tab, here are the preferences you can set (see figure 9.1):

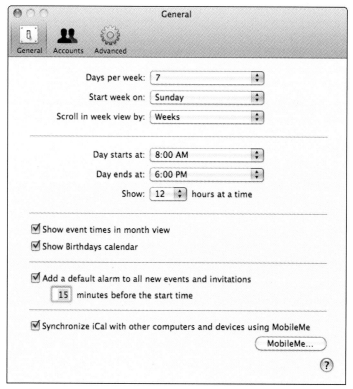

9.1 The General preferences enable you to configure how weeks and days are displayed.

- **Days per week.** On this pop-up menu, choose 7 if you want your calendars to include all 7 days in the week or 5 if you only want 5 days (the workweek) to be shown.

- **Start week on.** On this pop-up menu, choose the first day of the week.

- **Scroll in week view by.** This pop-up menu enables you to choose to scroll, when you are viewing iCal in the Weeks view, by weeks or days.

- **Day starts at, Day ends at, Show.** Use these pop-up menus to show when your work-day starts and ends and how many hours you want to be displayed on the calendar when you are viewing it in Day or Week view. The start and end times for your days don't really matter as iCal just shades hours outside of this period to indicate what you think the working part of each should be.

- **Show event times in month view.** When enabled, the times associated with events are shown. While useful, this can really clutter the Month view if you have several events on the same days.

- **Show Birthdays calendar.** Select this if you want iCal to display a calendar of birthdays for contacts you're managing in Address Book. This can be a helpful way to remember important people's birthdays because reminder events for those birthdays are added to iCal automatically.

- **Default alarms.** Because one of the important functions of iCal is to remind you of events, in most cases you want to have alarms set for your events by default. Select the Add a default alarm to all new events and invitations check box and enter the number of minutes before the event you want the alarm to activate.

- **iCal synchronization.** This check box takes you to the MobileMe pane so you can sync your calendars. More on this later.

The Accounts pane enables you to add calendars being managed elsewhere to iCal so you can view their events along with those that you create in iCal. iCal supports calendars from the following sources:

- **CalDAV.** CalDAV is a set of standards for calendars to enable applications on different devices to share calendar information. The good news is that iCal supports these standards so if you have access to accounts that include CalDAV calendar information, you can access that information in iCal.

- **Exchange 2007.** Perhaps the most useful kind, if you have a Microsoft Exchange 2007 account at your work or other organization, you can add your Exchange calendars to iCal. iCal also supports various Exchange functions, such as the ability to view the availability of other people when you are setting up meetings. Unfortunately, many organizations run older versions of Exchange that are not supported in iCal or don't allow external access to Exchange except through specialized network access. To see if your organization supports Exchange 2007 and client access from outside its firewall, contact your IT organization.

⬤ **Google.** You can set up and access Google calendars in iCal.

⬤ **Yahoo!** Same goes for Yahoo! calendars.

The steps to add calendar information from these sources are similar. A quick example showing how to add Google calendar information to iCal should be informative:

1. **Open the Accounts tab of the iCal Preferences window.**

2. **Click the Add (+) button at the bottom of the account list shown on the left side of the window.** The Add an Account sheet appears.

3. **In the Account type pop-up menu, choose Google.**

4. **Type your Google account email address and password (see figure 9.2).**

9.2 Add calendars from other sources, such as Google, to iCal.

5. **Click Create.** You are logged in to the account you configured. If successful, you return to the Preferences window where you see the new account on the Accounts list.

6. **Configure the options for the account, such as using the Refresh calendars pop-up menu to determine how often the calendar information from the account is updated.**

Genius

iCal doesn't support all options in all account types. For example, it doesn't support availability information from Google, whereas it does support that information for an Exchange 2007 account.

On the Advanced tab of the iCal Preferences window, you have the following options (see figure 9.3):

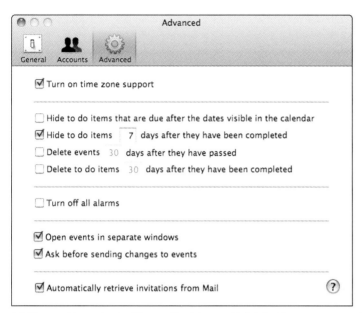

9.3 The most important setting on the Advanced tab is for time zone support.

- **Time zone support.** When you enable this, a time zone is associated with all of your iCal calendars and with each event you configure on those calendars. iCal automatically takes the time zone currently set for your MacBook Pro, but maintains the time zone associated with each event. This makes keeping events at the right time easier regardless of the time zone you happen to be in. For example, if you travel to a different time zone, you can simply choose that time zone in the iCal window and all event times are adjusted according to the difference between iCal's time zone and the events' time zones. You should enable this feature even if you don't travel outside of your current time zone because it can still help you coordinate with events that are outside your time zone.

- **Hide.** Use these check boxes and number field to hide to-do items that are due outside of the time shown on the calendar or that have been completed. For complete items, you can set how long they remain visible after they are completed.

- **Delete.** Use these check boxes and number fields to determine if and when events and to-do items are deleted from your calendar. I don't recommend you allow either to be deleted because you lose the historical information in iCal. This can be a valuable resource for you.

- **Turn off all alarms.** This feature is useful because when it is enabled, all alarms are temporarily disabled. Disable it to resume normal alarm functions.

- **Open events in separate windows.** When this is selected and you open an event, it appears in a separate window instead of as a sheet attached to the event on the calendar. I find this setting makes events much easier to work with so you might want to give it a try.

- **Ask before sending changes to events.** When you set up an event, you can invite others to it. This setting prompts you when you make a change to an event that has invitees. This prompt can help you prevent sending unnecessary or unintended messages to people you have invited, such as when you change the alarm setting on the event.

- **Automatically retrieve invitations from Mail.** With this enabled, when you receive an email message containing an invitation, iCal automatically grabs the invitation and you use iCal to manage it, such as to accept or reject it.

Creating calendars in iCal

There are two levels of calendars that you deal with when you use iCal. First, there is the overall calendar, which is what you see inside the iCal window. This calendar includes all the information being managed or shown by the application. On the second level are the individual calendars on which you create events and to-do items. There are many good reasons that you might want to create multiple calendars for your events and to-do items. The classic example is one calendar for work events and one calendar for personal events. When creating calendars, also consider publishing them. If there are some events you won't want to show in a published version, you can create a calendar for those events that you don't publish and another for those that you want to share.

On the other hand, you don't want to create so many calendars that they become unwieldy. In most situations, one to three calendars are ideal.

To create a calendar, follow these steps:

1. **Click the Add (+) button located in the bottom-left corner of the iCal window.**
2. **Type a name for the new calendar and press Return.**
3. **Open the calendar's contextual menu and choose Get Info.**
4. **Type a description of the calendar in the Description field.**
5. **Use the Color pop-up menu to associate a color with the calendar.**

6. **If you don't want alarms to be enabled for the new calendar, select the Ignore alarms check box.**

7. **Click OK.** The changes you made are saved and you see the calendar's name in the color you selected.

The calendars you are managing in iCal are shown in the upper-left pane of the window, organized into three sections. The CALENDARS section contains calendars you have created in iCal. The SUBSCRIPTIONS section shows calendars to which you've subscribed. You see other sections for any calendars coming from accounts you've added on the Accounts tab of the Preferences window. Figure 9.4 shows examples of each type (the wave icon indicates a calendar is being shared).

To include a calendar's events and to-do items in the calendar being displayed in the iCal window, select its check box. If you deselect a calendar's check box, its events and to-do items are hidden.

To remove a calendar, select it and press Delete. The calendar, along with all its events and to-do items, is removed from iCal. Most of

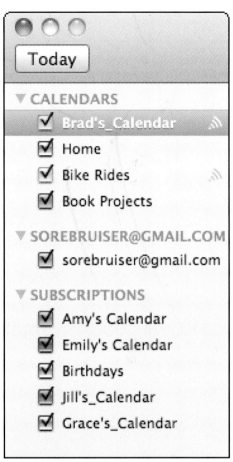

9.4 Calendars you create are shown in the CALENDARS section of the Calendars list.

the time, you're better off hiding a calendar because it won't appear in iCal anymore, but you can access its information at any time. When you delete a calendar, all its information goes with it.

Adding events to calendars

You can use iCal events to plan periods of time. If one of those periods of time is a meeting, you can invite others to join by sending them an invitation. In addition to the time and date, you can include all sorts of useful information in iCal events, such as file attachments, URLs, and notes. To add an event to a calendar, perform the following steps:

1. **Select the calendar on which you want the event to appear by clicking it.**

2. **Drag over the calendar to cover the time and date of the event.** A new event appears on the calendar with its title selected.

3. **Type the name of the event.**

4. **Press Return.** The event name is saved and it appears in the color of the calendar with which it is associated (see figure 9.5).

5. **Double-click the event.** What you see depends on the Open events in separate windows setting. If this is enabled, you see a separate window showing all of the event's current and potential information with the name ready to be edited. If you don't have this enabled, a window pops up from the event that shows the event's name, from and to dates and times, time zone, and alarm information. The rest of these steps assume the separate window setting is enabled.

9.5 At their most basic, events indicate a date, period of time, and title.

6. **Edit the name if needed and type the event's location in the Location text box.**

7. **Use the all-day check box, from, to, time zone, and repeat tools to set the time and date of the event and whether it repeats or is a one-time event.**

8. **Use the show as pop-up menu to set your availability during the event.** This enables other people who have access to your availability information to know if you are open for an event or not at this time.

9. **Use the calendar pop-up menu to associate the event with a calendar.**

10. **Use the alarm tools to configure one or more alarms for the event.** There are a number of actions you can choose for an alarm, such as a message with sound, email, sound only, and so on. The action you choose can present other tools to configure, such as to select an email address for an email alert. You can have as many alarms for an event as you want.

11. **To add other people to the event, click Add Invitees and type the name or email address of the person you want to invite; if iCal finds a match for what you type, click it to enter the associated email address.** Continue adding invitees by typing more email addresses in the Invitees box.

12. **To associate a file with the event, click Add File and use the resulting Open dialog box to browse and select the file you want to attach.**

Genius

13. **If a URL is associated with the event, type it in the url field or copy and paste it there.**

14. **Type text about the event in the notes field.**

15. **If you added people to the attendees list, click Send (see figure 9.6); if not, click Done.** After you click Send, an email is created in your default email application, the event is attached to it, and the email is sent. After you click Done, changes that you made to the event are saved.

Check out these tips for managing events that you create:

- You can change the calendar on which an event occurs by opening its contextual menu and selecting the event's new calendar.

- You can change the date on which an event occurs by dragging it from one date in the calendar to another date.

9.6 Events can contain lots of useful information.

- As you configure events, icons appear at the top of the event on the calendar to indicate when an alarm has been set, whether the event is a repeating event, if people have been invited, and so on.

- You can email an event to others by opening its contextual menu and selecting Mail Event. This is the same action that happens when you click Send for an event. The difference is that you can address the email that is created to anyone. When you use Send, the email is sent to only those people listed as attendees for the event. Your default email application opens and the event is included as an attachment. The recipient can then drag the attachment, which has the extension .ics, onto iCal to add it to her calendar.

● When you change an aspect of a repeating event, such as an alarm, you're prompted to make the change to all the events or only to the current one. If you choose only the current one, the current event is detached from the series and is no longer connected to the other instances of the same event. This is indicated by (detached event) being appended to the frequency shown in the repeat section for the event.

● If you use the Send command, you can use the event to track people's response to your invitation. The event's block on the calendar contains the icon of a person with a question mark, which indicates people have been invited, but have not responded to the event. As people add the event to their calendars, you'll see a green check mark next to their names when you open the event's Information window. This indicates that the attendee has accepted the event by adding it to his calendar. If an attendee hasn't added the event to his calendar, the name is marked with a question mark icon. This tracking doesn't occur when you use the Mail Event command.

Creating and completing to-do items

You can use iCal to-do items to track just about any kind of action for which you are responsible. In this section, you learn how to create to-do items and how to complete them (by that, I mean how to mark them as complete — you're on your own to actually do the work).

Creating a to-do item is similar to adding an event, as you see in the following steps:

1. **Select the calendar that you want the to-do item to be associated with.**

2. **Click in the To Do pane, open the contextual menu, and select New To Do, or press ⌘+K.** A new, untitled to-do item appears.

3. **Type the name of the to-do item and press Return.**

4. **Open the to-do item's contextual menu and select Get Info.** If you selected the open events in separate window preference, the to-do item's Information window appears.

5. **Edit the item's name as needed.**

6. **Use the priority pop-up menu to set the to-do item's priority.**

7. **If the to-do item has a due date, select the due date check box.** Use the date field that appears to set the due date.

8. **Use the alarm tools to set alarms for the to-do item.** Like events, you can configure multiple alarms with different options.

9. **Use the calendar pop-up menu to set the calendar with which the to-do item is associated.**

10. **If a URL is associated with the to-do item, type it in the url field.**

11. **Add notes in the note field (see figure 9.7).**

12. **Close the window.** The changes you made to the to-do item are saved.

Managing to-do items

You manage your to-do items in the To Do pane, which appears on the right side of the iCal window. (If you don't see this pane, click the pushpin button at the bottom of the window). As you work with to-do items, keep the following points in mind:

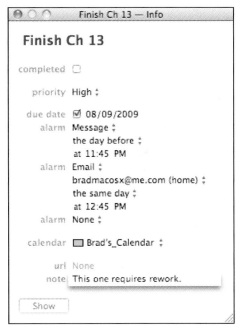

9.7 Configuring a to-do item is similar to configuring an event, although there are fewer options.

● The priority of a to-do item is indicated by the number of bars that appear to the right of its name on the To Do list. A high-priority item has three bars, a medium-priority item has two bars, and a low-priority item has one bar.

● You can perform a secondary click (such as Ctrl+click) on a to-do item to open its contextual menu. With the commands on that menu, you can duplicate it, change the calendar with which it is associated, mark its priority, email it, open its Information window, or change the sort order for the To Do pane.

● When you email an event or a to-do item to someone, the recipient can add the item to his calendar by clicking its link or by dragging it onto his iCal window. If the automatically retrieve preference is enabled and the recipient uses Mail, the to-do item information is added automatically.

● When you complete a to-do item, mark it as complete by selecting the check box next to its name on the to-do list or by selecting the completed check box on the Info window. Depending on the preferences you set, it might continue to remain on the list or it might be removed.

● When the due date for an item is the current date or the due date has passed, its complete check box becomes a warning icon to indicate that the item is due or overdue (see figure 9.8).

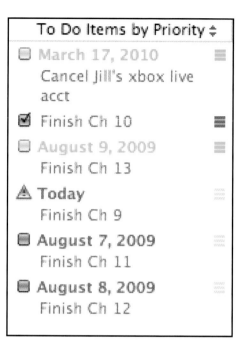

Managing Calendars, Events, and To-Do Items

9.8 To-do items marked with a caution icon are due today or are overdue; items marked with a check mark are complete.

As you build your calendars in iCal, there are many ways you can view and manage events and to-do items. You can also print calendar information in a number of ways for those times when you want a hard copy.

Check out the following list to learn what you can do with the iCal window to control how information is displayed:

● If you want to focus on specific events and to-do items, deselect the check boxes for the calendars that don't interest you, and their information is hidden.

● The Mini Months tool shows you one or more months at a glance. You can show or hide this section by choosing View ⇨ Show Mini Months, or View ⇨ Hide Mini Months, respectively, or by clicking the Calendar button in the center of the toolbar in the lower-left part of the iCal window. You can change the number of months being shown by dragging the Resize handle (which is the dot in the bar between the two sections) up or down.

- In the Mini Months area, the current day is highlighted in muted blue. The current dates being displayed (such as a week if the calendar is displaying a week at a time) are shaded in gray. When you click a day, the day is highlighted in bright blue to show you it is the date in focus and the calendar view jumps to that date if it isn't visible. You can move between months displayed by clicking the Forward or Backward arrows next to the top month's label.

- The line across the calendar with a pushpin at one end shows the current time.

- In the center pane is the actual calendar. There are three views for this: Day, Week, and Month. You can change the view by clicking the related button.

- You can jump to the current day by clicking the Today button. You can move ahead or back by clicking the Back or Forward arrows on each end of the view tool at the top of the iCal window.

- If Time Zone Support is enabled, you can change the current time zone by choosing a time zone on the pop-up menu above the Search tool. Open the menu and choose Other. The Change time zone sheet appears. Click the map near a city in the time zone you want, and then choose the specific time zone on the Closest city pop-up menu. Click OK. The times and dates are adjusted according to the new time zone. From that point on, the time zone you selected appears on the menu so you can choose it to switch to that time zone.

- If you click the Envelope button, the Notifications pane appears. This area shows you information about notifications, which you see only if you have set iCal to automatically receive invitations from Mail. When an invitation comes in, you can view it in the Notifications pane and accept, reject, or tentatively accept it.

- Use the Search tool to search for events, to-do items, notes, titles, or combinations of information. To search, click the Magnifying Glass pop-up menu in the Search bar and choose the kind of search you want to do. (If you don't select anything, all calendar items are searched.) Type your search text; as you do, items that match your search are found. When you type search text, iCal's Search Results pane opens at the bottom of the window automatically (see figure 9.9). This pane lists all events and to-do items that meet your search criterion. To see an event on the calendar, select it on the Search Results pane. You can sort the list by any of the columns, such as Date or Type. When you are done with a search, click the Clear (x) button in the Search tool. The search is cleared and the Search Results pane closes.

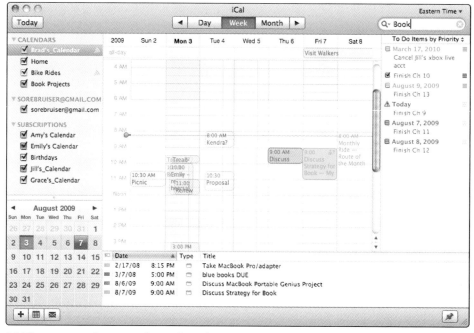

9.9 When you search, you see the results in the pane at the bottom of the iCal window.

Genius

To change the calendar view to by Day, by Week, or by Month, press ⌘+1, ⌘+2, or ⌘+3, respectively. To move to the next day, week, or month, press ⌘+right arrow; move back by pressing ⌘+left arrow. Press ⌘+T to jump to today, or Shift+⌘+T to move to a specific date. You can show or hide the To Do List by pressing Option+⌘+T. You can refresh all your calendars by pressing Shift+⌘+R.

Printing Calendars

While having your calendar in an electronic format is very useful and practical (because you can take your MacBook with you), there may be times when you'd like to have a hard copy of calendar information. You can use the iCal Print command to create paper versions of your calendar information by following these steps:

1. **Choose File ⇨ Print.** The Print dialog box appears (see figure 9.10).
2. **Choose the view you want to print on the View menu.**
3. **Use the tools in the Time range section to define the time period to include in the printed version.**

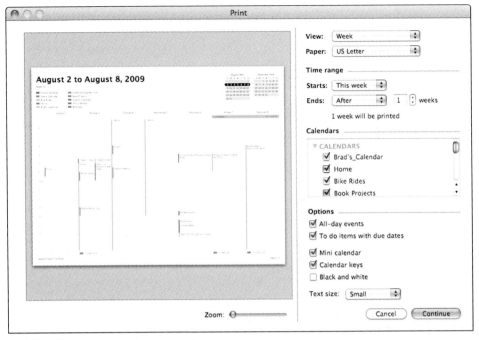

9.10 iCal offers a number of printing options.

4. **In the Calendars section, select the check box for each calendar whose information you want to be included in the printed version.**

5. **If you are printing to a black-and-white printer, select the Black and white check box.**

6. **On the Text size pop-up menu, choose the relative size of the text on the calendar.**

7. **Click Continue.** The Print dialog box for the current printer appears.

8. **Use the controls in the Print dialog box to configure the printer.**

9. **Click Print.**

Sharing Calendars

iCal is designed to be a collaborative calendar tool, and you can publish your calendars; other iCal users can subscribe to them to see your calendar information in iCal on their computers. You can also share your calendars with Windows users or even with Mac users who don't use iCal. Of course, you can subscribe to other people's calendars to add their information to your iCal window.

There are two basic ways to publish calendar information. If you have a MobileMe account and everyone with whom you want to share your calendar uses iCal, you can use the iCal Publish tool to make your calendar easy to add to their calendars. If you want to share your calendar with people who use Windows (or Mac users who don't use iCal) or you don't use MobileMe, it gets a little more complicated.

Sharing calendars via MobileMe

With your MobileMe account and iCal, it's simple to publish calendars for other people to view within their iCal application, as the following steps demonstrate:

1. **Select the calendar you want to publish.**

2. **Choose Calendar ⇨ Publish.** The Publish sheet appears (see figure 9.11).

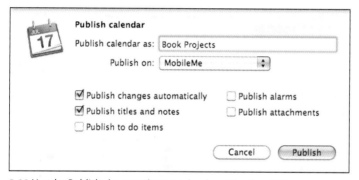

9.11 Use the Publish sheet to share a calendar with other iCal users.

3. **Type the name of the calendar as you want it to appear to someone with whom you share it.**

4. **Select MobileMe on the Publish on pop-up menu.**

5. **If you want changes that you make to your calendar to be published automatically, select the Publish changes automatically check box.** In most cases, you should select this option so that your calendar is always up to date.

6. **Use the other Publish check boxes to determine which elements of the calendar get published with it, including titles and notes, to-do items, alarms, and attachments.**

7. **Click Publish.** When the calendar has been published, you see the confirmation dialog box (see figure 9.12).

In the confirmation dialog box, you see the following:

⦿ The URL someone can use to subscribe to the calendar in iCal

- The URL to view the calendar on the Web

- The Visit Page button that takes you to the calendar on the Web

- The Send Mail button that creates an email message you can send to iCal users to enable them to subscribe to your calendar

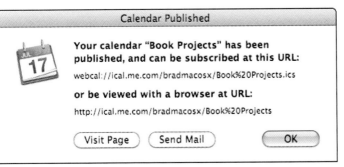

9.12 This calendar can be viewed on the Web or subscribed to in iCal.

Here are some additional points to consider when publishing your calendars:

- When a calendar is published, the published icon (which looks like a radiating wave) appears next to the calendar's name on the list of calendars.

- If you open a published shared calendar's contextual menu, you see several interesting commands. These include Unpublish, which removes the calendar from the Web; Send Publish Email, which enables you to send an email announcing the published calendar and its URL; Copy URL to Clipboard, which copies the calendar's URL to the Clipboard so you can paste it into documents; Refresh, which publishes any changes you have made to the calendar; Refresh All, which updates all of your published calendars; and Change Location, which enables you to move the calendar to a different site.

- You can view your own shared calendar at any time from any computer by moving to its URL. This is a great way to maintain access to your own calendar when you aren't at your Mac. To get the URL, use the calendar's contextual menu to select Copy URL to Clipboard. Paste the URL into a Web browser to move to the calendar on the Web.

- You can change a shared calendar by selecting the Get Info command. Use the tools in the calendar's Info sheet to make changes to the calendar's publishing and other settings.

Sharing calendars with non-iCal users

Using MobileMe to publish calendars has two drawbacks. One is that you must have a MobileMe account, which seems kind of obvious. The other limitation is that your shared calendar can only be subscribed to by iCal users, which leaves Windows users out of the picture.

For either of these scenarios, you can publish your iCal calendars to a different server so that people can access them over the Web, including Windows users. While this isn't as convenient as subscribing to shared calendars in iCal, it does work.

You need to find and use a calendar server service to be able to publish calendars. There are many of these available, and a number of them are free to use. After you find the service you're going to use, create an account and then configure iCal to publish your calendars using that account.

The following steps explain how to publish an iCal calendar using the iCal Exchange service located at www.icalx.com (other services work similarly):

1. **Go to www.icalx.com.**

2. **Create an account.** Use any username and password that you want, as you only use this information to access your icalx account.

3. **Move back to iCal.**

4. **Select the calendar you want to publish.**

5. **Choose Calendar ⇨ Publish.** The Publish sheet appears.

6. **Type the name of the calendar as you want it to appear to someone with whom you share it.** It's a good idea to remove spaces in the name by deleting them or replacing them with underscores.

7. **On the Publish on pop-up menu, choose A Private Server.** The Base URL, Login, and Password fields appear.

8. **In the Base URL field, type http://icalx.com/private/*your_icalx_username*/, where *your_icalx_username* is the username that you created in Step 2.** This assumes that you want to create a private calendar, meaning one that requires a password to be able to view. If you don't want to require a password, replace *private* with *public* in the URL.

9. **Type your icalx username in the Login field and your icalx password in the Password field.**

10. **If you want changes that you make to your calendar to be published automatically, select the Publish changes automatically check box.** In most cases, you should select this option so that your calendar is always up to date.

11. **Use the other Publish check boxes to determine which elements of the calendar are published with it, including titles and notes, to-do items, alarms, and attachments.**

12. **Click Publish.** When the calendar has been published, you see the confirmation dialog box (see figure 9.13).

9.13 This calendar has been published using the iCal Exchange service.

13. **Click OK.**

After you configure the calendar to be published in iCal, move back to icalx to complete the process:

1. **Log in to your icalx account.** You see the calendars that you've published on the Private Calendars or Public Calendars lists.

2. **Click the passwords link under the your account section on the left side of the screen.**

3. **Click add a password.**

4. **Type the username that you want to provide to people to enable them to access your calendar.**

5. **Type the password that you want to provide to people to enable them to access your calendar.**

6. **Select the calendars that you've published and want to share by selecting their check boxes.**

7. **Click Save Changes.** The calendar is protected with the password you created.

Subscribing to Calendars

When people share their calendars with you through the iCal Publishing tools, you can subscribe to those calendars to add them to your iCal window.

Subscribing to shared calendars

You can add published calendars to iCal by performing the following steps:

1. **Choose Calendar ⇨ Subscribe.** The Subscribe sheet appears.

2. **Type the URL for the calendar to which you want to subscribe.** URLs for calendars published with MobileMe start with webcal://ical.me.com.

3. **Click Subscribe.** The Subscribing configuration sheet appears, where you can name the calendar, assign it a color, and choose whether you want the calendar's associated alarms, attachments, and to-do items.

4. **If you want the calendar's information to be refreshed automatically, select the frequency at which you want the refresh to occur on the Auto-refresh pop-up menu.**

5. **Click OK.** The calendar is added to the Subscriptions section of your iCal window, and you can view it just like your own calendars. You can't add information to a calendar to which you've subscribed.

Subscribing to public calendars

Many public calendars are available to which you can subscribe. For example, most professional sports teams have calendars that show games and other events. You can also find DVD release calendars, TV schedules, and many other types of calendars to subscribe to. Just like shared calendars, when you subscribe to public calendars, the events on those calendars are shown in your iCal window. To find and subscribe to public calendars, do the following steps:

1. **Choose Calendar ⇨ Find Shared Calendars.** Your default Web browser opens and moves to the Apple Calendar library.

2. **Browse the available calendars by category, such as Most recent, Most popular, Alphabetical, or Staff picks.**

3. **Click the Download button for the calendar to which you want to subscribe.** You move into iCal and the Subscribe to calendar sheet appears. The calendar's URL is filled in automatically.

4. **Click Subscribe.** The Subscribe to configuration sheet appears, where you can name the calendar, assign it a color, and choose whether you want the calendar's associated alarms, attachments, and to-do items.

5. **If you want the calendar's information to be refreshed automatically, select the frequency at which you want the refresh to occur on the Auto-refresh pop-up menu.**

6. **Click OK.** The calendar is added to the Subscriptions section of your iCal window, and you can view it just like your own calendars. If you configured the calendar to be refreshed automatically, iCal keeps it current.

Moving iCal Calendars onto an iPhone

If you have an iPhone, you can synchronize your iCal calendars with the Calendar on the iPhone (this also works with an iPod touch). Here's how:

1. **Connect the iPhone to your MacBook.**

2. **Move into iTunes.**

3. **Select the iPhone on the Source list.**

4. **Click the Info tab (see figure 9.14).**

5. **Scroll down until you see the Calendars section.**

6. **Select the Sync iCal calendars check box.**

7. **Configure iCal to move all calendars or selected calendars onto your iPhone.**

8. **If you want to prevent older events from syncing, select the Do not sync events older than check box and type the number of days in the box.**

9. **Click Apply.** Each time you sync your iPhone, its calendar is updated with changes that you make in iCal, and changes that you make on the iPhone calendar are moved into iCal.

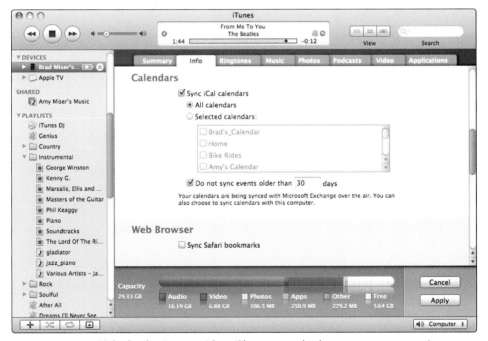

9.14 Keeping your iCal calendars in sync with an iPhone can make them even more convenient.

Genius

If you have a MobileMe account, you can sync your calendars on your iPhone wirelessly. Just configure your MobileMe account on the iPhone and ensure the Calendars setting is ON. This is very similar to syncing contacts on an iPhone through MobileMe. See Chapter 6 for the details.

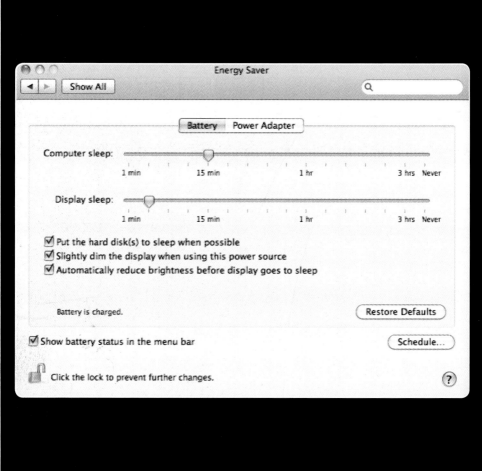

Like all devices with batteries, a MacBook can operate only as long as its battery continues to provide power; fortunately, with the current models this is quite a long time. Still, once your battery runs out, your trusty MacBook becomes so much dead weight to carry around. To get the most working time while you're mobile, you should practice good energy-management habits. These include a combination of using the Mac OS X battery management tools, conserving battery power, and being prepared to connect to an external power source whenever you have the opportunity.

Monitoring Battery Status

You can use the Battery menu to keep an eye on where your MacBook power level is so that you know how much working time you have left and can take action if it's clear you are going to run out of power soon.

You can configure the Battery menu on your MacBook by performing the following steps:

1. **Open the Energy Saver pane of the System Preferences application.**

2. **Select the Show battery status in the menu bar check box if it isn't selected already.**

3. **Open the Battery menu.**

4. **Select Show, and choose one of the following display options (see figure 10.1):**

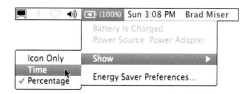

10.1 Configure the Battery status menu to provide the most meaningful indicator for you.

   - **Icon Only.** This displays the battery icon at the top of the menu when you are on battery power or charging the battery. The amount of the icon that is dark represents the battery's current power level.

   - **Time.** This displays the battery icon and time at the top of the menu. When you are operating on a battery, the time indicates the approximate amount of working time remaining at the current power use level.

   - **Percentage.** This displays the battery icon and the percentage of power remaining.

Genius

You can check the current state of a battery by turning the MacBook over and pressing the button on the battery. The number of lights indicates the state of the battery's charge.

As you work with your MacBook, keep an eye on the Battery menu (see figure 10.2). At the top of the menu, you see the parameter you configured, such as percentage. If you open the Battery status menu, the first item is the percentage of power remaining if you selected the Time view, or the time remaining if you selected the Icon or Percentage view. You also see the current source of power, those being either Battery or Power Adapter.

When the battery gets close to being discharged, warnings appear that provide an estimate of the remaining time and recommend that you save your work. If you keep going, the MacBook eventually goes into Sleep mode and you won't be able to wake it until you connect it to a power source or insert a charged battery.

10.2 Monitor the Battery menu as you work so that your MacBook doesn't suddenly come to a grinding halt.

While it can remain in Sleep mode for a long time, a MacBook eventually runs out of even the low level of power required to keep that going and shuts off. If you have any open documents with unsaved changes, there is a slight chance they may be lost when this happens; the MacBook goes into a hibernation mode, and any open documents are saved to the hard drive, which, in most cases, will enable you to recover them as soon as you power your MacBook again. Beyond the very minor possibility of losing unsaved changes, there really isn't any risk to you to let the MacBook run completely out of power.

When you connect the MacBook to a power source, the Battery menu displays information about the charging process instead of time remaining. The battery icon contains the lightning bolt symbol to indicate that it's currently being charged. The time displayed on the menu is the time until the battery is fully charged; when it is fully or close to fully charged (mid-90 percent or higher), the battery icon contains the electrical plug symbol to show that you are operating from the power adapter.

Genius

When you connect the adapter to the MacBook, its status light is amber when the battery is charging. When fully charged, the status light turns green.

Making the Battery Last Longer

You can use the Energy Saver to minimize power use while operating on battery power. You can also adopt simple practices to minimize the amount of power your MacBook uses so that you get the most time possible from its battery.

Using the Energy Saver

Use the Energy Saver pane of the System Preferences application to tailor how the computer uses power so that you can extend the working life of the battery as long as possible. There are two basic ways to configure power usage on a MacBook: You can use the default settings, or you can customize your settings. You configure settings for operating on battery power and for operating on the power adapter. Once your settings are configured, the MacBook automatically uses the settings for the power source you are currently using.

Use the following steps to set up your MacBook for minimum energy use and maximum working time:

1. **Open the Energy Saver pane of the System Preferences application.**

2. **Click the Battery tab to configure energy use while operating on battery power (see figure 10.3).**

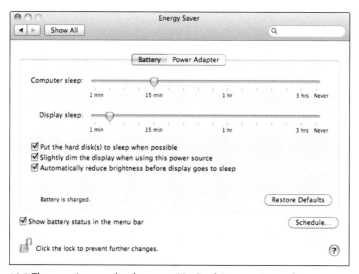

10.3 These options apply when your MacBook is operating on battery power.

3. **Use the top slider to control the amount of inactive time before the entire system goes to sleep.** The MacBook uses the least amount of power when it is asleep, using only slightly more than when it is shut off. Of course, it wakes up a lot faster than it starts up so sleep is a good thing. You want to set a time that conserves power, but that doesn't go to sleep so frequently that it interrupts what you are doing.

4. **Use the bottom slider to set the amount of inactive time before the display goes dark.** The display is one of the highest drains on your battery's power so you can extend your battery life by having the display sleep after shorter periods of activity. Of course, if it goes to sleep too quickly, it can be intrusive and annoying so you need to find a good balance between these effects.

5. **In most cases, you should leave the Put the hard disk(s) to sleep when possible check box selected.** If you notice that you have to pause frequently when what you are doing has to save data to the hard drive, try deselecting this check box.

6. **Select the Slightly dim the display when using this power source check box if you want your display to have a lower brightness when operating on the battery.** Dimming causes the screen to go to a lower brightness setting before the display sleeps (when it goes totally dark). In my experimentation, it appears that this function reduces screen brightness by about two ticks on the brightness indicator.

7. **Select the Automatically reduce brightness before display goes to sleep check box if you want your display's brightness to be reduced automatically before it goes to sleep.** This saves a little power but is more useful because you have some warning before the MacBook goes to sleep.

8. **Click the Power Adapter tab.** You see slightly different options in the pane (see figure 10.4).

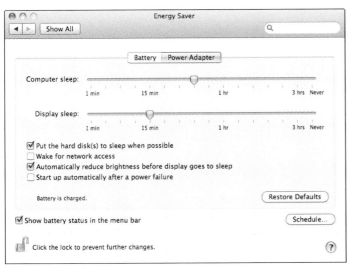

10.4 These options apply when your MacBook is connected to the power adapter.

9. **Configure the settings like you did for operating on the battery.** Usually, you are less concerned about saving energy when you are operating on the power adapter so you can extend sleep times to prevent interruptions.

10. **Select the Wake for network access check box if you want the MacBook to wake up when network activity is detected.** (This setting replaces the Automatically dim display setting for battery power option.)

Automatically Starting or Stopping MacBook

You can configure MacBook to automatically start up, sleep, restart, or shut down according to a schedule. To do this, perform the following steps:

1. **Open the Energy Saver pane of the System Preferences application.**
2. **Click Schedule.** The Schedule sheet appears.
3. **To set an automatic startup or wake time, select the Start up or wake check box and set the time you want this event to occur using the pop-up menu and time box.**
4. **To set an automatic sleep, restart, or shutdown time, select the lower check box on the sheet, select Sleep, Restart, or Shut Down on the pop-up menu, and set the time you want the selected event to occur using the pop-up menu and time box.**
5. **Click OK.** The sheet closes and the schedules you set take effect.

11. **Select Start up automatically after a power failure if you want your MacBook to start up after it has lost power.** This setting is more applicable for desktop Macs because your MacBook has a battery. However, if the power remains out so long that the battery is completely drained, your MacBook will automatically restart when power is restored.

To return the energy configuration to what Apple considers optimal for most users, click Restore Defaults.

Genius

If the MacBook's lid is shut, the schedule has no effect.

Note

Adopting low energy habits

Although configuring the energy use of your MacBook has some impact on how long you can operate it on its battery, you can also adopt low energy habits to maximize the amount of time your MacBook operates on its battery. Here are some ideas to consider:

- **Lower the brightness of your display.** Because it is one of the higher demands on your battery's power, you want to set your display's brightness at the lowest brightness level that is still comfortable to see to maximize battery life. To dim your screen, use the Brightness slider on the Displays pane of the System Preferences application, or press F1 to decrease it or F2 to increase it.

- **Set automatic brightness adjustment.** Open the Displays pane of the System Preferences application and ensure Automatically adjust brightness as ambient light changes is enabled. This automatically dims the display in lower-level light conditions and increases it in brighter conditions. If you use the MacBook in bright conditions for an extended period, you might want to disable this and instead manually set the brightness level to the dimmest you can tolerate.

- **Avoid applications that constantly read from the hard drive.** While you probably won't have much choice on this, some applications have settings that impact hard drive use, such as autosave features (you can increase the amount of time between automatic saves to reduce hard drive use, and thus energy use).

- **Avoid applications that constantly read from a CD or DVD.** If you can copy files you need onto your hard drive and use them from there, you use power at a lower rate than if your MacBook is constantly accessing its removable media drive. For example, when you want to listen to music or watch movies, you can add the content to your iTunes library so you don't need to use the CD or DVD drive.

- **Use an iPod.** Playing content in iTunes requires a lot of hard drive activity and is a heavy user of battery power. Using an iPod for these tasks saves your MacBook for the tasks you can only do on it.

- **Put your MacBook to sleep whenever you aren't actively using it by closing the lid.** When you open the lid or press a key, the MacBook wakes up quickly, so putting it to sleep frequently doesn't cause a lot of wasted time for you.

Genius You can also set a hot corner for display sleep on the Exposé subtab of the Exposé & Spaces pane of the System Preferences application. If you aren't going to be using your MacBook for a little while, move the pointer to the hot corner to make the display sleep.

Powering Your MacBook while Traveling

If you are traveling for a long period of time, the odds are good that you're going to run out of battery power, even if you have tweaked your MacBook for maximum operating time and you practice low energy habits. You can reduce the chances of running out of power by being ready to power your MacBook while you are on the move.

Note Most airports have power outlets available in the gate areas, but they aren't always obvious to see and can be hidden by chairs or other obstacles. Some airports have charging stations that are a handy way to top off your MacBook's battery.

Following are some recommended items that can help you manage your power on the move:

- **Standard power adapter.** Whenever there's a power outlet available, you can use the included adapter to run the MacBook and to charge its battery.

- **MagSafe Airline Adapter.** With this adapter, you can connect your MacBook to the power outlet that is available in some kinds of seats on airlines. The requirement is that the seat must have an EmPower or 20mm power port.

- **International adapters.** If you travel internationally, get a set of power adapters so that you can connect the MacBook power adapter to power outlets in a variety of countries.

Caution While the airline adapter looks like it might be compatible with the DC power port in automobiles, it isn't.

Maintaining Battery Life

Over time, the accuracy of the battery charge indicator decreases along with the battery's ability to hold a charge. However, you can improve your battery's capability again by calibrating it every so often. Here's how:

1. **Charge the battery so it's full.**

2. **Leave the battery in the fully charged state for at least two hours by leaving the power adapter connected.**

3. **Disconnect the power adapter.**

4. **Use the MacBook on battery power until you see the second or third low power warning.**

5. **Save all your open documents and quit all applications.** Eventually, your MacBook goes to sleep.

6. **Let the MacBook sleep or shut it down for five hours.**

7. **Reconnect the power adapter and fully recharge the battery.**

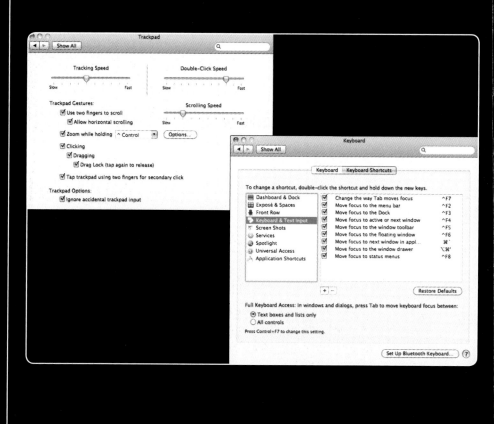

To get the most from your MacBook, you should customize the keyboard and trackpad so that they work according to your preferences. And learning to use keyboard shortcuts effectively will help you work more quickly and efficiently. You might want to add a mouse or external keyboard to your toolkit, especially for those times when you are using the computer at a desk; Bluetooth mice and keyboards enable you to do this without being tethered with cables.

Using the Trackpad Effectively

A trackpad is an ideal input device for a mobile computer because it provides a similar degree of control that a mouse does but doesn't require anything external to the computer. The MacBook trackpad provides all the basic capabilities you need to enable you to point and click, but it certainly doesn't stop there. The MacBook's trackpad supports gestures, which go way beyond just pointing and clicking. Using combinations of your fingers and motion, you can scroll windows, zoom in, zoom out, and so on. You can use the trackpad much more effectively by tweaking its options over time.

You can configure the trackpad to work according to your preferences with the Trackpad pane of the System Preferences application. Here's how:

1. **Open the Trackpad pane of the System Preferences application.** The trackpad's configuration options appear (see figure 11.1).

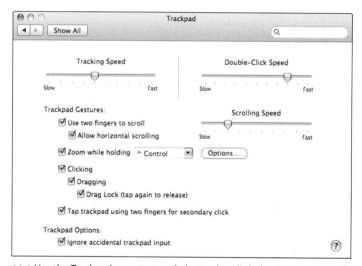

11.1 Use the Trackpad pane to tweak the trackpad's behavior to your preferences.

2. **Use the three Speed sliders at the top of the pane to set the tracking, double-click, and scrolling speeds.** The faster you set the tracking and scrolling speeds, the farther the pointer moves on the screen for the same motion of your fingers on the trackpad. The faster you set the double-click speed, the less time between "clicks" on the trackpad to register as a double-click.

3. **To be able to scroll by dragging two fingers on the trackpad, select the Use two fingers to scroll check box; when enabled, you can also select the Allow horizontal scrolling check box to be able to scroll horizontally and vertically.**

4. **To be able to zoom by dragging two fingers on the trackpad, select the Zoom while holding check box and on the pop-up menu, choose the modifier key that you want to press to activate zooming; then click Options.** You see the Zoom Options sheet (see figure 11.2). (If you don't enable zooming, skip to Step 8.)

> When zoomed in, the screen image moves:
> ○ Continuously with pointer
> ⦿ Only when the pointer reaches an edge
> ○ So the pointer is at or near the center of the image
>
> ☑ Smooth images (Press ⌥⌘\ to turn smoothing on or off)
>
> (Done)

11.2 You can further configure Zoom options on this sheet.

5. **Use the radio buttons to configure how the image scrolls while you are zoomed.** You can have it move with the pointer, move only when the pointer reaches the edge of the screen, or so that the pointer is always near the center of the image.

6. **If movement seems sluggish when zoomed, deselect the Smooth images check box.**

7. **Click Done.** The sheet closes.

8. **To be able to perform a single mouse-click by tapping the trackpad, select the Clicking check box.** If you don't enable this, skip to Step 11.

9. **If you performed Step 8 and want to be able to drag objects by dragging your finger on the trackpad, select the Dragging check box.**

10. **If you enabled Dragging and want to be able to lock the pointer so an object continues to be attached to the pointer until you tap the trackpad again, select the Drag Lock check box.**

11. **To be able to perform a secondary click by tapping two fingers on the trackpad, select the Tap trackpad using two fingers for secondary click check box.** A secondary click is equivalent to a right-click with a two-button mouse or a Ctrl+click. This typically activates a contextual menu when you are working in the Finder, for example.

12. **To make the trackpad less sensitive to keep accidental inputs from occurring, select the Ignore accidental trackpad input check box.** If you find commands or actions happening when you don't intend them to, make sure this is enabled.

You may have to intentionally use some of the gestures for a little while, such as using dragging, but soon you'll find them becoming second nature and you'll be able to control things on the desktop quickly and easily. If you find some unexpected actions happening, check the gestures you have configured again. Some of them might cause you a problem if they mimic a natural motion of your fingers; either disable the gesture or simply be aware of it until you get used to it.

Using the Keyboard Effectively

Your MacBook's keyboard is used not only for typing but also for controlling your computer, particularly through keyboard shortcuts. In this section, you first learn how to configure the basic functions of the keyboard and then how to control the language it uses. In the latter parts, you learn how to use the keyboard to efficiently control your MacBook.

Configuring the keyboard

Start with the Keyboard pane of the System Preferences application, as shown in the following steps:

1. **Open the Keyboard tab of the Keyboard pane of the System Preferences application (see figure 11.3).**

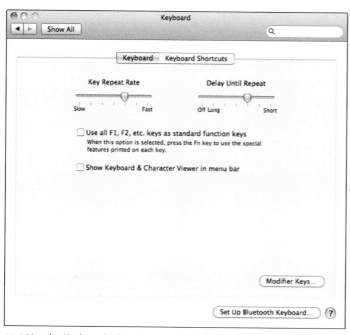

11.3 Use the Keyboard tab to tune your MacBook's keyboard.

2. **Drag the sliders at the top of the pane to configure how keys repeat when you hold them down.** The Key Repeat Rate slider controls how fast the corresponding character repeats while the Delay Until Repeat slider controls how long you hold the key down to start repeating.

3. **If you want the function keys to behave as standard function keys instead of the default actions they are programmed to perform (such as F2 to brighten the display), select the Use all F1, F2, etc. keys as standard function keys check box.** If you select this option, you must hold the Fn key down and press the appropriate key to perform its action (such as F10 to mute your MacBook).

4. **To display the Input menu, including the Keyboard Viewer and Character Viewer commands, on the menu bar, select the Show Keyboard & Character Viewer in menu bar check box.**

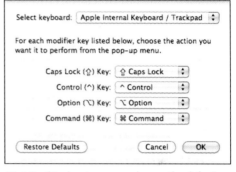

5. **Click Modifier Keys.** The Modifier Keys sheet appears (see figure 11.4).

6. **For each of the four modifier keys, use the pop-up menu to select the action that you want to occur when**

11.4 On this sheet, you can change the default modifier keys.

you press that key. If your keyboard preference is such that the Control key is more convenient for you, you might want to set it to be the Command key, because you use that key more frequently. You can select No Action to disable a key, in which case it is grayed out on the sheet.

7. **Click OK to set your preferences and close the sheet.**

Genius

I have never discovered a real use for the Caps Lock key, but I have accidentally turned it on thousands of times and found myself TYPING IN ALL CAPS, which is very annoying. You can disable this key by choosing No Action on its pop-up menu. Ah, now you don't have to yell as you type just because you accidentally hit this key.

Configuring language settings and the Input menu

You can configure the languages you use for the keyboard, along with other input preferences, using the Language & Text pane of the System Preferences application.

To configure languages, follow these steps:

1. **Open the Language tab of the Language & Text pane of the System Preferences application (see figure 11.5).**

11.5 You can configure your MacBook's keyboard to use any or all of the languages.

2. **Click Edit List.**

3. **On the resulting sheet, click the check box for any language you don't want to be available and click OK.** The sheet closes and the languages whose check boxes are not selected are removed from the list. You also see a warning that you have to log out and log in for the changes to take effect in applications.

4. **Drag the languages up or down the list to change their order with the one you want to be the default at the top of the list.**

5. **On the Order for sorted lists pop-up menu, choose the language that should be used to sort lists.** This is used regardless of the language you happened to be using at any point in time. For example, if you choose English on the list and have Italian as the current keyboard language, lists are still sorted according to English.

To configure global symbol and text substitution, use the following steps:

1. **Open the Text tab of the Language & Text pane of the System Preferences application (see figure 11.6).**

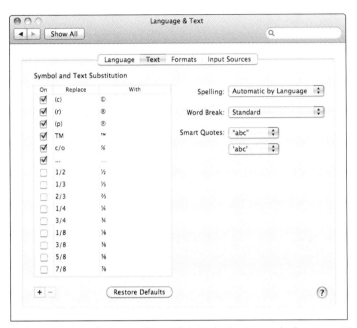

11.6 On the Text tab, you configure global substitutions and other text settings.

Note

The settings on the Text tab are global, meaning that your MacBook uses them unless overridden by an application. For example, if you use Word and have autocorrect set such that "(c)" gets corrected to the word "copyright," that setting overrides the global text substitution setting, which happens to be the copyright symbol © by default.

2. **Select the On check box for any text substitutions you want to enable or deselect the On check box to disable a substitution.**

Genius

You can create custom substitutions by clicking the Add (+) button at the bottom of the substitution list. A new entry appears on the list and is enabled by default. Type the characters that will be replaced, press the Tab key, and then type what those characters will be replaced with. The substitution is added to the list and can be used just like the defaults. You can remove a substitution by selecting it and clicking the Remove (–) button (or you can just disable it by deselecting its On check box).

3. **On the Spelling pop-up menu, choose how you want Mac OS X's Spell Check function to work.** The default is Automatic by Language, which means your current language is used. You can open the menu to choose a specific language or choose Setup to do an advanced configuration of the spell checker.

4. **On the Word Break pop-up menu, choose how you want word breaks to be applied.** You can choose Standard (the default) or you can choose a specific language on the pop-up menu.

5. **Use the Smart Quotes pop-up menu to determine what is entered when you press either single or double quotes.**

You can configure format options like so:

1. **Open the Formats tab of the Language & Text pane of the System Preferences application (see figure 11.7).**

11.7 On the Formats tab, configure date, time, and currency formats.

2. **Choose the region whose formats you want to use on the Region pop-up menu.**

3. **Use the pop-up menus to configure options for the various formats, such as the calendar you want, currency, and so on.**

4. **To specifically configure a format, click its Customize button, use the controls on the resulting sheet to customize the format, and click OK to use the new settings.**

You can also configure the Input menu, which enables you to quickly choose among languages and select some other handy keyboard tools. Here's how:

1. **Open the Input Sources tab of the Language & Text pane of the System Preferences application.**

2. **If you want the Keyboard & Character Viewer to be available, select its On check box.** The menu appears on the Finder's menu bar.

3. **Select the check box next to each input source you want to have available to you.**

4. **If you selected at least two input sources, select the Use the same one in all documents radio button or the Allow a different one for each document radio button to choose whether more than one input source can be available at the same time.**

5. **Select the Show input menu in menu bar check box.** The Input menu appears on the menu bar; its icon is the flag for the currently selected input source.

Using keyboard tricks

It's worth taking some time to learn some of the ways you can control your MacBook using its keyboard; there's a lot of power hidden behind those mild-mannered keys.

Controlling your MacBook with function keys

The MacBook includes a number of built-in functions on the function keys that are quite useful (see Table 11.1).

Table 11.1 MacBook Default Function Keys

Function Key	What It Does
F1	Decreases display brightness.
F2	Increases display brightness.
F3	Uses Exposé to show thumbnails of all windows open in all applications; click a window to make it active.
F4	Opens or closes the Dashboard.
F7	Rewind/Previous in various applications, such as iTunes.
F8	Play/Pause in various applications, such as iTunes.
F9	Fast-forward/Next in various applications, such as iTunes.
F10	Mutes sound.
F11	Decreases volume.
F12	Increases volume.
Eject	While technically not a function key because it's not labeled that way, this single-purpose key is useful nonetheless for ejecting a selected item, such as a DVD, a network volume, and so on.

By default, you can perform these functions by simply pressing the appropriate function key. As you'll learn, you can remap these keys to different functions if you so choose. Remember, you can select the Use all F1, F2, etc. keys as standard function keys check box to make the standard function keys available; if you do this, hold the Fn key down and press the function keys shown in Table 11.1 to perform their default functions.

Genius
The F5 and F6 keys don't have default actions preprogrammed for them and so are especially useful for assigning specific actions that you want to be able to activate by pressing a single key.

Controlling your MacBook with default keyboard shortcuts

Mac OS X includes support for many keyboard shortcuts by default. For example, you've probably used ⌘+Q to quit applications. There are many more keyboard shortcuts available to you. The only challenge to using keyboard shortcuts is learning (and remembering) which ones are available to you. Fortunately, there are a number of ways to discover keyboard shortcuts, as described in the following list:

- **The Keyboard Shortcuts tab of the Keyboard pane of the System Preferences application.** If you click this tab, you see a list of Mac OS X keyboard shortcuts. Select the type of shortcuts in which you are interested and the current shortcuts appear in the right pane of the window (see figure 11.8). You can also use this pane to change the current shortcuts and to create new ones.

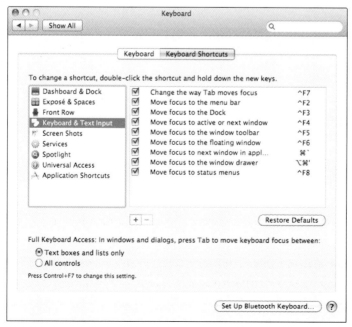

11.8 You should become familiar with the keyboard shortcuts for the commands you use most frequently.

- **Menus.** When you open menus, keyboard shortcuts are shown next to the commands for which they are available.

- **Mac Help.** Open the Help menu and search for shortcuts for the Finder and for your favorite applications.

Configuring keyboard shortcuts

Using the Keyboard Shortcuts tab of the Keyboard pane, you can configure keyboard shortcuts. You can enable or disable the default keyboard shortcuts, change them, and add your own keyboard shortcuts.

To configure default keyboard shortcuts, perform the following steps:

1. **Open the Keyboard Shortcuts tab of the Keyboard pane of the System Preferences application.** You see a list of standard OS keyboard shortcuts in various categories, such as Dashboard & Dock, Front Row, Screen Shots, and so on.

2. **Select the category containing the shortcuts you want to change.** The current commands and associated shortcuts are shown in the right pane.

3. **Disable or enable any of the listed shortcuts by deselecting or selecting the shortcut's check box.**

4. **To change the key combination for a shortcut, double-click the current shortcut and press the new key combination you want to use for that command.**

Creating your own application keyboard shortcuts

You can create your own keyboard shortcut for any menu command in any application. To add your own keyboard shortcuts, perform the following steps:

1. **Identify the specific command for which you want to create a keyboard shortcut.** If it is a command specific to an application, note the exact name of the command, including whether it includes an ellipsis. You can find commands on application menus or by accessing an application's Help system.

2. **Open the Keyboard Shortcuts tab of the Keyboard pane of the System Preferences application.**

3. **Click the Add (+) button at the bottom of the list of shortcuts.** The Add Shortcut sheet appears.

4. **On the Application pop-up menu, choose All Applications if you want the shortcut to be available for all applications, or choose a specific application to create the shortcut only within it.**

5. **In the Menu Title box, type the name of the command for which you want to create a shortcut exactly as it appears on its menu.** If the command contains an ellipsis, you also need to include that because the text has to exactly match the name of the command.

6. **In the Keyboard Shortcut field, press the key combination for the shortcut that you want to use to access the command (see figure 11.9).**

7. **Click Add.** The sheet closes and when you return to the Keyboard Shortcuts tab, the shortcut you added is shown under the related application located in the Application Shortcuts category or under All Applications if you configured the shortcut to be available under all applications.

11.9 You can use this sheet to create your own keyboard shortcuts in any application or in all applications.

8. **Open the application in which you created the shortcut.** The keyboard command you created appears next to the command on the application's menu.

9. **Test the shortcut.** Sometimes applications already have a shortcut mapped to the shortcut you create, which can cause a conflict. You can resolve these either by disabling the application's shortcut or choosing a different keyboard shortcut.

Navigating with the keyboard

One of the least used, but most useful, aspects of using keyboard shortcuts is keyboard navigation. You can use the keyboard to access almost any area on your MacBook in any application, including the Finder. For example, you can open any menu item by using only keys, even if that item does not have a keyboard shortcut assigned to it.

To see what the default keyboard navigation tools are, open the Keyboard Shortcuts tab of the Keyboard pane in the System Preferences application and select Keyboard & Text Input. You see the commands explained in Table 11.2. A quick explanation shows you how these work.

Table 11.2 Keyboard Navigation

Description	What It Does	Default Shortcut (hold the Fn key down if the standard function key preference is not enabled)
Change the way Tab moves focus	By default, pressing the Tab key in windows and dialog boxes moves you only between text boxes and lists. This command toggles between that mode and having the Tab key take you to every element in a dialog box or window.	Ctrl+F7
Move focus to the menu bar	Highlights the Apple menu; use the Tab or arrow keys to move to other menus and commands on the menu bar.	Ctrl+F2
Move focus to the Dock	Makes the Finder icon on the Dock active; use the Tab or arrow keys to move to icons on the Dock.	Ctrl+F3
Move focus to the active window or next window	Moves into the currently active window or takes you to the next window if you are already in a window.	Ctrl+F4
Move focus to the window toolbar	If you are using an application with a toolbar, this makes the toolbar active. Use the Tab or arrow keys to select a button on the toolbar.	Ctrl+F5
Move focus to the floating window	If you are using an application that has a floating window, this takes you into the floating window.	Ctrl+F6
Move focus to the next window in the active application	Moves you among the open windows in the current application.	⌘+`
Move focus to the status menus in the menu bar	If you have enabled additional menus, such as the Displays menu, in the Mac OS X menu bar, this command highlights the first one; use the arrow or Tab keys to move to and select menus and their commands.	Ctrl+F8
Select the previous input source	When you have multiple input sources configured, this returns you to the one you used most recently.	⌘+spacebar
Select next source in Input menu	When you have multiple input sources configured, this moves you to the previous source on the menu.	Option+⌘+spacebar

When something, such as a menu, is ready for your action (it is selected in other words), Mac OS X calls that being in focus. For example, the shortcut for putting the menu bar in focus is Ctrl+F2; if you haven't set your keyboard to use the standard function keys, hold down the Fn key and press Ctrl+F2. The apple marking the Apple menu is highlighted to show it is in focus. Once it is in focus, you can move to any menu and commands by pressing the right- and left-arrow keys until the menu you want to use is highlighted; then use the down-arrow key to open the menu. Once open, use the down-, up-, left-, and right-arrow keys to select the command you want. When that is selected, press the Return key to activate it. It takes a little effort to get the hang of this, but once you do, you can quickly move to any menu command.

Using the Input menu

The Input menu enables you to change the current language you are using or to activate specific tools, such as the Character Viewer. A flag representing the language you have made the default is shown at the top of this menu on the menu bar. When you open it, you see the items you configured there (see figure 11.10).

You can change the current input source, which is indicated by the check mark, to a different one by selecting a different source on the menu. When you do this, the keyboard is converted to the layout appropriate to the source you selected.

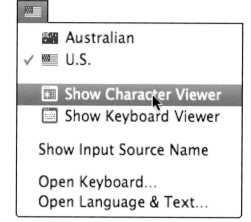

11.10 The Input menu enables you to change input sources and open other tools, such as the Character Viewer.

Using the Character Viewer

The Character Viewer is a tool to help you find special characters in various languages and quickly apply those characters to your documents. You can open the Character Viewer by doing either of the following:

- **Open the Input menu and select Show Character Viewer.**

- **In the Finder, choose Edit ⇨ Special Characters.**

When the viewer opens, you see that it has two tabs (see figure 11.11). The By Category tab enables you to select and insert categories of characters you need. When you find a character you use regularly, you can add it to the other tab, which is the Favorites tab, so you can grab it easily and quickly.

To find and use a special character, perform the following steps:

1. **Open the Character Viewer.**

2. **On the View pop-up menu, select the language sets you want to access.** For example, to see Roman characters, select Roman. To see all possible characters, select All Characters.

3. **Click the By Category tab.**

4. **Select the category of character you want to view in the left pane.** For example, select Math to view mathematical symbols. The characters in the category you select appear in the right pane.

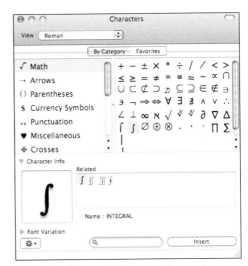

11.11 The Character Viewer enables you to configure and select special characters.

5. **Select the character with which you want to work by clicking it.**

Genius

You can search for special characters by description or code using the Search tool that appears at the bottom of the Character Viewer window.

6. **Expand the Character Info section by clicking its expansion triangle at the bottom of the window.** You see a large version of the selected character along with its name. You also see characters to which the selected one is related. You can choose to work with one of the related characters by clicking it. The one you click becomes selected, even if it is not in the currently selected category.

7. **To apply different fonts to the character, click the expansion triangle next to the Font Variation tab.** When you expand the Font Variation section, a preview pane appears that shows a preview of the character you have selected along with its name. You can see a version of the character in each font family in the collection selected on the Collections pop-up menu.

8. **Select the font collection you want to use on the Collections pop-up menu.**

9. **Click the version of the character you want to use.**

10. **Continue adjusting the character until it is the way you want it.**

11. **Click Insert with Font.** The character is pasted into the active document at the insertion point.

Note

If you don't apply a font to the character, the Insert with Font button is just the Insert button.

12. **Close the viewer.** Because it remains on top of all other windows, you'll probably want to keep it closed whenever you aren't using it.

Genius

After you configure a character and want to reuse it, save it as a favorite. Open the Action menu at the bottom of the window and select Add to Favorites. This copies the character onto the Favorites tab. You can use it again by selecting the Favorites tab and clicking the character.

Using the Keyboard Viewer

The Keyboard Viewer is a simple tool that shows you the layout of the keyboard in specific situations. To use it, select Show Keyboard Viewer on the Input menu. The Keyboard Viewer appears (see figure 11.12). You see what each key on the keyboard represents for the current input source. Hold down the modifier keys to see their impact.

11.12 If you want to see what pressing a key does, check out the Keyboard Viewer.

Configuring Bluetooth on a MacBook

Bluetooth support is built in to your MacBook, so you can wirelessly connect to and use any Bluetooth device.

Bluetooth communication is set up between two devices through a process called pairing, where each device recognizes the other and they are paired so that they can communicate with each other. A single device can communicate with more than one other Bluetooth device at the same time. Each device with which your MacBook communicates over Bluetooth must be paired separately.

To be able to pair two devices together, they must be able to "find" one another. To accomplish this automatically, the devices must be discoverable, meaning that they are broadcasting their Bluetooth signals to other devices in the area so that those devices can find and pair with the discoverable device. If you don't want your MacBook to be discoverable by other devices, you can turn this off, but pairing devices will be a bit more difficult.

Bluetooth communication requires hardware (transmitter/receiver) and software. Both of these are part of your MacBook, but you need to configure Bluetooth services on your MacBook before you try to connect Bluetooth devices to it. Here's what to do:

1. **Open the Bluetooth pane of the System Preferences application.** The Bluetooth pane appears. In the center part of the Bluetooth pane, you see the devices with which your MacBook is currently communicating or the "No Devices" message if you haven't paired it with any devices yet (see figure 11.13).

11.13 Use the Bluetooth pane to configure Bluetooth services on your MacBook.

2. **Select the On check box.** Bluetooth services start.

3. **Select the Discoverable check box.** This makes your MacBook discoverable by other devices because your MacBook transmits signals that other devices can detect. You can still connect to your configured Bluetooth devices when this box is not selected; your MacBook just won't be able to be detected by other devices automatically.

4. **Select the Show Bluetooth status in the menu bar check box.**

263

5. **Click Advanced.** The Advanced sheet appears.

6. **Leave the Open Bluetooth Setup Assistant at startup when no input device is present check box unselected.** This is for desktop computers that might only have Bluetooth input devices; because your MacBook has a built-in keyboard and trackpad, it always has input devices.

7. **Select the Allow Bluetooth devices to wake this computer check box.** When you use a Bluetooth mouse or keyboard, you'll be able to wake your MacBook with one of those devices.

8. **Select the Prompt for all incoming audio requests check box if you want to be warned when Bluetooth audio devices attempt to communicate with your MacBook.**

9. **To share your MacBook Internet connection using Bluetooth, select the Share my Internet connection with other Bluetooth devices check box.** Because it's slower than Wi-Fi, you should use AirPort or Ethernet instead of Bluetooth to share an Internet connection with other computers. However, sharing through Bluetooth can be useful for PDAs or other handheld Internet devices that only support Bluetooth communication.

10. **Click OK.** The sheet closes. Your MacBook is ready to connect to Bluetooth devices.

Adding a Bluetooth Mouse

Using Bluetooth, you can easily connect a mouse to your MacBook.

The rest of this section focuses on Bluetooth mice, but using a wireless USB mouse is similar in many respects. The main differences are that you have to connect the USB transmitter to a USB port, and you don't have to go through the pairing process.

To set up a new Bluetooth device by pairing it with your MacBook, you use the Bluetooth Setup Assistant. Follow these steps:

1. **If the mouse is not auto-discoverable, and most mice are not, then press its discoverable button.** These are usually small buttons located on the bottom of the mouse. When you push this button, the mouse goes into Discoverable mode, which causes the device to start broadcasting a Bluetooth signal that your MacBook can detect. To make an Apple Wireless Mighty Mouse discoverable, turn it on by moving the switch on the underside so the sensor is exposed; the green power light illuminates.

2. **Open the Bluetooth menu and choose Set Up Bluetooth Device.** The Bluetooth Setup Assistant opens.

3. **Click Continue.**

4. **Click Mouse.**

5. **Click Continue.** Your MacBook searches for available Bluetooth mice and presents the mice it finds on the list (see figure 11.14).

11.14 My MacBook has found a Bluetooth mouse called bradm's mouse.

6. **Select the mouse you want to pair.**

7. **Click Continue.** When the pairing is successful, you see the Conclusion screen.

8. **Click Quit.** The Bluetooth mouse is ready to configure.

Following are the steps to configure an Apple Wireless Mighty Mouse (mice that have other features are configured for those specific features, but the general process is the same):

1. **Open the Mouse pane of the System Preferences application.**

2. **Use the sliders to determine tracking, double-clicking, and scrolling speeds.**

3. **Choose the action that happens when you press the left or right side of the mouse on the pop-up menus with lines pointing to the respective sides.** A common configuration is to select Primary Button (click) on the left menu and Secondary Button (right+click) on the right menu.

4. **Use the top pop-up menu to select the action that occurs when you press the scroll ball.**

5. **Use the pop-up menu connected to the side buttons to set the action that happens when you "squeeze" the buttons on the sides of the mouse.** Though there is a button on each side of the mouse, they are connected and perform only a single action.

6. **Use the Scrolling pop-up menu to configure the Scroll ball, such as to allow both vertical and horizontal scrolling.**

7. **To use the Scroll ball to zoom, select the Zoom using scroll ball check box, choose the modifier key to activate scrolling on the pop-up menu, and click the Options button to configure zooming options.**

Adding a Bluetooth Keyboard

There may be times when you prefer to use an external keyboard instead of the MacBook's built-in keyboard. Just like it is with a mouse, it is easy and convenient to add a Bluetooth keyboard. Follow these steps:

1. **If the keyboard is not auto-discoverable, press its discoverable button.** These are usually small buttons located on the bottom of the keyboard. When you push this button, the keyboard goes into Discoverable mode, which causes it to start broadcasting a Bluetooth signal that your MacBook can detect.

Note
Some keyboards, such as the Apple Wireless Keyboard, have a power button. Of course, you need to press this button to turn on the keyboard before you can pair it. In most cases, this also puts the keyboard into Discoverable mode.

2. **Open the Bluetooth menu and choose Set Up Bluetooth Device.** The Bluetooth Setup Assistant opens.

3. **Click Continue.**

4. **Click Keyboard.**

5. **Click Continue.** Your MacBook searches for available Bluetooth keyboards and presents all those it finds on the list (see figure 11.15). Each keyboard is indicated by its name or a series of numbers, depending on whether your MacBook can decipher the keyboard's signal to include its name.

6. **Select the keyboard you want to pair.**

7. **Click Continue.** The pairing process starts and you see the Keyboard setup screen. Here, you type the passkey shown on the keyboard to complete the pairing process.

8. **On the Bluetooth keyboard, type the passkey shown in the Assistant's window.**

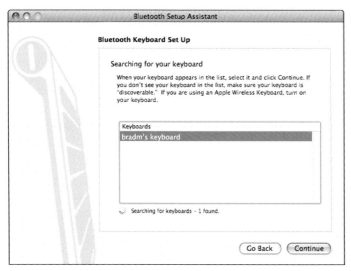

11.15 The keyboard called bradm's keyboard is actually an Apple Wireless Keyboard.

9. **Press Return.** If the pairing is successful, you see the Conclusion screen.

10. **Click Quit.** The Bluetooth keyboard is ready to configure.

After you pair a Bluetooth keyboard with your MacBook, configure it using the Keyboard pane in the System Preferences application. You see controls for the specific keyboard you are using. These might or might not be the same as the MacBook's internal keyboard, but in most cases, they are similar. Steps for configuring a typical keyboard appear earlier in the chapter.

Note   If you use different preferences for the Bluetooth keyboard than what you prefer with the MacBook internal keyboard, you need to reconfigure the Keyboard preferences each time you change keyboards.

How Do I Make Better Use of My MacBook's Audio?

Sound is an important part of the MacBook experience. If you use iTunes, iDVD, Front Row, GarageBand, or any other Mac digital media application, audio is a major part of the experience. And so understanding how to get the most from your MacBook audio capabilities is fundamental to enjoying your MacBook to the fullest. On its own, a MacBook has reasonable audio capabilities. If you want to invest in a bit of hardware and some additional software, you can transform your MacBook into an audio powerhouse.

Getting Sound Out of a MacBook

Many applications that you use, including iTunes, iDVD, iPhoto, DVD Player, QuickTime, and iChat, involve the use of sound. In this section, you can learn about sound output options that are available to you, and how to choose and use those options to ensure that you have a great audio experience as you work with your MacBook.

Understanding sound output options

When it comes to audio, there are two fundamental options: analog or digital. Like seemingly everything else, digital is better than analog from the quality perspective, but taking advantage of digital sound is more expensive and requires a bit more work than does analog sound. With your MacBook, you can use both options in different situations.

On the analog side, you have the following methods for getting sound out of your MacBook:

- **Built-in speakers.** MacBooks include built-in stereo speakers that actually do a decent job considering their small size and basic capabilities. However, if the quality of sound is important to you when you listen to music or watch movies or television shows, it's unlikely that the internal speakers will satisfy you. They are a bit on the tinny side and their bass certainly isn't impressive compared to a home theater or car audio system.

- **Headphones.** You can connect any analog headphones to the MacBook headphones/digital minijack located on the left side of the computer (it's marked with the headphones icon).

- **External speakers.** You can connect any set of powered (also called computer) speakers to your MacBook's optical digital input/analog line out minijack.

When it comes to digital music, you need to add an external speaker system, such as a 5.1 surround sound speaker system, to be able to experience the best in sound quality for movies, television shows, and music. Fortunately, your MacBook has the internal hardware required to support digital speaker systems so that all you need to add is the system itself.

Using external speakers

To be compatible with your MacBook, you must use a powered speaker system because the optical digital input/analog line out minijack on the MacBook doesn't provide enough power to drive a speaker, so you can't just use standard audio speakers. The good news is that there are many kinds of powered speaker sets available.

Connecting an analog speaker system

Analog speakers are the simplest to install. If you have a two-speaker set, place one speaker on your right and one on your left. If you have a three-speaker system, place the bass unit on the ground or on your desktop. Connect the input line for the speaker set (which is usually connected to one of the satellite speakers or to the bass unit) to the optical digital input/analog line out minijack on the MacBook. Connect the speakers to the bass unit and power the system. That's all there is to it, and you're ready to control the sound (more on this later in this section).

Connecting a digital speaker system

Your MacBook has only one sound out port, which is the headphones/digital audio out port. While this looks like a typical stereo minijack port, its appearance is deceiving. When you connect a typical stereo minijack plug, it behaves like a regular stereo minijack, just like the headphones port on an iPod, and you get stereo sound output. To access the digital output from the port, you need a special adapter that connects to a digital audio cable and fits into the port in order to make the correct connections for digital audio. This is called a Mini Toslink adapter; when you buy a digital audio cable, look for one that includes this adapter (see figure 12.1). You can also purchase the cable and adapter separately.

12.1 To connect to a digital sound system, you use a digital cable with a Mini Toslink adapter, such as this example from Belkin.

The input connectors on your speaker system determine the specific type of audio cable you need. There are two basic options: digital coax or Toslink (which is more commonly called optical digital). If you use a 5.1 system, it probably includes a central control unit with the input jacks; the jacks available on this control unit determine the cable you need. It probably has more than one input, including a digital optical input, digital coax input, and analog stereo input.

After you place the speakers, you need to connect their wires together at a central point; typically, you connect them to the bass speaker along with power. Then you connect the bass input wire to the control unit and use the cable you purchased to connect the control unit's input jack to your MacBook headphones/digital audio out minijack.

Note Some speaker systems connect via one of your MacBook's USB ports. These speakers work like other external systems, with the exception that they don't disable the MacBook's internal speakers like any system connected to the optical digital input/ analog line out minijack does.

Controlling sound output

When it comes to sound output, be aware that there are up to three types of volume levels:

- **System volume level.** Sets the base level of volume output for the MacBook.

- **Relative volume of applications.** When you adjust volume levels within applications, such as iTunes or a DVD player, you change their volume relative to the system volume level.

- **Physical volume level of an external speaker system.** You control this with the system's volume controls. Like the system volume level, changes you make impact all of the audio coming from your MacBook.

To configure your MacBook output sound, follow these steps:

1. **If you are using headphones or an external speaker system, connect them to the MacBook headphones/digital audio out minijack.**

2. **Open the Sound pane of the System Preferences application.**

3. **Click the Output tab (see figure 12.2).** On this tab, you see the available output devices on the list at the top of the pane. When you select an output device, you see controls for the selected device below the list.

4. **Select the output device over which you want your MacBook to play sound.** The most common options are:

   - Internal Speakers

   - Headphones, which is used for headphones or for external, analog speaker systems

   - Digital Out, which is used for an external, digital speaker system

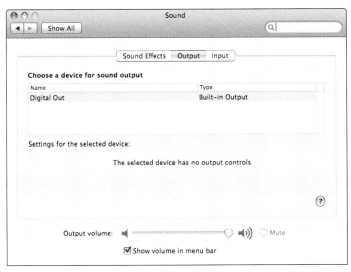

12.2 Use the Output tab of the Sound pane of the System Preferences application to configure how you hear audio.

5. **Use the controls that appear for the selected device to adjust its sound.**

6. **If enabled, drag the Output volume slider to near its center point.** This sets the system volume level at midlevel.

7. **Select the Show volume in menu bar check box.**

Note

When you use the slider on the Volume menu (its icon is the speaker with waves emanating from it) or the volume function keys to adjust volume, you are changing the system volume level. Most applications have keyboard shortcuts to enable you to adjust the application's volume level; in iTunes, press ⌘+↑ or ⌘+↓.

8. **If you are using an external speaker system, set its volume at a relatively low level.**

9. **Open an application that you use to play audio, such as iTunes.** Use that application's volume slider to set its relative volume level (see figure 12.3).

12.3 Use the volume slider on iTunes to set the application's volume relative to the system volume level.

10. **Play the audio and adjust the system volume level accordingly.** Typically, you want to set the system volume at a

273

level such that you can control the volume at each level to the amount you want, such as making it as loud as you want or being able to make it as quiet as you want. This sometimes requires experimentation to get the right balance between system volume level and application volume level. (When you are using external speakers, their volume control is yet a third level to balance.)

Note

If you are using a digital system and see the message "The selected device has no output controls" when Digital Out is selected, you use only the speaker system's controls to set system volume levels and to make other adjustments, such as the bass level, balance, surround sound field, and so on.

Genius

To mute all sound, select the Mute check box or press F10. To unmute the sound, deselect the Mute check box or press F10. (Remember, when you are using a digital speaker system, these controls are disabled.) To increase the system volume level, press F12; to decrease it, press F11.

Working with Sound Effects

Mac OS X includes a number of sound effects that the system uses to alert you or to provide audible feedback for specific events. You control these effects on the Sound Effects tab of the Sound pane of the System Preferences application.

Configuring sound effects

To configure sound effects, perform the following steps:

1. **Open the Sound pane of the System Preferences application.**
2. **Click the Sound Effects tab (see figure 12.4).**
3. **Click a sound on the alert sound list.** The sound plays and becomes the current alert sound.
4. **If your MacBook can output sound through different devices simultaneously, such as through internal speakers and a sound system connected to a USB port, then select the system on which you want the sounds to be played on the Play alerts and sound effects through pop-up menu.**

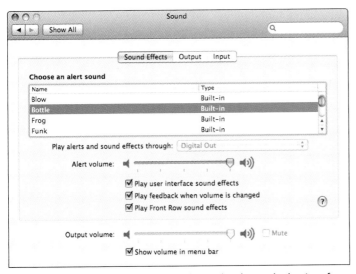

12.4 Use the Sound Effects pane to configure the alert and other interface sounds.

5. **Drag the Alert volume slider to the right to make it louder, or to the left to make it quieter.** This sets the volume of the alert sound relative to the system sound level. The default alert sounds have a relatively low volume level so you'll probably have to set the slider to a high level to hear the alert sound above music or other audio you are listening to.

6. **If you don't want to hear sound effects for system actions, such as when you empty the trash, deselect the Play user interface sound effects check box.**

7. **If you don't want audio feedback when you change the volume level, deselect the Play feedback when volume is changed check box.**

8. **If you don't want to hear Front Row's sound effects, deselect the Play Front Row sound effects check box.** These include sounds when you launch Front Row and when you make menu selections.

Using your own alert sounds

You can also create and use your own alert sounds if you want your MacBook to sport a unique way of communicating with you.

Under Mac OS X, system alert sounds are in the Audio Interchange File Format (AIFF). You can use iTunes to convert or record almost any sound into an AIFF file and use that sound as a custom alert sound.

There are two basic ways in which you can add custom alert sounds: You can add them to specific user accounts so only those users can access them, or you can add them to the system so they are accessible to everyone who uses your MacBook. The steps to add alert sounds are slightly different for each option.

Creating an alert sound

There are many ways to create a custom alert sound, including the following:

- **iMovie.** Use iMovie to create an audio track and save it as an AIFF file. Or you can save part of a movie's audio track as an AIFF file. You can also record narration or other sounds to use as an alert sound. (You learn about getting sound into your MacBook later in this chapter.)

- **iTunes.** You can use iTunes to convert any sound in your library to an AIFF file.

- **GarageBand.** Create a music snippet and save it as an AIFF file.

- **Record audio playing on your MacBook.** Using an application like WireTap Pro from Ambrosia Software, you can record any audio playing on your MacBook and use what you record as an alert sound.

I have included an example showing how to use iMovie to create and save a sound as an alert sound from audio stored in your iTunes library. This technique enables you to add just about any sound as an alert sound. Here's how:

1. **Move the audio you want to use as an alert sound into your iTunes library.** You can add it from the iTunes Store, download it from the Internet, or record it in another application.

2. **Launch iMovie.**

3. **Choose File ⇨ New Project.** The New Project sheet appears.

4. **Name your project.** The Aspect Ratio and Theme settings don't matter because you are only going to use the audio.

5. **Click Create.** The new project is created and appears in the project library.

6. **Click the Titles button (the button with the capital "T").** The Titles Browser appears in the lower-right corner of the window.

7. **Drag a title into the project window.** It doesn't matter which title you choose because it's not going to be seen anyway. You should do this step because iMovie needs some video in a project to be able to work with audio content.

8. **Click the Music and Sound Effects button (the musical note icon).** The Music and Sound Effects Browser appears in the lower-right corner of the window.

9. **Choose iTunes on the pop-up menu.** The content of your iTunes library appears.

10. **Search or browse for the audio you want to use as the alert sound.**

11. **Drag the audio from the Music and Sound Effects Browser and drop it in the project window.**

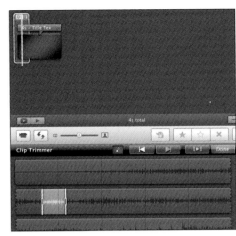

12.5 Use the Clip Trimmer to edit your alert sound.

12. **Open the audio clip's Action pop-up menu and choose Clip Trimmer.** The Clip Trimmer opens in the lower-left corner of the window.

13. **Edit the clip so it contains only the alert sound, and click Done (see figure 12.5).**

14. **Edit the title clip so it is the length of the alert sound.**

15. **Choose Share ➪ Export using QuickTime.** The Save exported file as dialog box appears (see figure 12.6).

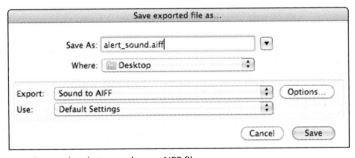

12.6 Export the alert sound as an AIFF file.

16. **On the Export pop-up menu, choose Sound to AIFF.**

17. **Name the sound file; append an "f" to the existing filename extension so it is .aiff (it is .aif by default).**

18. **Choose a location in which to save the alert sound and click Save.** The file is exported from iMovie and is ready to use as an alert sound.

Adding an alert sound for a specific user

To add a custom alert sound to a specific user account, follow these steps:

1. **Log in to the user account under which you want to make the alert sound available.**

2. **Place the alert sound file in the user's Sounds folder that is located in the Library folder within the Home folder.**

3. **If the System Preferences application is open, quit it, then open it.**

4. **Click the Sound Effects tab.**

5. **Select and configure the custom alert sound just like one of the default sounds (see figure 12.7).** Note that the type of alert sound you create is Custom to differentiate it from default sounds, which have Built-in as the type.

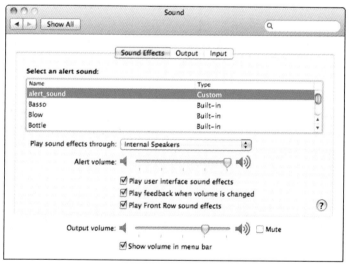

12.7 If this book had a soundtrack, you'd hear this awesome custom alert sound.

Adding an alert sound for all users

You can also add alert sounds to the system so they are available to all of the user accounts on your computer. To do this, you must authenticate yourself as an administrator.

To add alert sounds to your system, follow these steps:

1. **Drag the AIFF file into the folder *startupvolume*/System/Library/Sounds, where *startupvolume* is the name of your Mac OS X startup volume.**

2. **At the prompt, provide an administrator account username and password and click OK.**

3. **If the System Preferences application is open, quit it, then open it.**

4. **Click the Sound Effects tab.**

5. **Select and configure the custom alert sound just like one of the default sounds.**
   Alert sounds that you add to the system have the type Built-in and also behave the same as the default alert sounds, so any user can access them.

Getting Sound into a MacBook

There are many situations in which you may want to put sound into your MacBook. For example, you might want to add narration to iMovie projects; you need to have audio input for audio and video chats in iChat; if you use GarageBand, you'll want to record instruments and vocals; or you might want to add narration to a slide show you create in iPhoto.

On the simplest side, you can use the MacBook's built-in microphone to record voice narration or other sounds, and it is certainly good enough for most audio and video chats. Toward the more complex, you can add an external MIDI (Musical Instrument Digital Interface) keyboard or other device that enables you to record sound from musical instruments and other sources.

Caution

The MacBook audio line in/optical digital audio in minijack is not powered. This means that you can't just plug a standard analog microphone into it and record sound. Whatever you connect to the minijack must provide amplification to be able to record sound from it. To be able to connect a microphone to it, there must be a power source for the microphone.

Recording sound with the MacBook's internal microphone

Using the MacBook's internal microphone is easy and is probably good enough for a number of purposes, such as audio and video chats, recording narration for iMovie and iPhoto projects, and other relatively simple projects.

Configuring the internal microphone

To record audio with the built-in microphone, first configure the internal microphone by following these steps:

1. **Open the Sound pane of the System Preferences application.**

2. **Click the Input tab.** On the Input tab, there are two default options: Internal microphone or Line In. Under the device list, you see the controls you use to configure the device selected on the list.

3. **Select Internal microphone.** As your MacBook receives audio input through the microphone, the relative volume of the input is shown on the Input level gauge (see figure 12.8).

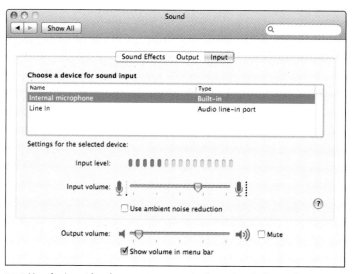

12.8 Use the Input level gauge to assess the input level of sound coming in to the MacBook.

4. **As you speak or play the sound, monitor the input on the level gauge.** The maximum level freezes briefly so that you can see where it is.

5. **If the gauge shows input when you aren't speaking or playing a sound, select the Use ambient noise reduction check box.** This applies a filter that screens out background sound.

6. **Drag the Input volume slider to the left to reduce the level of input sound, or to the right to increase it.** The microphone should be ready to use to record sound in an application.

Recording sound with the internal microphone in iMovie

A common use of recorded sound is as narration in iMovie projects. Here's how to add your own narration to an iMovie project:

1. **Launch iMovie.**

2. **Select the project in which you want to record sound using the internal microphone and put the playhead where you want to start recording.**

3. **Click the Voiceover button (the microphone).** The Voiceover dialog box appears (see figure 12.9).

4. **On the Record From pop-up menu, choose Built-In Microphone.**

5. **Click the clip for which you want to record narration.** The timer starts a countdown. When the countdown stops, the project starts to play and iMovie starts recording.

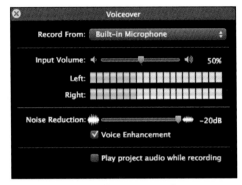

12.9 Here, I'm recording narration for an iMovie project.

6. **Speak in a normal conversational voice as the project plays.** As you speak, monitor the sound levels using the two input gauges under the Input Volume slider. You want the sound level to be as high as possible without going into the red. If it isn't, use the tools in the Voiceover dialog box to adjust the input volume. A red bar fills the clip you are recording over, and you see a large red dot and the "Recording" message in the Preview pane.

7. **When you finish speaking, press the spacebar.** The recording stops, and an audio clip appears under the clip on which you recorded sound. The recording also stops when you reach the end of the project.

8. **Edit the recorded audio clip just like other audio clips.** For example, you can make it fade in, adjust its volume, and move it earlier or later in the project. Narration is shown in purple and is labeled as "Voice Clip."

Recording sound with a USB headset

If you are going to be recording a lot of narration or you want better quality when you have video or audio chats, a USB headset is a good option. Like other audio input devices, you configure the USB headset to record its input and then use it to record sound in applications.

Configuring a USB headset is similar to configuring the internal microphone, as you see in the following steps:

1. **Connect the headset to a USB port.**

2. **Open the Sound pane of the System Preferences application.**

3. **Click the Input tab (see figure 12.10).** You should see the USB headset on the list of devices.

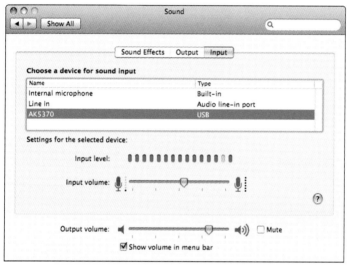

12.10 Configuring a USB headset improves the quality of its sound in applications.

4. **Select the USB headset.** As the MacBook receives audio input through the headset, the relative volume of the input is shown on the Input level gauge.

5. **As you speak or play the sound, monitor the input on the level gauge.** The maximum level freezes briefly so that you can see where it is.

6. **Drag the Input volume slider to the left to reduce the level of input sound, or to the right to increase it.** The USB headset should be ready to use to record sound in an application.

Recording sound from a USB headset is similar to recording sound with other input sources. For example, the steps to record sound in iMovie are the same as the steps described earlier for the internal microphone, except that you select the USB headset instead of Built-in Microphone.

Recording sound with a video camera

While it might not be obvious, a video camera can be a great way to record sound for your projects. You can then use iMovie to save that sound as a file to use in projects, to add to your iTunes library, and for other purposes. Here's how to move sound that you've recorded using a video camera into your iTunes library:

1. **Use the video camera to capture the sound you want to use in an application.**
2. **Connect the camera to your MacBook.**
3. **Launch iMovie.**
4. **Add the clips containing the audio to the event library.**
5. **Choose File ⇨ New Project.** The New Project sheet appears.
6. **Name your project.** Again, the options don't matter because you are only using the audio.
7. **Click Create.** The new project is created and appears on the project list.
8. **Add the clips with audio you want to save to the new project.**
9. **Edit the clips until the audio track is what you want to use.**
10. **Choose Share ⇨ Export using QuickTime.** The Save exported file as dialog box appears.
11. **On the Export pop-up menu, choose Sound to AIFF.**
12. **Choose a location and save the file.** The file is exported from iMovie.
13. **Launch iTunes.**
14. **Choose File ⇨ Add to Library.** The Add To Library dialog box appears.
15. **Move to and select the sound file you created in iMovie.**
16. **Click Open.** The sound is added to your iTunes library where you can listen to it, or you can select it from other applications using the Media Browser (for example, you can select it as a soundtrack for an iPhoto slide show).

Recording sound from external microphones and musical instruments

If you want to record sound from external microphones and musical instruments, you need an interface between the devices and the MacBook. These devices can use either the audio line in/optical digital audio in minijack or USB port to connect to your MacBook, but USB is a more common interface that is easier to work with in most situations.

There are a variety of USB audio devices that you can use for this purpose. Some devices include a MIDI instrument, such as a keyboard, as part of the interface device; these are convenient because you get an input source (the instrument) and the interface in one unit.

To use devices like these, connect the device to a USB port on your MacBook. You then connect microphones or instruments from which you want to record sound into the various ports.

Once the device is configured, you can choose it as the input device in audio applications, such as GarageBand, so that you can record the output of the microphones and instruments in those applications.

Recording sound with an iPhone

iPhones have the Voice Memos application that you can use to record sounds. It's intended and works best for sounds spoken into the phone or into the headset mic. To capture sound, do the following:

1. **Tap Voice Memos.** The application launches.
2. **Tap the Record button.**
3. **Start speaking.**
4. **When you finish recording, tap the Stop button.** The sound you recorded is captured as a clip.

To move the sound onto your MacBook, connect the iPhone to the MacBook, select it on the iTunes Source list, click the Music tab, and select the Include Voice Memos check box. Click Apply. The iPhone is synced and the sound clips you recorded are moved into your iTunes library (the default name of each clip is the date and time you recorded it). You can work with those clips just like other audio in iTunes; you can add it to iMovie and other projects through the Media Browser.

How Do I Store and Maintain My Data?

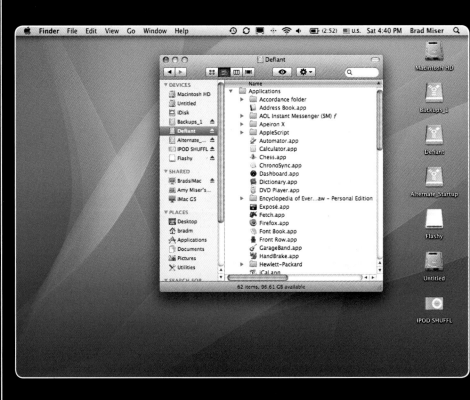

There are two primary reasons to add more data storage space to your MacBook, and both of them are important. One is to back up the data on your MacBook; one of the easiest ways to do this is to use Time Machine, which requires that you use an external hard drive. The other is that over time, you end up with a lot of data, especially if you create iMovie projects or you download movies or other video. Your MacBook's hard drive is only so big; adding more storage space enables you to work with more information. Also, you may want to carry some data with you even when you don't have your MacBook; a flash drive or iPod is a great choice for this purpose.

Using External Hard Drives

Adding an external hard drive to your MacBook system is an easy and relatively inexpensive way of making more storage space available; it is also a requirement if you want to use Time Machine for backing up your MacBook. In this section, you learn how to add more space to your MacBook by adding, configuring, and using an external hard drive.

When it comes to choosing a hard drive to add to your MacBook, consider the following factors:

- **Which interface will you use to connect the drive to your MacBook?** External drives use FireWire, FireWire 800, or USB 2 to connect to computers. The good news is that your MacBook supports both USB 2 and FireWire, so you can use a wide variety of external hard drives. From the performance perspective, FireWire is about the same speed as USB 2, and unless you are going to be writing to the external drive constantly while you work on projects, the communication speed is not likely to be an important factor in any case. More important will probably be the number of devices you already use with your MacBook. If you already use two or more USB devices, you might want to consider a FireWire drive because a hard drive is probably the only FireWire device you'll use. Because USB 2 is the more common technology, USB 2 drives tend to be less expensive, all other things being equal. Some external drives use both FireWire and USB 2. These multiple-interface drives are more expensive, but also provide more flexibility.

- **What size drive do you need?** Drives come in various sizes; generally, you should get the largest drive you can afford. Hard drive prices continue to fall, and even large drives with 1TB or more of storage space are fairly inexpensive. Smaller drives, such as 750GB, are even less expensive. For backup purposes, I don't recommend you ever purchase a drive smaller than 750GB, but in all cases, a drive with more capacity is better than one with less storage space.

- **Does the drive need to meet specific performance requirements?** If you intend to use the drive for high data rate work, such as for digital video, you need to get a drive that spins at least 7200 RPM. Some drives spin even faster, which means they can transfer data at a greater rate. However, if you are primarily going to use the external drive for backing up and for less data-intense projects, its speed isn't really important. Because faster drives are more expensive, you can save some money by choosing a relatively slow drive.

- **What format is the drive?** There are a variety of formats available, and all drives come formatted for one system or another. Fortunately, it doesn't really matter which format the drive comes in because you can always reformat it to work with your MacBook using the Disk Utility application, which you learn about later in this section. Drives that are formatted for Windows are generally less expensive than those that have been formatted for Macs. It's usually better to get a less expensive drive formatted for Windows and then use Disk Utility to prepare the drive to work with your MacBook.

● **How much can you afford to spend?** As with all things digital, you get more by spending more (assuming all other things being equal). For most purposes, such as backing up, you should decide how much you can afford to spend and then get the largest drive you can afford for that amount of money. If you're willing to shop around a bit, you'll be amazed how much the cost of external hard drives varies from retailer to retailer, and hard drives are also something that many retailers put on sale frequently.

Installing an external hard drive

Installing an external hard drive is about as simple as it gets. Follow these steps:

1. **Connect the power supply to the drive and to an electrical outlet.**

2. **Connect the USB 2 or FireWire cable to the drive and to the appropriate port on your MacBook.**

3. **Power up the drive.** If the drive is formatted so that it is compatible with your MacBook, it mounts on your desktop and you see it on the sidebar in Finder windows (see figure 13.1). If not, you won't see the device. In either case, you should reformat and initialize the drive before you start using it.

13.1 A mounted external hard drive appears in the DEVICES section of the sidebar, just like the internal hard drive.

Note

If the drive is formatted so that your MacBook can access it, you might be prompted to configure Time Machine. Just click Cancel and proceed to the next section. Time Machine is covered in Chapter 14.

Using Disk Utility to prepare an external hard drive

Before you use a hard drive, you should initialize and format it. You can also partition a hard drive to create multiple volumes on a single drive so that it behaves as if it is more than one drive.

Genius

I recommend that you reformat your external drive to ensure that you have the most storage space available and that the drive is formatted in the best way for your MacBook. Some drives include software, especially if the drive is intended for Windows computers, in which case that software is a waste of space and you should get rid of it.

When you partition a hard drive, logical volumes are created for each partition on the drive. For most practical purposes, a logical volume looks and acts just like a separate hard drive. There can be some small performance advantages to partitioning a drive, or you might choose to partition it to help you keep your data organized. For example, you might want to create one partition on the hard drive for your backups and another to install Mac OS X as an alternate startup drive.

One of the results of partitioning a drive is that all the volumes outside of the startup volume are outside of the default Mac OS X organization scheme. This can be a benefit or a problem depending on what you are doing. For example, documents you store on a separate volume aren't secured using the Mac OS X default permissions, like documents you store within your Home folder are. If you want to provide broader access to files, this is a good thing. If you don't want people to be able to access these documents outside the control of the Mac OS X security, it isn't.

Generally, you should keep your partitions pretty large unless you create one for a very specific purpose, such as to install Mac OS X for an alternate startup drive. If you run out of space on a partition, you have to delete files from it or repartition the drive, which means that you must start over and reformat the disk (resulting in all files being erased). Unless you have a very specific reason to do so, you typically shouldn't partition a drive into more than two volumes. In many cases, especially if you are only using the drive for backups, one partition is the best option.

Caution

When you follow these steps, all the information currently on the drive is erased. If the hard drive came with software installed on it, check out the software to make sure you don't have any use for it (you probably won't). If you do find some that you want to keep, copy it from the external drive onto a DVD, CD, or your MacBook's internal drive before formatting the drive.

To initialize, format, and partition a drive, perform the following steps:

1. **Launch the Disk Utility application, which is located in the Utilities folder within the Applications folder.** In the Disk Utility window, you see two panes. In the upper part of the left pane, you see the drives with which your MacBook can communicate, along with the MacBook's internal hard and optical drives. Under each disk, you see the volumes with which that disk has been partitioned. Below the drives, you see any disk images that are currently mounted on your MacBook. In the right pane, you see information and tools for the drive or volume that is selected in the left pane.

2. **Select the drive you want to format.** At the top of the right pane are five tabs; each tab enables you to view data about a drive or to perform a specific action. At the bottom of the window, you see detailed information about the drive with which you are working, such as its connection bus, type, capacity, and so on.

3. **Click the Partition tab (see figure 13.2).** In the left part of this tab, you see a graphical representation of the partitions on the disk. If the drive is currently partitioned, you see its current partitions. If you are working with a new drive or one with a single partition, you see one partition called "Untitled" (if you've not named it before). In the right part of the pane, you see information about the selected volume, such as its name, current format, and size.

4. **Select the number of partitions you want to have on the drive using the Volume Scheme pop-up menu.** You can choose Current, which leaves the partitions as they are, or the number of partitions you want from 1 to 16. After you choose the number of partitions, each partition is represented by a box in the disk graphic shown under the Volume Scheme pop-up menu. The partitions are called Untitled 1, Untitled 2, and so on.

5. **Select a partition by clicking its box in the graphical representation of the drive.** The volume's partition is highlighted and information for that volume is shown in the Volume Information area.

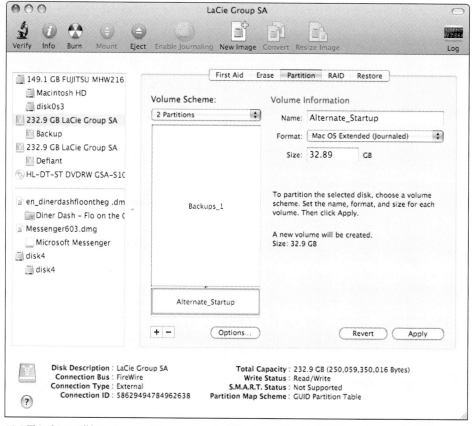

13.2 This drive will have two partitions: one called "Backups_1" with 200GB, and one called "Alternate_Startup" with 32.89GB.

Genius

Instead of a space in a partition name, use an underscore or just run the words together so the space isn't replaced by 20% in a path name.

6. **Name the selected volume by typing a name in the Name box.** As you type the name, it is shown in the partition's box. You can name the partition just about anything you want. This name is how you identify the partition's volume in the sidebar and other locations, so use a meaningful name. In most cases, you want to use a name that indicates the purpose of the partition.

7. **Select the format for the partition on the Format pop-up menu.** In most cases, you should choose Mac OS Extended (Case-sensitive, Journaled) to take advantage of the most sophisticated format option.

8. **Type the size of the partition in the Size box.** You can enter a size up to the maximum capacity of the drive, but it also depends on the number of other partitions on the drive and how much space is allocated to each.

Genius

You can also set the size of a partition by dragging its Resize handle in the Volumes pane.

9. **Select, name, and set a size for each partition on the drive; once you've configured all the partitions on the disk, click Options.** The Options sheet appears.

10. **If it isn't selected already, click the GUID Partition Table radio button.** The other options don't apply when you are using the disk with a MacBook.

Caution

If you purchase a drive that's been formatted for Windows computers using the Master Boot Record format option, it won't mount on your MacBook and will be unusable. You must format the disk with the GUID Partition Table format before you can use it.

11. **Click OK.** The format option is set and the sheet closes.

Caution

Before proceeding, make sure that the drive doesn't contain any data you need. Performing the next steps erases all the data from the drive.

12. **Click Apply.**

13. **If you are sure that you want to initialize and partition the drive, click Partition in the Warning sheet.** In this sheet, you see a summary of what will be done to the drive. After you click Partition, you return to the Disk Utility window and a progress bar appears in the lower-right corner of the window. You can use this to monitor the process. Once this process is completed, you should see the partitions you created under the drive's icon, and the drive and its partitions are ready to use.

Working with external hard drives

After you configure an external hard drive, you can use it in the following ways:

- **Store files.** You can use the drive just like the internal hard drive.

- **Backing up to the drive with Time Machine.** I discuss Time Machine in Chapter 14.

- **Stop using the drive.** Before you stop using a hard drive and any of its partitions, you need to eject the drive. This makes sure that all data has been written to the drive and all processes impacting it are stopped so that when you disconnect the drive, the data isn't damaged. To eject a drive, select one of its partitions and click the Eject button. If the drive has only one partition, it is unmounted and disappears from the Finder window. If the drive has more than one partition, you are prompted to eject only the selected partition by clicking the Eject button or eject the entire disk by clicking the Eject All button. You should always click the Eject All button at which point all the drive's partitions are unmounted and disappear from the Finder window. You can then disconnect the drive from the MacBook.

- **Start using the drive again.** To start using the drive again, simply reconnect the drive to your MacBook. After a few moments, the drive is mounted, you see all of its partitions in the sidebar, and it is ready to use.

Sharing an External Hard Drive

An external hard drive is a great way to share files among multiple computers. You can do this in a number of ways:

- **Physically connect the drive to different computers.** After a drive has been formatted, you can connect it to any Mac to be able to access its files or to write files to it.

- **Share the drive over a network.** Like other resources, you can share the partitions and files on them with other computers over a local network.

- **Share the drive from an AirPort Base Station.** If you connect a USB external hard drive to an AirPort Base Station, any computer that can access the Base Station's network can also access the drive.

Maintaining Hard Drives

Keeping your hard drives, whether internal or external, in good working condition goes a long way to making your MacBook reliable. In this section, you learn about some of the more important disk maintenance habits you should practice to keep your drives in top form.

Caution
You should regularly maintain your hard drives to keep them operating as long as possible. If you hear a drive making an odd noise, such as becoming louder, you should expect the drive to fail soon if not immediately. Unusual sounds typically precede a hard drive's failure (but not always). Make sure you get any data you need off the drive right away, or it will be very expensive and a hassle to recover it. Never store important data in only one location.

Managing a hard drive's free space

You can do a lot for the performance of your drives by simply keeping them cleaned up. The more data on your drive, the less room you have to store new files. If your drives get too full, their performance slows down significantly. You can also run into all kinds of problems if you try to save files to drives that are full to the brim; how full this is depends on the size of the files with which you are working.

As you use a hard drive, keep an eye on its available space by selecting the drive in the sidebar and looking at the space available shown at the bottom of the Finder window (see figure 13.3). If the space available falls below 10GB, you can start running into problems when you try to save files or perform other tasks. If the space available drops below 1GB, you can count on having problems.

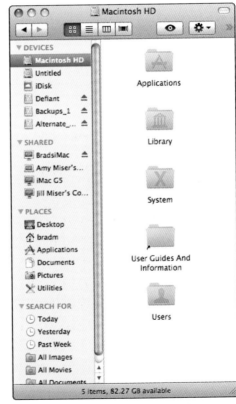

13.3 This MacBook internal hard drive has more than 80GB available, so it is in good shape.

Genius

Application installers waste a lot of disk space. If you're sure that the application version you want will continue to be available on the Web, you can delete its installation files. If you have to pay for an application, it's better to archive its files on CD or DVD in case you need to reinstall it again. Some companies remove older versions as newer versions are released, in which case you might have to pay an upgrade fee to download the application again. With a version safely archived, you can always get back to the version you purchased.

Learn and practice good work habits such as deleting files you don't need, uninstalling software you don't use, keeping your files organized (no duplicates), and archiving files you are done with (such as on a DVD). Regularly removing files that you no longer need from your hard drives will go a long way toward keeping them performing well for you, not to mention maximizing the room you have to store files you do need.

Using Activity Monitor to check a drive's available space

You can use Activity Monitor to get more information about how you are using a specific drive. Follow these steps:

1. **Launch the Activity Monitor application located in the Utilities folder within the Applications folder.**

2. **Click the Disk Usage tab located at the bottom of the window.**

3. **On the pop-up menu, choose the disk or partition whose information you want to view.** You see a pie chart showing the amount of free space (in green) versus the amount of space used (in blue), along with the specific values within each category (see figure 13.4).

Note

Each partition and drive has its own Trash. If you empty the Trash while an external drive that has files in its Trash is disconnected, the Trash icon becomes full again when you reconnect the drive because the Trash associated with that drive still has files in it. Just empty the Trash again once you've reconnected the drive to get rid of the trashed files.

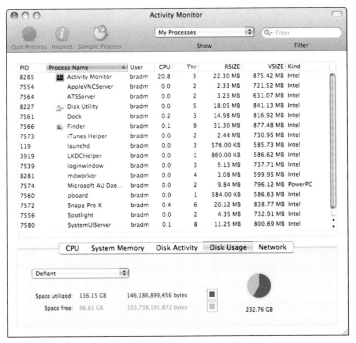

13.4 The drive called Defiant has about 136GB of files stored on it.

Using Disk Utility to check or repair an external drive

Two of the tasks for which you can use Disk Utility are to check or repair an external hard drive. If you start having problems with a disk, first make sure that it has plenty of available space. If it doesn't, get rid of files until it does. If it does have plenty of free space, use Disk Utility to check or repair it, as in the following steps:

1. **Launch Disk Utility.**

2. **Select a drive or partition you want to check or repair.** In most cases, you should select a drive so that the entire drive is checked or repaired, rather than just one of its partitions.

3. **Check the bottom of the Disk Utility window for information about the drive, volume, disc, or image you selected.** If you select a hard drive, you see the disk type, connection bus (such as ATA for internal drives or FireWire for an external drive), connection type (internal or external), capacity, write status, S.M.A.R.T. status, and partition map scheme. If you select a partition on a drive, you see various data about the volume, such as its mount point (the path to it), format, whether owners are enabled, the number of folders it contains, its capacity, the amount of space available, the amount of space used, and the number of files it contains.

4. **Click the First Aid tab to see some information explaining how Disk Utility works.**

5. **Click Repair Disk.** The application checks the selected disk for problems and repairs any it finds. When the process is complete, a report of the results appears (see figure 13.5).

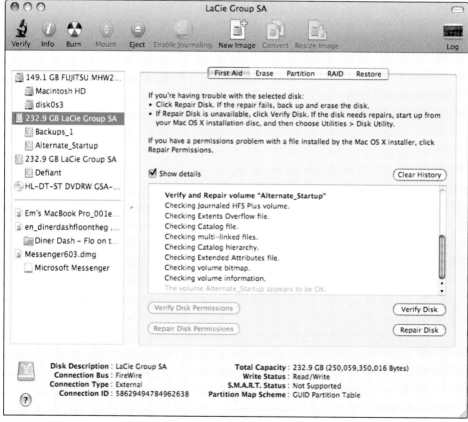

13.5 Disk Utility has checked this disk, which seems to be okay.

You can choose to verify a drive by clicking Verify Disk, rather than to repair it by clicking Repair Disk. When you do so, the application finds problems with the drive and reports back to you. You then have to tell the application to repair those problems.

Note For most drives, the S.M.A.R.T. (Self-Monitoring, Analysis, and Reporting Technology) status provides an indication of the drive's health. This is Verified if the drive is in good working condition, or About to Fail if the drive has problems. If you see About to Fail, immediately copy important data onto another drive or CD/DVD. If a drive doesn't support S.M.A.R.T., the status will be Not Supported. Your MacBook internal drive supports S.M.A.R.T., but many external drives do not.

Erasing an external hard drive with Disk Utility

You can use Disk Utility to quickly erase and reformat an external hard drive by performing the following steps:

1. **Launch Disk Utility.**

2. **Select a partition you want to erase.**

3. **Click the Erase tab.**

4. **Choose the format you want to use for the volume on the Volume Format pop-up menu.** The format options are Mac OS Extended (Journaled), Mac OS Extended, Mac OS Extended (Case-sensitive, Journaled), Mac OS Extended (Case-sensitive), or MS-DOS (FAT).

Genius You can use the Erase Free Space button to remove files that you have deleted from a drive or partition to make them harder or impossible to recover using data recovery tools.

5. **Click the Security Options button.** The Secure Erase Options sheet appears (see figure 13.6).

6. **Select one of the following options:**

   - **Don't Erase Data.** This makes the data unviewable from the Finder but leaves the data physically on the drive. As your MacBook needs to write more files to the drive, it overwrites the erased space. Until the data is overwritten, it can be recovered (unerased) using an application designed to recover data. This is the fastest, but least secure option.

Secure Erase Options

These options specify how to erase the selected disk or volume to prevent disk recovery applications from recovering it.

 Don't Erase Data

This is quick and provides the least security. It erases just the information used to access your files and leaves the data in the files unchanged. Many commonly available disk recovery applications can restore that data.

○ **Zero Out Data**

This is quick and provides good security. It erases the information used to access your files and writes zeros over the data once.

○ **7-Pass Erase**

This option takes 7 times longer than "Zero Out Data," and meets the US Department of Defense (DOD) 5220-22 M standard for securely erasing magnetic media. It erases the information used to access your files and writes over the data 7 times.

○ **35-Pass Erase**

This option takes 35 times longer than "Zero Out Data" and provides the best security. It erases the information used to access your files and writes over the data 35 times.

(?)

13.6 Use this sheet to select how you want data you are erasing to be handled.

● **Zero Out Data.** This option writes zeros in all sectors on the drive. This is secure because it overwrites the entire drive, which makes the data harder to recover, but is slower than the first option.

● **7-Pass Erase.** This option writes data over the entire drive seven times. This takes a long time, and makes the data virtually impossible to recover (hey, if it's good enough for the U.S. Department of Defense, it should be good enough for you).

● **35-Pass Erase.** This option overwrites the drive 35 times, taking even longer and making the data more than virtually impossible to recover.

7. **Click OK.** The option you selected is set and the sheet closes.

8. **Click Erase.** The confirmation sheet appears.

9. **If you are sure you want to erase the drive, click Erase in the sheet.** The drive's or partition's data is erased and is formatted with the options you selected.

Installing Mac OS X on an External Hard Drive

You can install Mac OS X on an external hard drive and then start up under that drive; this is very useful for troubleshooting. To install Mac OS X on an external hard drive, perform the following steps:

1. **Configure a partition or drive on which you want to install Mac OS X.**

2. **Insert the System Software disc included with your MacBook or the Mac OS X Install disc.**

3. **Double-click the Install Mac OS X application.**

4. **Click Continue, and then agree to the license.**

5. **Click Show All Disks.**

6. **Select the partition or hard drive you configured in Step 1.**

7. **Click the Install button, click Install again at the prompt, and then authenticate yourself.** The installation process starts; your MacBook will restart at some point. When complete, you're prompted to restart it.

8. **Click Restart.** The MacBook starts up from the external drive.

9. **Work through the screens of the assistant to complete the installation.** This is the same process as when you first started your computer.

10. **Run the Software Update application (see Chapter 16).** The system on the external drive is ready for you to start up from.

Note

The purpose of the three overwrite options is to prevent data on the drive from being restored after you erase it. For example, if you were transferring a drive to someone else, you want to select one of these options so that the data you had on the drive cannot be recovered. If you are maintaining control of the drive, you probably don't need to choose one of the secure erase options, but using the Zero Out Data option doesn't add a lot of time to the process, so it isn't a bad choice.

Using Disk Utility to check or repair the internal drive

Because you can't use Disk Utility to repair a drive with open files and your startup disk always has open files, you can't use Disk Utility to repair the internal hard drive while you are started up from it.

Genius

While you can't repair the current startup disk, you can verify it. Although this won't fix any problems, it does identify that there is a problem.

If it appears that your internal hard drive has problems, you need to start up from a different disk to repair them. You can use one of the following options to accomplish this:

- **Start up from an alternate drive and run Disk Utility from there.** If you have installed Mac OS X on an external drive, you can start up from that drive and run Disk Utility to repair the internal drive. (See Chapter 16 to learn how to start up from an alternate startup disk.) Once you're booted up, use the steps in the section about checking or repairing an external drive to select and repair the internal hard drive.

- **Start up from the system software disc.** Insert the system software disc that came with your MacBook. Restart the computer and hold the C key down while it restarts. When it does, the Mac OS X Installation application launches. On the Utilities menu, choose Disk Utility. The Disk Utility application launches; use the steps in the section about checking or repairing an external drive to select and repair the internal hard drive.

The alternate drive option is better because you use the current version of Mac OS X and its applications (including Disk Utility) instead of the versions included on the system software disc. But in some cases, the system software option can work if you don't have an alternate external drive configured.

Using an iPod as an External Drive

In addition to being a fantastic digital media device, your iPod can also be used as a portable external drive on which you can store files, just like a hard drive connected to your MacBook.

Configuring an iPod Classic as a drive

An iPod Classic packs a lot of data storage in a small package. To configure an iPod Classic to be used as an external hard drive, perform the following steps:

1. **Connect the iPod to the MacBook.** If it isn't open already, iTunes launches and connects to the iPod.

2. **Select the iPod on the Source list.**

3. **Click the Summary tab if it isn't selected already.**

4. **Select the Enable disk use check box.** You see a warning prompt that explains that because the iPod will be acting as a hard drive, you must manually eject it before disconnecting it from the computer.

5. **Click OK at the prompt.**

6. **Click Apply.** The iPod is ready to be used as a drive.

Configuring an iPod shuffle as a drive

iPod shuffles don't actually have hard drives; their memory is flash memory, which means that it doesn't require any moving parts. This is why iPod shuffles can be so small and also why they have limited memory. Still, the up to 4GB they offer provides space for documents and other small files. To set up an iPod shuffle for drive use, do the following:

1. **Connect the iPod shuffle to your MacBook.** If it isn't open already, iTunes launches and connects to the iPod shuffle.

2. **Select the iPod shuffle on the Source list.**

3. **Click the Settings tab if it isn't selected already.**

4. **Select the Enable disk use check box.** You see a warning prompt that explains that because the iPod shuffle will be acting as a hard drive, you must manually eject it before disconnecting it from the computer.

5. **Click OK at the prompt.**

6. **Drag the slider to the right to allocate more space for data or to the left to allocate less space for data (see figure 13.7).** Because you are limited to the total memory in the iPod shuffle, you have to trade off memory for music versus that for data. The number of songs you set on the slider determines the number that iTunes places on the iPod shuffle when you use the AutoFill tool.

7. **Click Apply.** The iPod shuffle is ready to be used as a drive.

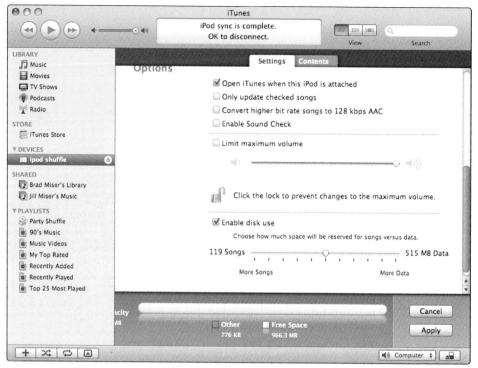

13.7 This iPod shuffle will have 515MB dedicated to data storage, which means it can hold about 119 songs.

Working with an iPod as a hard drive

Once configured, using an iPod as a drive is like using other kinds of drives. When you select an iPod on the DEVICES list, you see the folders and files it contains (see figure 13.8).

When you select an iPod Classic, you see four folders that are used for content that is synced: Calendars, Contacts, Notes, and Photos. You should leave these folders as they are, but you can create new folders and store files within them on the iPod, just as you can other kinds of hard drives. Of course, any storage space you use for data won't be available for content in your iTunes library.

Genius

An iPod makes a great portable backup drive when you travel with your MacBook. Just move files that you want to back up from the MacBook onto the iPod.

Caution

Make sure you eject iPods before disconnecting them or you risk damaging their data. You can eject iPods from the desktop or within iTunes.

Because there is no data synced for iPod shuffles, they don't have default folders. You can store as much data on the iPod shuffle as you've allocated. However, this setting only impacts the amount of music that is moved onto the iPod shuffle using the AutoFill tool. If you move more data onto the iPod shuffle than the slider setting implies, but you have moved less music onto it, you can store more data than the slider shows. If you manually manage music on the iPod shuffle, the slider setting has no effect. It only limits you when you use the AutoFill tool.

13.8 On the DEVICES list, you see the selected iPod and an iPod shuffle; both can be used for data storage.

Working with Flash Drives

USB flash drives are a popular way to move files around. Because they have flash memory, they are very small and easy to carry. The capacity of these drives continues to increase rapidly; at press time, you can get them in up to 16GB. A flash drive can be a good way to transfer files between computers or to back up data when you are on the move.

To use a flash drive on your MacBook, simply plug it into one of the USB ports. The drive is mounted on your MacBook and you can work with it. (However, for best results, you should prepare the drive for use by reformatting it with Disk Utility using the same process as with a hard drive.)

Genius

If you also want to use the drive on Windows computers, select the MS-DOS (FAT) format. This makes it easy to move files between Macs and Windows PCs.

Software Update

New software is available for your computer.

If you don't want to install now, choose Apple menu > Software Update when you're ready to install.

Install	Name	Version	Size
☑	GarageBand Update	5.1	145.9 MB

This update addresses general compatibi... fixes a number of other minor issues. T...

- GarageBand track effects and Au...
- Improved support for Apogee au...
- Faster switching to full screen in...
- Improved access to audio monito...

This update is recommended for all use...

Note: Use of this software is subject to t... that accompanied the software being up... here: http://www.apple.com/legal/sla/.

(Hide Details)

Security

◀ ▶ (Show All)   Q

General   FileVault   Firewall

☑ Require password (1 hour ⬦) after sleep or screen saver begins

For all accounts on this computer:

☐ Disable automatic login

☐ Require a password to unlock each System Preferences pane

(set Warnings)

(Pair...)

?

Time Machine

◀ ▶ (Show All)   Q

Name: Valiant

Available: 18.06 GB of 500.11 GB

Oldest Backup: June 13, 2009

(Select Disk...) Latest Backup: Today, 1:34 AM

(Options...) Backing Up: ▪▪▪▪▪▪▪▪▪▪▪▪▪▪▪▪ ⊙
                59.3 MB of 59.9 MB

Time Machine

OFF [   ] ON

Time Machine keeps:

- Hourly backups for the past 24 hours
- Daily backups for the past month
- Weekly backups for all previous months

The oldest backups are deleted when your disk becomes full.

☑ Show Time Machine status in the menu bar

🔒 Click the lock to prevent further changes.   ?

Your MacBook is valuable; protecting it is important, but this chapter is about protecting the data on your MacBook, which is even more valuable. If you've purchased music, movies, or other content from the iTunes Store, you've invested hard-earned dollars in that content. If you use iPhoto, you can't replace those photos stored there at any price. Then there's personal data such as financial information that you need to safeguard. For all these reasons, you should take precautions to secure your MacBook and its data.

Keeping Software Current

There are two good reasons why you should keep the software that you use current. One is that software developers frequently develop revisions to improve the features of their applications and to remove bugs. The other, and the reason this topic is included in this chapter, is that many applications, and most definitely Mac OS X itself, have a large role in how secure your MacBook and its data are. The bad guys, people who develop viruses and attempt to hijack your computer or steal your data, are always working on new ways to penetrate your computer. Most software developers try to limit your exposure to attacks in their software as much as possible; to keep up with the new attempts to compromise your computer, you need to take advantage of security improvements that are part of software updates.

There are two basic categories of software that you need to keep current. The first is Apple software, which includes Mac OS X along with Apple applications you have. The second category is the third-party software you have installed.

Keeping Apple software current

Because it is the largest factor in how secure your MacBook and its data are, Mac OS X is the most important software you need to keep current. The good news is that Mac OS X includes the Software Update tool that makes it easy to keep Mac OS X and your Apple applications current. You can update software manually, and you can also configure Software Update so that it checks for and downloads updates automatically.

Updating Apple software manually

You can update your Apple software manually by performing the following steps:

1. **Choose Apple menu ⇨ Software Update.** The Software Update application launches, connects to the Internet, and compares the versions of Apple software installed on your MacBook to the current versions. If it finds that updates are available, you see a dialog box informing you of this; continue to Step 2. If no updates are found, you see a dialog box informing you that your software is up to date; click Quit to close the Software Update application and skip the rest of these steps.

2. **Click Show Details.** The dialog box expands so that you see each of the updates that were found (see figure 14.1).

3. **To install an update, select its check box.** To prevent an update from being installed, deselect its check box.

4. **Click Install** *numberofupdates*, **where** *numberofupdates* **is the number of updates you've selected to install.**

5. **If prompted to do so, type your Administrator username and password and click OK.**

6. **Click Restart if prompted to do so.**

14.1 Software Update has found an update to GarageBand.

If a restart is required, your MacBook restarts and continues the installation process. When the desktop reappears, you are using the updated software.

If a restart isn't required, after the update process is complete, you see a dialog box letting you know; click OK to close it. The Software Update application checks for additional updates (the updates you installed are marked with a check mark in a green circle); if it doesn't find any new updates, quit the Software Update application by clicking Quit.

Genius

Updating Apple software automatically

Checking for software updates is easy enough, but why not have your MacBook handle this for you automatically? Here's how:

1. **Open the Software Update pane of the System Preferences application.**

2. **Click the Scheduled Check tab if it isn't selected already.**

3. **Select the Check for updates check box.**

4. **On the Check for updates pop-up menu, choose the frequency with which your MacBook checks for updates (see figure 14.2).**

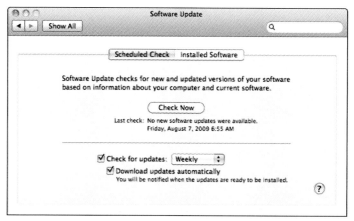

14.2 Use the Software Update pane to configure your MacBook to update its Apple software automatically.

5. **If you want important updates to be downloaded automatically, select the Download updates automatically check box.** Important updates are those that affect your system and have the most impact on its security. I recommend that you select this check box so these vital updates are downloaded as soon as they are found. If you don't select this check box, you're prompted to download the updates when they are available.

6. **Quit the System Preferences application.** When the specified amount of time passes, Software Update checks for new software. When it finds new versions, it downloads them automatically and then prompts you to allow them to be installed or prompts you to allow them to be downloaded and then installed.

You can check for updates manually by clicking Check Now; this does the same thing as choosing Apple menu ⇨ Software Update.

Genius

Viewing installed updates

You can use the Software Update pane to view information about updates you've installed by doing the following:

1. **Open the Software Update pane of the System Preferences application.**

2. **Click the Installed Software tab.** You see a list of all updates you've downloaded and installed on your MacBook (see figure 14.3).

14.3 You can see from this list that updates are not an infrequent occurrence.

3. **Sort the list by clicking any of the column headings.** You can change the sort direction by clicking the column heading again.

Keeping non-Apple software current

Support for updates to non-Apple software isn't built in to Mac OS X. Instead, each application provides its own tools to download and install updates. Most of these support manual or automatic updates. The details of updating a third-party application depend on the specific application. The following sections show how to update Microsoft Office applications manually and Snapz Pro X from Ambrosia Software automatically; other third-party applications are updated similarly.

To Install or Not to Install?

Updates are also software, and like other kinds of software, updates can have bugs, security problems, and other issues. Some experts recommend that you delay installing updates until it's clear that the updates don't cause more problems than they solve. There is some logic to this approach as there have been occasions in which an update was problematic. However, those occasions are rare, especially for Apple software. And if an update is released to correct a potential security issue, you continue to be exposed to that issue until you install the update. Personally, I install updates to Apple software as they become available and do so automatically. In the rare cases that an update with problems is released, the problematic update is typically immediately followed by one that corrects its problems. If you prefer a more cautious approach, you should disable automatic software updates and use the manual approach. You'll need to keep up on Mac-related news to determine when updates are released and to discover if there are problems with those releases before you install them. This is too much work for too little return for most people though.

Note

Ever since Mac OS X was released many years ago, I've hoped that Apple and third-party companies would develop an approach whereby the Software Update tool works on all software installed on your MacBook, whether it's from Apple or not. Alas, that's not happened yet.

Updating Microsoft Office applications manually

Most Mac users are also Office users; to update an Office application manually, do the following:

1. **Launch the Office application.**

2. **Choose Help ⇨ Check for Updates.** The Microsoft AutoUpdate application opens and checks for updates (see figure 14.4).

3. **Select the update you want to install.**

4. **Click Install.**

5. **Follow the on-screen instructions to complete the update.**

Genius

You can configure Microsoft Office applications to check for updates automatically by choosing Help ➪ Check for Updates. In the Microsoft AutoUpdate window (if an update is found install it and then select the command again), click the Automatically radio button and select the frequency at which you want to check for updates on the Check for Updates pop-up menu.

14.4 An update to Microsoft Office has been found.

Updating Snapz Pro X automatically

Snapz Pro X from Ambrosia Software (www.ambrosiasw.com) is the best screen capture application for the Mac (almost all the figures in this book were captured with it). To configure it to check for updates automatically, perform the following steps:

1. **Launch Snapz Pro X.**

2. **Click the Preferences tab.**

3. **Select the Check for new versions at launch check box.** Each time you launch the application, it checks for newer versions. When one is found, you are prompted to download and install it.

Can't Find an Update Command?

While most modern applications provide either a manual update command or an automatic update setting, not all of them do. If an application doesn't support updates via a command, you have to manually determine if an update is available. Move to the Web site for the software and determine the current version. Compare the version installed on your MacBook with the most current one shown on the Web site. If a new version is available, download and install it.

For most applications, when you download and install them, you have an option to sign up for emails related to the application. These emails are a good way to know when updates are released because information about those updates and links to them are usually included in the email. (Some emails are just for marketing purposes so determine the purpose of emails before agreeing to receive them.)

Preventing Internet Attacks

When you use your home network, you should shield your MacBook from Internet attacks through an AirPort Extreme Base Station or Time Capsule. When you use networks outside of your control, such as one available in public places, you should use the Mac OS X firewall to prevent unauthorized access to your computer.

Caution

Never connect your MacBook directly to a cable or DSL modem without first enabling the Mac OS X firewall.

Using a base station to shield your MacBook

You can protect the computers on your local network from attack by placing a barrier between them and the public Internet. You can then use a Dynamic Host Configuration Protocol (DHCP) server that provides network address translation (NAT) protection for your network, or you can add or use a hub that contains a more sophisticated firewall to ensure that your network can't be violated. A benefit to these devices is that you can also use them to share a single Internet connection.

One of the easiest and best ways to protect machines on a local network from attack and simultaneously to share an Internet connection is to install an AirPort Extreme Base Station or Time Capsule. These devices provide NAT protection for any computers that obtain Internet service through them, and for most users, this is an adequate level of protection from hacking. That's because the addresses of each computer on the network are hidden from the outside Internet. The only address exposed is the one that is assigned to the base station by the cable or DSL modem. This address is useless to hackers because there isn't any data or functionality exposed to the Internet from the base station.

To learn how to configure a base station to protect your network and the computers on it, see Chapter 3.

Using the Mac OS X firewall to shield your MacBook

Whenever your MacBook isn't protected by a base station or other firewall, make sure you config- ure its firewall to protect it from Internet attacks. Common situations are when you travel and connect to various networks, such as in public places and hotel rooms. In most cases, these net- works are configured to limit access to your computer (similar to how a base station shields it), but you shouldn't count on this. Instead, protect your MacBook with its firewall by performing the fol- lowing steps:

1. **Open the Security pane of the System Preferences application.**

2. **Click the Firewall tab.**

3. **Click Start.**

4. **Click the Advanced button.** The Advanced sheet appears (see figure 14.5).

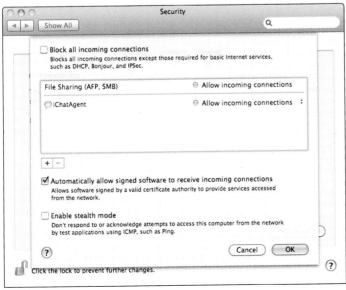

14.5 Use the Mac OS X firewall to protect your computer from Internet attacks.

5. **To provide the maximum protection, select the Block all incoming connections check box.** This prevents all connections except those very basic connections required for network access, such as DHCP and Bonjour. If an action you try doesn't work the next time you try it after configuring the firewall, you need to deselect this check box and perform Step 6 instead.

6. **Add any applications you are sure you want to allow to have incoming connections or block all incoming connections by clicking the Add (+) button below the action list, selecting the application you want to add, and configuring its pop-up menu to Allow incoming connections or Block incoming connections.** Applications that are allowed have a green status while those that are blocked have a red status. Any blocked applications are unable to receive incoming traffic, and functions associated with receiving communication from outside your MacBook are prevented. (When you've not allowed a specific application through the firewall and it tries to communicate, you're prompted to allow or prevent it.)

7. **To allow applications that have a valid security certificate to receive incoming connections, select the Automatically allow signed software to receive incoming connections check box.**

8. **Select the Enable stealth mode check box.** This further protects your MacBook by making sure that uninvited connection requests aren't acknowledged in any form so that the existence of your computer is hidden.

9. **Click OK.** Your settings are saved and the sheet closes. Your MacBook is protected by the firewall.

Genius

If you have trouble with some network or Internet services after configuring the firewall, make sure you check the firewall configuration to ensure it isn't configured to prevent the kind of service you are trying to use. As long as the service is configured within Mac OS X, this shouldn't be the case, but it's a good thing to check if you have a problem.

Protecting MacBook with General Security

Mac OS X includes a number of general security settings that are particularly useful if you use your MacBook in a variety of locations, some of which might allow it to be accessed by someone else. To configure these settings, do the following:

1. **Open the Security pane of the System Preferences application.**

2. **Click the General tab (see figure 14.6).**

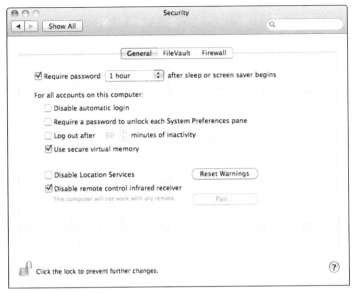

14.6 The General tab helps you to protect your MacBook from unauthorized access.

3. **Select the Require password after sleep or screen saver begins check box to require that a user type his account's login password to stop the screen saver or wake up the MacBook from sleep and then choose the amount of time the computer is asleep or in screen saver mode before the password is required on the pop-up menu.**

4. **To prevent someone from being able to use your computer just by starting it, select the Disable automatic login check box.**

5. **To restrict a user's ability to change system settings, select the Require password to unlock each System Preferences pane check box.**

6. **To cause user accounts to be automatically logged out after periods of inactivity, select the Log out after check box and set the amount of inactive time using the time box.**

7. **To protect the contents of your MacBook's virtual memory, select the Use secure virtual memory check box.** When this feature is active, data written to disk is stored securely when virtual memory is required.

8. **To prevent location services from identifying the MacBook's current location, select the Disable Location Services check box.**

9. **To prevent your MacBook from being controlled through an infrared remote control, select the Disable remote control infrared receiver check box.**

Viruses: Big Deal or Not?

I believe that viruses are less of a problem than they appear to be from the tremendous amount of media hype they receive, especially for Mac users. Most of the time, you can protect yourself from viruses by being very careful about the files you receive in email or download from the Web. Because the only way for a virus to get onto your machine is for you to accept a file in which it is contained, you can protect yourself from most viruses by using common sense. For example, if you receive an email containing an oddly titled attachment (such as the famous I Love You file), you should either request more information from the sender before you open the file or simply delete the message.

Adding and using an antivirus application makes your machine even safer, but if you are very careful about downloading files, you might find that you can get by just fine without one. It's mostly a matter of whether you are consistently careful about moving files onto your computer or whether you would benefit from an application helping you avoid viruses. An antivirus application is also a good idea if you share your computer with inexperienced users who are more likely to accept viruses.

Genius

When you allow access to your MacBook through a remote control, you can click Pair and follow the on-screen instructions to pair your MacBook with a remote.

Protecting Data with Time Machine

The most important thing you can do to protect your MacBook and its data is to back it up. Backing up simply means having at least one copy of all the data on your computer in case something should happen to the data. What could happen? Lots of things, such as an accidental deletion of files, a hardware or software problem that makes the data unavailable, liquid being spilled on the MacBook, and so on. There shouldn't be any question in your mind that something like this will happen, because no matter how careful you are, at some point data you want to keep is going to disappear from your computer. If you have everything backed up properly, this is a minor nuisance. If you don't have good backups, this could be a disaster.

To drive this point home, think about how much money you've spent on content from the iTunes Store. You can only download this content once. After that, if you need to download it again, you have to pay for it again. Going beyond money, consider photos that you manage in iPhoto. Many of those are irreplaceable; without a backup in place, you could lose them and never be able to get them back. Then there are documents you've created, financial records, and so on.

The good news is that with an external hard drive, you can use the Mac OS X Time Machine to back up with minimal effort on your part; in fact, once you set it up, the process is automatic. Time Machine makes recovering files you've lost easy and intuitive.

Time Machine backs up your data for as long as it can until the backup hard drive is full. It stores hourly backups for the past 24 hours. It stores daily backups for the past month. It stores weekly backups until the backup drive is full. Once the drive is full, it deletes the oldest backups to make room for new backups. To protect yourself as long as possible, use the largest hard drive you can, and exclude files that you don't need to back up (such as system files if you have the Mac OS X installation disc) to save space on the backup drive.

To use Time Machine, you need to gain access to an external hard drive and then configure Time Machine to use it. And you should know how to use Time Machine to restore files, should (I mean when) you need to.

Preparing a backup drive

To use Time Machine, you need to be able to store data on an external drive. To accomplish this, you have the following options:

- **Time Capsule.** This Apple device is a combination AirPort Extreme Base Station and hard drive (see figure 14.7). With capacity options of 1TB or 2TB, you can gain a lot of backup storage space. Additionally, a Time Capsule is also a fully featured AirPort Extreme Base Station, so it makes an ideal backup drive for any computer connected to the AirPort network it provides. The downside of Time Capsule is that it is more expensive than a standard hard drive, but if you don't already have an AirPort Extreme Base Station, it is slightly less expensive than buying the base station and hard drive separately.

- **Hard drive connected through USB or FireWire.** You can use a hard drive directly connected to your MacBook as a backup drive. This provides the fastest performance of any option, and hard drives are inexpensive and easy to configure. (See Chapter 13 for detailed information about connecting your MacBook to an external hard drive.)

- **Shared hard drive.** You can back up to a hard drive that you can access through File Sharing over a local network.

Caution It's best if you don't use a backup hard drive for any purpose beyond backing up your data. You want to keep as much space available for your backups as possible and using the drive for other purposes makes less room available for backing up, which means that your backups don't go as far back in time as they might. You can share a backup drive among multiple computers, but if you do this, make sure it is a very large drive.

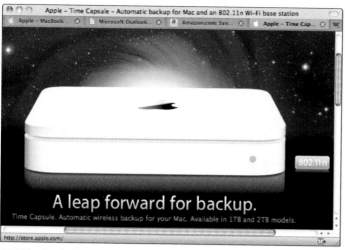

14.7 The Apple Time Capsule is useful as a backup drive for your MacBook, and it is also an AirPort Base Station.

Backing up with Time Machine

After you gain access to a backup hard drive, you can configure Time Machine to back up your data. In an ideal world, your backup hard drive is large enough so that you can copy your MacBook's entire drive onto the backup so you can restore any file on your machine. However, unless you have a relatively small amount of data on your computer or a very large backup hard drive, making a complete backup will limit the time for which backup data is stored. So you might want to exclude certain files, such as system software files that are on the installation disc, to make your backups smaller so that they can be stored longer.

Caution Is Time Machine perfect? It's close, but there are some things you need to be aware of. Hard drives can fail, and if your backup drive fails, it is no longer protecting your data. If you don't discover this until you need to restore files, you're out of luck. You should also back up important files in a second way, such as on DVD. You can burn files to a disc from the Finder and from within some applications. You should store your backup DVDs and CDs in a separate location just to be even more safe.

To configure Time Machine, perform the following steps:

1. **Open the Time Machine pane of the System Preferences application.**

2. **Drag the slider to the ON position.** Time Machine activates and the select drive sheet appears (see figure 14.8).

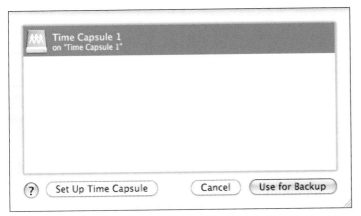

14.8 Use this sheet to select the drive Time Machine uses to store your backed-up data.

3. **Select the drive on which you want to store the backed-up information.**

4. **Click Use for Backup.**

5. **If you selected a Time Capsule protected by a password, type the password and click Connect; if not, you don't need to do anything for this step.** The sheet closes and you return to the Time Machine page. The drive you selected is shown at the top of the pane, and the timer starts the backup process, which you see next to the text "Next Backup."

6. **Click the Stop button next to the text "Next Backup."** This stops the backup process so that you can configure it more specifically.

7. **Click Options.** The Do not back up sheet appears. This sheet enables you to exclude files from the backup process. For example, you can exclude the System Files and Applications if you have the Mac OS X installation disc available because you can always restore the system from the disc.

8. **Click the Add (+) button.** The select sheet appears.

9. **Move to and select the folders or files you want to exclude from the backup and click Exclude.**

10. **If you selected system files, click Exclude System Folder Only to exclude only files in the System folder, or Exclude All System Files to exclude system files no matter where they are stored.**

11. **If you don't want the backup process to run when you are operating on battery power, deselect the Back up while on battery power check box.**

12. **If you want to be warned as old backups are removed from the backup drive, select the Warn after old backups are deleted check box.** This is a good idea, as it lets you know when your backup drive fills up.

13. **Click Done.** You return to the Time Machine pane, which displays information about your backup (see figure 14.9). The timer starts and when it expires, the first backup is created. From then on, Time Machine automatically backs up your data to the selected hard drive. New backups are created every hour.

14. **Select the Show Time Machine status in the menu bar check box.**

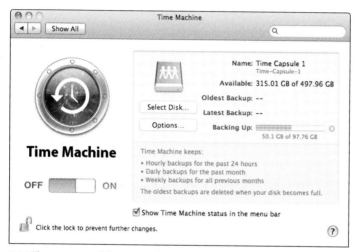

14.9 The progress of the current backup is shown in the Backing Up progress bar.

Genius

After you disconnect the external hard drive you use as the backup drive or move out of range of the Time Capsule you use, the next time you reconnect to it, a backup is performed automatically. Make sure you connect to the hard drive or Time Capsule frequently because your backups are only as "fresh" as the last time you connected to the backup drive.

Time Machine backups happen automatically, but you should ensure things are working properly by following a few simple suggestions:

● **Every so often, open the Time Machine pane of the System Preferences application and check the status of your backups.** This includes the name of the current backup drive, the amount of disk space available, the oldest backup stored on the drive, the latest backup, and the time at which the next backup will be performed. The latest backup date and time tell you how fresh your current backup is; it shouldn't be more than one hour old unless there is a problem, you've disabled Time Machine, or haven't connected the backup drive to your MacBook in a while.

- **As the backup drive gets full, you see warnings when old backups are deleted.** You need to make sure that there aren't files in the old backups that you might need at some point. This can happen if you delete a document or folder from your MacBook but don't restore it for a long time. Eventually, the only copy left might be in the oldest backup that gets deleted when the hard drive gets full.

- **When your backup system has worked for a while, check the status of the hard drive you are using.** If it is filling up rapidly, consider removing some of the system and application files that might be part of it to reduce the space required. The most important files to protect over a long period of time are those you've created, changed, or have purchased. Files that are already on a disc, such as Mac OS X software, are relatively easy to recover.

- **If there are files you want to keep, but don't use any more, consider moving them onto a DVD or CD for archival purposes.** Then delete them from your MacBook's hard drive, and over time they'll be removed from the backups or you can exclude them from Time Machine to reduce the amount of drive space required.

- **Test your backups periodically to make sure things are working properly by attempting to restore some files (explained in the next section).** If you don't discover a problem until you need to restore important files, it is too late, so make sure your backup system is working properly. Create a couple of test files for this purpose and let them exist long enough to get into your backups (at least one hour assuming you are connected to your backup drive). Delete some of the files and empty the Trash. Make and save changes to some of the test files. Then try to restore both the deleted files and the original versions of the files you changed. If you are able to restore the files, your data is protected. If not, you have a problem and need to get it solved so that your data isn't at risk.

- **Use the Time Machine menu on the Finder menu bar to quickly access commands and information.** At the top of the menu, you see the date and time of the most recent backup. You can use the Back Up Now command to start a backup at any time. Select Enter Time Machine to restore files. Select Open Time Machine preferences to move to the Time Machine pane of the System Preferences application.

Restoring files with Time Machine

If you only have to use the information in this section to test your backups, it's a good thing. However, there may come a day when you need to use this information "for real" to recover files that are important to you. These might be photos from your last vacation, favorite songs you purchased from the iTunes Store, or even documents you've put a lot of work into. You might have accidentally deleted the file or realized you wanted a previous version. Or something might have gone haywire on MacBook and you lost some important files.

The reason this function is called Time Machine is that you can use it to go back in time to restore files that are included in your backups. You can restore files and folders from the Finder, and you can recover individual items from within some applications (such as photos from within iPhoto).

Restoring files in the Finder

If the folders or files you want to restore are included in your backups and are available in the Finder, you can restore them by performing the following steps:

1. **Open a Finder window showing the location where the files you want to recover were stored.** This can be the location where files that have been deleted were placed, or it may be where the current versions of files are stored (in the event you want to go back to a previous version of a file).

2. **Launch the Time Machine application by:**

   - Clicking its icon (the clock with the arrow showing time moving backward) on the Dock.
   - Double-clicking its icon in the Applications folder.
   - Choosing Time Machine menu ➪ Enter Time Machine.

   The desktop disappears and the Time Machine window fills the entire space (see figure 14.10). In the center of the window, you see the Finder window that you opened in Step 1. Behind it, you see all the versions of that window that are stored in your backup, from the current version to as far back in time as the backups go.

   Along the right side of the window, you see the timeline for your backups, starting with today and moving back in time as you move up the screen. At the bottom of the screen, you see the Time Machine toolbar. In the center of the toolbar, you see the time of the window that is currently in the foreground. At each end, you see controls that you use to exit Time Machine (Cancel) and the Restore button (which is active only when you have selected a file or folder that can be restored).

3. **Move back in time by:**

   - Clicking the time on the timeline when the files you want to restore were available.
   - Clicking the back arrow (pointing away from you) located just to the left of the timeline.
   - Clicking a Finder window behind the foremost one.

4. **When you reach the files you want to restore, select them.**

5. **Click Restore.** The files and folders you selected are returned to their locations in the condition they were in the version of the backup you selected, and Time Machine quits. You move back to the Finder's location where the restored files were saved. You can resume using them as if you'd never lost them.

14.10 You can use Time Machine to travel back in time to when files you want to restore were available.

Genius

To restore a previous version of a file and keep the current version, rename the file before you launch Time Machine. Then restore the version of the file you want and you'll have both versions of the file in the Finder window.

Restoring files in applications

Some applications that work with individual files, such as iPhoto and iTunes, provide Time Machine support so that you can restore files from within the application instead of by selecting the files in the Finder. This makes restoring files from certain kinds of applications easier because you can find the files to restore using the application's interface instead of using the Finder (which is difficult for iPhoto files because of the way that application names and organizes your photos).

The following steps show you how to restore photos in iPhoto (restoring files in other compatible applications is done similarly):

1. **Open iPhoto.**

2. **Launch the Time Machine application by doing one of the following:**

   - Clicking its icon (the clock with the arrow showing time moving backward) on the Dock

   - Double-clicking its icon in the Applications folder

   - Choosing Time Machine menu ⇨ Enter Time Machine

   The desktop disappears and the Time Machine window fills the entire space. In the center of the window, you see the iPhoto window. Behind it, you see all the versions of that window that are stored in your backup from the current version as far back in time as the backups go.

3. **Move back in time by:**

   - Clicking the time on the timeline when the photos you want to restore were available. The higher on the timeline you click, the farther back in time you go.

   - Clicking the back arrow (pointing away from you) located just to the left of the timeline.

   - Clicking an iPhoto window behind the foremost one.

   As you move back in time, you see the versions of the window that are saved in the backup you are viewing, and the date and time of the backup in the center of the toolbar.

4. **Use the iPhoto controls to move to the photos you want to restore.**

5. **Select the photos you want to restore.**

6. **Click Restore.** The files are returned to iPhoto, and you can use them as if they'd never been lost.

Genius

A portable hard drive is an ideal accessory for your MacBook so you can back up your data when you are on the move. A flash drive, SD card, or iPod is a good option to back up specific files when you can't access your regular backup system. If you have a MobileMe account, you can copy files to your iDisk to back them up.

Protecting Data with Encryption

If you travel with your MacBook, the data it contains is vulnerable because your computer can be carried away by other people. If you store important data on your computer, you can encrypt the data in your Home folder so that it can't be used without an appropriate password. Even if someone is able to mount the hard drive in your MacBook, he must have the password to be able to access data in your Home folder.

Caution

If you use your MacBook in public, you should disable automatic login whether you use FileVault or not. With automatic login enabled, anyone who starts your computer can use it. With this feature disabled, a password is needed to access it, which provides some level of protection. You should also require a password to wake up or come out of the screensaver if you leave your MacBook for any period of time without logging out.

The Mac OS X FileVault feature encrypts your Home folder using a password that you create so that this data can't be accessed without the appropriate password. To do this, Mac OS X has to create a copy of your Home folder during the encryption process, which means that you need to have free space that is at least the size of the information in your Home folder before you can enable FileVault.

Caution

To use FileVault, the associated user account must have a password. If you didn't configure a password for your user account, or for any other user account, you need to do so before you can activate FileVault. Also, only one user account can be logged in to activate FileVault.

To activate FileVault, perform the following steps:

1. **Open the Security pane of the System Preferences application.**

2. **Click the FileVault tab (see figure 14.11).**

3. **Click Set Master Password.** The master password sheet opens. The master password enables you to decrypt encrypted files for all users. You must create a master password before you can activate FileVault. If you are an administrator of the computer and no one else knows your password, you can use the same password that you use for your user account.

4. **Type the master password in the Master Password field and the Verify field, and then click OK.** The sheet closes and the Set Master Password button becomes the Change button.

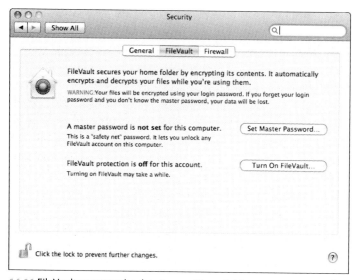

14.11 FileVault encrypts the data in your Home folder to prevent unauthorized access to it.

Caution

FileVault can interfere with backup applications, including Time Machine. You must be logged out of your user account for Time Machine to be able to back up your Home folder. I recommend that you disable FileVault when you use your MacBook in a secure location so that your backups aren't disrupted.

5. **Click Turn On FileVault.** The FileVault service starts up, and you are prompted to type your password.

6. **Type your user account's login password.**

7. **Click OK.** You see a warning sheet that explains what you are doing and that activating this service can take a while (you can't log out of your account until the service has been turned on).

8. **If you also want the data that is being encrypted to be erased securely when the encrypted version is created, select the Use secure erase check box (which overwrites deleted data so that it can't be recovered as easily).**

9. **Click Turn On FileVault.** The FileVault window appears; you can't do anything else on your MacBook until FileVault starts. When the process is complete, you see the Login window.

Caution

FileVault must be activated for each user account to secure each user's Home folder. Also, it only protects data stored in the encrypted Home folder. Any data stored outside of an encrypted Home folder is vulnerable.

10. **Log back in to your account.** You shouldn't notice any difference, except that your Home folder's icon is now marked with the secure icon (a lock). All your Home folder files are encrypted and aren't accessible unless a valid encryption password has been entered.

When you log in to your account (or any other account protected by FileVault), the files in your Home folder are decrypted automatically so you won't need to do anything else to access them. The value of FileVault is for those times when you aren't logged in to your account and someone else has access to your computer. For example, suppose someone steals your MacBook. Although she can't access your user account without your login password, she could connect the computer to a FireWire drive with Mac OS X installed and start up from that volume. Because the files on your MacBook startup volume are not protected anymore (the OS on the computer to which the MacBook is connected is running the show), they are accessible. If FileVault is not on, these files are not encrypted and can be used, but if FileVault is on, these files are encrypted and are useless unless the password is known.

Genius

If another user turns on FileVault and subsequently forgets his password, you can use your FileVault master password to decrypt the files in that user's Home folder. You can provide the master password to the other user so he can decrypt his files. Then change the master password to make sure only the authorized people have it. Or reset the user's FileVault password without providing the master password.

Protecting Information with Keychains

Many times, you can select a check box that causes Mac OS X to remember the passwords you type. These passwords are remembered in the keychain associated with your account. Just by using the remember check box, you get a lot of value from the keychain because it stores the various usernames and passwords for you. All you have to remember is the password for your user account that unlocks the keychain, which in turn applies the appropriate usernames and passwords so you don't have to type them manually.

When you have applications, such as Safari, remember usernames and passwords (such as those for Web sites you visit), they are also stored in your keychain so that you don't have to type this information each time you need to log in. Each kind of username and password is stored as a specific type in your keychain.

Before you can use a keychain, it has to be created; a keychain is created automatically for each user account you create. However, you can create additional keychains for specific purposes if you need to.

To use a keychain, it must be unlocked. To unlock a keychain, type its password when you are prompted to do so. When you log in to your user account, the default keychain for that account is unlocked automatically because its password is the password for the user account with which it is associated.

While typing a keychain's password can be annoying because it is a fairly common requirement, you should remember that at least you only have to remember the keychain's password instead of remembering a separate password for each resource.

Many types of resources can be added to your keychain to enable you to access them, including the following:

- **AirPort network passwords.**
- **File sharing passwords.**
- **Internet passwords.**
- **MobileMe password.**
- **Secure notes.** You can store information that you want to protect using secure notes. For example, if you want to store your credit card information so that it can't be accessed unless you are logged in to your user account, you can add it to your keychain. When you need that information, you can open the secured note containing your credit card information in your keychain.

Viewing and configuring your keychains

You can view and configure your keychain with the following steps:

1. **Open the Keychain Access application located in the Utilities folder within the Applications folder (see figure 14.12).** In the top-left pane is a list of all keychains that your account can access. In the lower-left pane is a list of categories for all the keychains that are installed under your user account. Select a category and the keychain items it contains appear in the lower-right pane of the window. You see information related to each keychain item, such as its name, its kind, the date it was last modified, when it expires, and the keychain in which it is stored. When you select a keychain item, detailed information about that item appears in the upper part of the window.

Note Your default keychain is called the login keychain. The Passwords category contains several subcategories. To view them, expand that category by clicking its expansion triangle.

14.12 You can see that a number of items have been stored in my keychain.

2. **To see what items are included in your default keychain, select login.**

3. **Select the All Items category.** Each item in your keychain appears in the list.

4. **To get summary information about a keychain item, select it.** A summary of the item appears at the top of the window, including the kind of item it is, the user account with which it is associated, where the location to which it relates is, and the modification date.

5. **With the item still selected, click the Information button (the i located at the bottom of the Keychain Access window).** The Information window appears. Depending on the item's type, its Information window contains various kinds of information that you can explore.

6. **Close the Information window.**

7. **Double-click a keychain item.** Its window appears. This window has two tabs: Attributes and Access Control. The Attributes tab presents information about the item, such as its name, its kind, the account, the location of the resource with which it is associated, comments you have entered, and the password (which is hidden when you first view an item). The Access Control tab enables you to configure how the item is used.

8. **To see the item's password, select the Show password check box.** You are then prompted to confirm the keychain's password.

9. **Confirm the password by typing it at the prompt and choosing to allow access to the item.** When you return to the Attributes tab, you see the item's password.

10. **Click the Access Control tab.** Use the access controls in the pane to control which applications can access this keychain item and how they can access it.

11. **To allow access to the item by all applications, click the Allow all applications to access this item radio button.** If you want to configure access for specific applications, continue with the rest of these steps.

12. **To allow access by specific applications but require confirmation, click the Confirm before allowing access radio button, and select the Ask for Keychain password check box if you want to be prompted for your keychain's password before access is allowed.**

13. **To enable an application not currently on the list to access the keychain item, click the Add (+) button located at the bottom of the list and select the application to which you want to provide access.**

14. **Click Save Changes.** Your changes are saved, and you return to the Keychain Access window.

Adding items to a keychain

You can add items to a keychain in several ways, including the following:

- **When you access a resource that can provide access to a keychain, such as a file server, look for the Add to Keychain check box.**

- **Drag a network server onto the Keychain Access window.**

- **Drag the Internet Resource Locator file for a Web page onto the Keychain Access window.**

- **Manually create a keychain item.**

Genius

If a particular application or resource doesn't support keychains, you won't be able to access that resource automatically. However, you can still use Keychain Access to store such an item's username and password for you, thus enabling you to recall that information easily.

One useful thing you can add to a keychain is a secure note. This protects the information you enter with a password so that it can only be viewed if the appropriate password is provided. To add a secure note to a keychain, use the following steps:

1. **Open Keychain Access.**

2. **Select the keychain to which you want to add the note.**

3. **Choose File ⇨ New Secure Note Item.** The New Secured Note sheet appears (see figure 14.13).

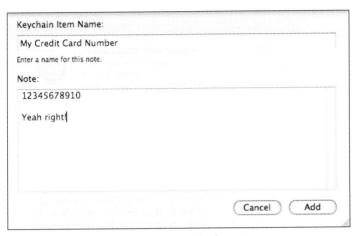

Keychain Item Name:

My Credit Card Number

Enter a name for this note.

Note:

12345678910

Yeah right!

Cancel   Add

14.13 Here's a secure note containing vital information.

4. **Type a name for the note in the Keychain Item Name box.**

5. **Type the information you want to store in the Note box.**

6. **Click Add.** The note is added to your keychain and you return to the Keychain Access window where you see the new note you added.

To view a secure note, do the following:

1. **Select the Secure Notes category.** Your secure notes appear.

2. **Double-click the note you want to read.** The note opens.

3. **Click the Show note check box.** You see the note in the window.

Working with keychains

When an application needs to access a keychain item and it is not configured to always allow access, you see the Confirm Access to Keychain dialog box that prompts you to type a keychain's password and choose an access option (see figure 14.14). When prompted, you have the following three options:

- **Deny.** Access to the item is prevented.

- **Allow.** A single access to the item is allowed.

- **Always Allow.** Access to the item is always allowed, and you don't see the prompt the next time it is used.

Keychain Access wants to use your confidential information stored in "My Credit Card Number" in your keychain.

To allow this, enter the "login" keychain password.

Password: [   ]

▼ Details

Keychain: ☐ login.keychain ↕

Application: 👤 Keychain Access ↕

(?)   (Always Allow)   (Deny)   (Allow)

14.14 At a prompt, you can choose the kind of access you allow to an item.

If you want to become a keychain master, check out the following information:

- **Your keychains are stored in the Library/Keychains folder in your Home directory.** You can add a keychain from one account to another account by moving the keychain file to a location that can be accessed by the second account. (For example, you can copy your keychain into the Public folder of your Home directory to enable other users to add that keychain to their own accounts.) To add a keychain to a user account, open Keychain Access under that account and choose File ➪ Import Items. This is useful if you want to use the same keychain from several accounts.

- **Delete a keychain by selecting it and choosing File ➪ Delete Keychain** *keychainname*, **where** *keychainname* **is the name of the keychain.** All the items in the keychain and the keychain itself are deleted.

- **If you choose Edit ➪ Change Settings for Keychain** *keychainname*, **where** *keychainname* **is the name of the keychain, you can set a keychain to lock after a specified period of time or lock when the MacBook is asleep.**

- **You can synchronize keychains on different computers by using MobileMe syncing (see Chapter 5).** This ensures that once you add information to your keychain, such as a secure note, it is available on all of your Macs.

- **If you choose Edit ➪ Change Password for Keychain** *keychainname*, **where** *keychainname* **is the name of the keychain, you can change a keychain's password.**

334

- **Choose Keychain Access ➪ Preferences.** On the General tab, select the Show Status in Menu Bar check box. This adds the Keychain Access menu to the menu bar. From this menu, you can lock or unlock keychains and access security preferences and the Keychain Access application.

- **If you choose Edit ➪ Keychain List, you see the Configure Keychain sheet.** You can use this sheet to configure keychains for a user account or the system. For example, you can select the Shared check box to share a keychain between user accounts.

- **If you choose Keychain Access ➪ Keychain First Aid, you see the Keychain First Aid dialog box.** You can use this dialog box to verify keychains or repair a damaged keychain.

How Can I Run Windows Applications?

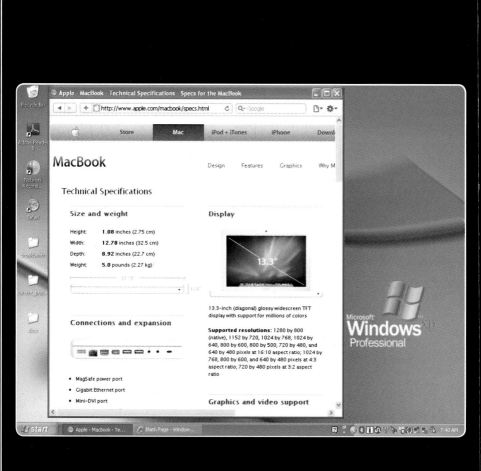

Some of us live in two worlds. One is the Mac world we know and love. The other world is that of Windows computers. For Mac fans, Windows isn't the operating system of choice for many reasons. However, Windows computers do dominate certain areas, particularly midsize and large organizations, and there are a number of applications that run on Windows only. The good news is that with your MacBook, you can run the Mac OS and Windows on the same computer, which means you really do have the best of both worlds.

Choosing a Windows Option

When the Mac platform switched to Intel processors, two options for running Windows on Macs became available: Boot Camp and virtualization. Each method has its advantages and disadvantages. More good news is that you can use both of these methods when you need to.

● **Boot Camp.** Boot Camp is the Apple technology that transforms Mac hardware into a fully capable Windows PC. You can choose to boot up your MacBook in the Mac OS or in Windows. When you boot up in Windows, you have a fully functional Windows PC on your hands.

   The strengths of Boot Camp include great performance (your MacBook can outperform many laptops designed to run Windows only), maximum compatibility for hardware and software, and a lower cost because your only expense is a copy of Windows. A minor downside is that it can be a bit more complicated to share data between the two operating systems because they can't be running at the same time. And you have to restart your computer to switch between the operating systems.

● **Virtualization.** Under virtualization, an application provides a virtual environment (also called a virtual machine) in which you install and run Windows. You install the virtualization application and then install a version of Windows in a virtual machine. When you want to run Windows, you launch the virtualization application, and within its windows you run Windows and Windows applications.

   The virtual approach has a number of benefits, including being able to run Windows and the Mac OS at the same time because the virtualization software is just another application running on your MacBook, good performance (it isn't noticeably slower than running it under Boot Camp), and easy data sharing because the Mac OS and Windows are running at the same time.

   Virtualization does have two points against it. One is the cost of the virtualization software (the Parallels Desktop for Mac application that I recommend for this is currently about $80). The other is that a virtual approach might not be compatible with all the hardware and software you want to run.

While I've explained Boot Camp and virtualization as two distinct options, if you choose the virtualization application I recommend (Parallels Desktop for Mac), you can use both options and switch between them easily.

Obtaining Windows

To run Windows on a Mac, you have to purchase a full copy of Windows to install, whether you use Boot Camp or a virtualization application (or both). The cost for this varies, depending on the version of Windows you purchase and how you purchase it. When you purchase Windows, try to get a version that is designed for builders, also called the Original Equipment Manufacturers (OEM) version. This version is significantly less expensive than the full retail version and is ideal for installing Windows on a MacBook.

If you are getting Windows only to run specific applications, see if the applications you need are supported on Windows XP SP2. If so, you might be better off. At press time, Microsoft Windows XP Home Edition SP2B for System Builders was selling for about $90. If you want the most current version of Windows, a full version of Windows Vista Home Basic Edition costs about the same. Windows 7, when it is released, will be yet a third option for you to consider. If you're only going to use Windows to run Windows applications, the basic edition should be sufficient. Make sure you get a full version; an upgrade version won't work.

Within each version of Windows are various subtypes, such as Home, Professional, and other categories between which the differences are difficult to understand. For most MacBook users running Windows as a second operating system, the Home or Basic versions are likely to be sufficient.

Using Boot Camp to Run Windows

To get Windows running under Boot Camp, use the Boot Camp Assistant, which creates a partition on your hard drive for your Windows installation. Once the Assistant is done with its work, you install Windows in the partition it creates. Finally, use the Mac OS X Installation DVD to add drivers for your MacBook hardware.

Once the installation is complete, you can run Windows at any time.

Configuring Boot Camp and installing Windows

Running the Boot Camp Assistant is mostly a matter of following the on-screen steps to work through the assistant and then using the Windows installer. The next set of steps demonstrates how to install Windows XP; if you install Windows Vista or Windows 7, the details might be slightly different, but the overall process is the same.

1. **Launch the Boot Camp Assistant application located in the Utilities folder in the Applications folder.** You see the first screen of the assistant.

2. **Click Continue.** You see the Create a Partition for Windows screen. On the left, you see the partition for Mac OS X, while on the right you see the partition for Windows, which is a minimum of 5GB.

3. **Set the size of the Windows partition by doing one of the following:**

    - **Drag the Resize handle (the dot) between the two partitions to the left to increase the size of the Windows partition (see figure 15.1).** You can set the partition to be any size you want. I recommend that you allocate at least 10GB to Windows.

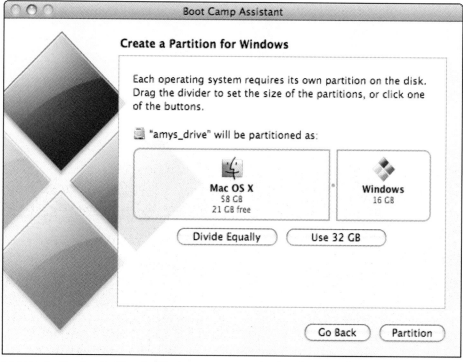

15.1 Use the Create a Partition for Window screen to set the size of your Windows environment.

    - **Click Divide Equally to divide the drive into two equally sized partitions.** I don't recommend this option, as it significantly reduces the amount of space available to you under Mac OS X.

    - **Click Use 32 GB to set the Windows partition at 32GB.** The 32GB option is a reasonable size for many Windows environments, and this option is a good choice if your MacBook's hard drive has plenty of free space.

4. **Click Partition.** When the process is complete, you're prompted to insert your Windows installation disc.

5. **Insert the Windows installation disc.**

6. **After it is mounted on your MacBook, click Start Installation.** The Mac restarts and boots from the Windows installation disc. The installation application starts installing files; you see the progress at the bottom of the blue Windows Setup screen.

7. **When the Welcome To Setup screen appears, press the Return key (which is equivalent to the Enter key in Windows).**

8. **Press F8 to agree to the Windows license information.**

9. **Select the BOOTCAMP partition and press the Return key.**

Caution Make sure you select the correct partition to install Windows on. If you don't, you might overwrite a partition with Mac OS X or your data on it, in which case that data is lost.

10. **Select either the FAT (Quick) or NTFS (Quick) format option.** Choose NTFS if you want Windows to be more secure and reliable. Choose FAT if you want to be able to save files to the Windows partition while using Mac OS X.

11. **Double-check to make sure you have the BOOTCAMP partition selected and press F8.** When the format process is complete, the MacBook restarts, running Windows instead of Mac OS X. The Windows Setup Wizard runs.

12. **Work through the various screens of the Setup Wizard to configure Windows.** For example, you need to type the Windows product key, set time and date, name the computer, and configure how you'll connect to the Internet. You can expect this process to take 30 or 40 minutes. When the process is complete, the Mac restarts. This time, it starts up in Windows and you see the Windows Setup application.

13. **Follow the on-screen prompts to do some basic configuration, including selecting security settings and creating one or more user accounts.**

14. **When you complete the Setup application, click Finish.** The Windows Desktop appears.

15. **Eject the Windows installation disc.**

16. **Insert the Mac OS X installation disc.**

17. **Follow the on-screen instructions to complete the installation of various drivers that Windows needs to work with the MacBook hardware.**

18. **At the prompt, restart your MacBook.** It starts up in Windows.

19. **If you're prompted by New Hardware wizards, follow the on-screen prompts to work through them.** Most of the time, the default selections work, so just approve all the suggested actions.

20. **To return to the Mac OS, choose Start menu ⇨ Shut Down ⇨ Turn Off Computer (see figure 15.2).**

21. **Click Turn Off.**

22. **Restart the MacBook and hold the Option key down while it starts up.**

23. **Select the Mac OS X startup volume and press the Return key.** The Mac starts up under Mac OS X again.

15.2 To shut Windows down, use the Turn Off Computer command on the Start menu.

Running Windows using Boot Camp

After you install Windows, you can transform your MacBook into a Windows PC by performing the following steps:

1. **Open the Startup Disk pane of the System Preferences application (see figure 15.3).**

2. **Select the Windows startup disk.**

15.3 Use the Startup Disk pane of the System Preferences application to choose a default operating system.

Genius

Right-clicking is a fundamental part of using Windows. To right-click with your MacBook when you are running Windows, hold two fingers on the trackpad and click the trackpad button.

3. **Click Restart.**

Caution

Windows is constantly under attack from viruses, Trojan horses, and other nasty attempts to steal or damage data. Running Windows on a MacBook doesn't protect you from these threats when you are using the Windows environment; it's as susceptible to the same attacks that Windows running on PC hardware is. You should install and use security software under Windows as soon as you get your Windows environment running, especially if you're accessing the Internet under Windows.

4. **At the prompt, click Restart again.** The Mac restarts and the Windows Desktop or Login screen appears.

5. **When you're ready to switch back to the Mac OS, choose Start menu ⇨ Control Panel.**

6. **Click the Switch to Classic View link.** The Control Panel folder is reorganized so that the control panels are shown together in one window instead of being organized by categories.

7. **Double-click the Boot Camp control panel.**

8. **Select the Mac startup volume.**

9. **Click Restart.**

10. **Click OK at the prompt.** Your MacBook starts up under Mac OS X.

Windows Activation

You must activate a copy of Windows to keep it running for more than 30 days. When you do this, the copy of Windows you run is registered to the specific computer on which you activate it as a means to limit illegal copies of Windows. Don't activate your copy of Windows until you've used it long enough to ensure that you've got it configured the way you want and can run it under Boot Camp, in a virtual environment, or both. Once activated, if you make a significant change, there's a chance you'll have to reactivate it, in which case you'll have to pay for a new copy of Windows to activate it under a different scheme or try to explain the situation to Microsoft to get the previous activation "undone" so you can activate it under a different environment. Running a "nonactivated" version of Windows doesn't limit you in any way, although you do get annoying reminders that it needs to be activated along the way. Once you hit the 30-day mark, you have to activate it to continue using Windows.

Running Windows Virtually

As you learned earlier, running Windows under a virtual environment has the significant advantage that you can run Windows and the Mac OS at the same time, making it fast and easy to switch between the two environments. The general steps to get Windows running under a virtual environment are as follows:

1. **Purchase, download, and install the virtualization software.**

2. **Configure a virtual environment and install Windows.**

3. **Run Windows in the virtual environment.**

There are several virtualization applications available, but the one that works best for me is Parallels Desktop for Mac. This application is simple to install and configure, and it performs very well. It has a lot of great features, including the ability to easily share data and files between the Mac OS and Windows. You can download and try it before you purchase the application; at press time, it cost about $80 to continue using the application beyond the 15-day trial period. It also has the benefit of being able to use Windows installed under Boot Camp, in which case you don't need to install Windows again, and you retain the option of running Windows under Boot Camp any time you want to. The remainder of this section focuses on using Parallels Desktop for Mac using a Boot Camp installation of Windows; if you choose a different application or install a version of Windows directly under Parallels Desktop for Mac, your details may vary.

Installing Parallels Desktop for Mac

To download and install Parallels Desktop for Mac, perform the following steps:

1. **Move to www.parallels.com and click the Parallels Desktop for Mac link.**

2. **Click the Download Trial link.** You move to the My Account page.

3. **Create a Parallels user account by following the on-screen instructions.**

4. **Download Parallels Desktop for Mac.**

5. **While you wait for the download to complete, click the Get trial key link.**

6. **When the download process is complete, move back to the desktop and run the Install Parallels Desktop application (see figure 15.4).**

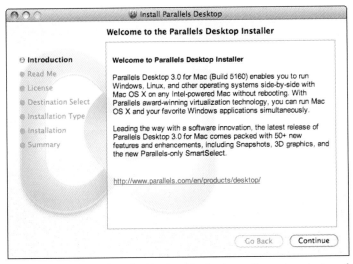

15.4 The Parallels Desktop for Mac Installer leads you through each step of installing the application.

7. **Follow the on-screen instructions to complete the installation.** When the process is done, you see the completion screen.

8. **Click Close to quit the installer.** You're ready to launch Parallels and configure a virtual environment.

Configuring Parallels Desktop for Mac

The first time you start Parallels, you configure the Windows environment you want to run. Because you've already installed Windows under Boot Camp, all you have to do is select that version of Windows to create a virtual Windows environment. Here's how:

1. **Launch Parallels Desktop (by default, it is installed in the Applications folder).** You're prompted to type an activation code.

2. **Click Enter Activation Key.** The Enter Activation Key sheet appears.

3. **Type the activation key and your name, and click Activate.** You see the OS Installation Assistant window. This Assistant leads you through the creation of the virtual environment.

4. **Select Custom.**

5. **Click Next.**

Note

If Parallels detects your Boot Camp installation and finds no virtual machines configured on your MacBook, it selects Boot Camp automatically. Follow the on-screen instructions to complete the configuration of the virtual environments.

6. **Leave Windows selected on the OS Type pop-up menu.**

7. **Leave Windows XP selected on the OS Version pop-up menu.**

8. **Click Next.**

9. **Choose the amount of RAM you want to allocate to the virtual machine. In most cases, the default should work.** Use the slider to increase or decrease the amount of RAM available to the virtual machine.

10. **Click Next.** You see the Select a virtual hard disk option screen (see figure 15.5).

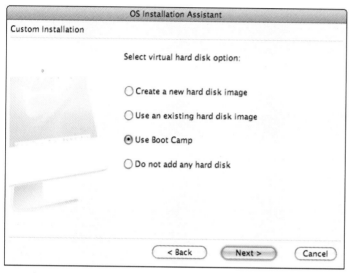

15.5 Choose Boot Camp to use your Boot Camp installation for the virtual Windows environment.

11. **Select the Use Boot Camp option.**

12. **Click Next.**

13. **Select Shared Networking.**

14. **Click Next.**

15. **Name your virtual environment.**

16. **Select the Enable file sharing check box.**

17. **Expand the More Options section.**

18. **Select the Share virtual machine with other Mac users check box.**

19. **Click Next.**

20. **Select the Virtual machine (recommended).**

21. **Click Next.**

Note One of the great things about Parallels Desktop is that the Windows environment gets its network settings from the Mac. So if the Mac on which you install Parallels is connected to a network and the Internet, the Windows environment is also connected without any additional configuration by you. Also, because the Windows environment gets its connection from the Mac, any protection from hacking through the network (such as NAT protection from an AirPort Extreme Base Station) is also applied to the Windows environment.

22. **Click Finish.** Windows starts up in the virtual environment.

23. **When the warning prompt disappears, log in to Windows.** If your Windows environment has only one user account, you log in automatically.

24. **Choose Actions ⇨ Install Parallels Tools.**

25. **Click OK in the prompt.** The installer begins to install Parallels Tools, and you see a warning on the screen. When the process is complete, Windows restarts.

26. **After Windows restarts, turn it off by clicking the Turn Off Computer link.**

27. **At the prompt, click Turn Off; Windows shuts down.** You then see the Parallels Desktop Configuration screen (see figure 15.6).

28. **Quit Parallels Desktop.**

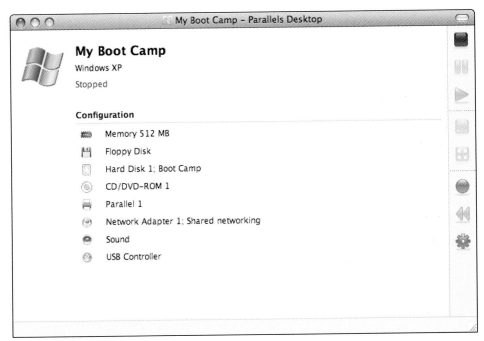

15.6 This screen provides information about, and controls for, your virtual Windows environment.

Running Windows under Parallels Desktop for Mac

After you install Parallels Desktop for Mac and configure a virtual environment, running Windows is a snap. Follow these steps:

1. **Launch Parallels Desktop.** The application launches and you see information about the virtual machine in the window.

2. **Click the Start button (the green right-pointing arrow).**

3. **If prompted to, type your Mac OS X username and password and click OK.** Windows starts up in the Parallels window.

4. **Run Windows.**

There isn't much difference between running Windows in a virtual machine and running it on a Windows PC.

Here are some points of interest to consider:

- You can move from Windows applications to Mac applications by pressing ⌘+Tab, by clicking in an application's window, choosing it on the Dock, and all the other standard ways of switching between applications.

- As you move your pointer over the Windows window, it changes to the Windows pointer and starts controlling Windows elements. When you move it out to the Mac desktop, it becomes a Mac pointer again.

- You can copy files from Windows to the Mac or vice versa by dragging them from one environment to the other.

- Only one environment can be using a CD or DVD at the same time. If you've inserted a CD or DVD, but don't see it on the Mac desktop, the odds are that Windows is running and the disc is mounted there, which makes it unavailable to the Mac. Stop the Windows environment and the disc appears on the Mac desktop.

- You can use the Coherence mode so that the Parallels window disappears and all you see on the Mac desktop is the Windows Start menu and any Windows applications you are running. To try this, choose View ➪ Coherence.

- You can also run Parallels in Full Screen mode, which is especially useful if you have two displays connected to your MacBook because you can run the Mac OS on one display and have the Windows environment fill the other. To try this, choose View ➪ Full Screen.

How Do I Solve MacBook Problems?

While MacBooks are among the most reliable and easiest-to-use computers available, they are still complex systems that involve advanced technology, complex software, and connections to networks, the Internet, and other devices. To put it in analog terms, there are a lot of moving parts. You can expect that every once in a while, something is going to go wrong. With a bit of preparation and some basic troubleshooting, you should be able to recover from most common problems relatively easily.

Looking for Trouble

You should build a MacBook toolkit that you can use to troubleshoot and solve problems. This way, you aren't wasting a lot of time and energy trying to locate or create the tools you need to solve problems when you need them but instead can simply put them into action. Here are a few of the important tools you should have in your toolkit in case of an emergency:

- **Current backups.** Backups are a critical part of your toolkit because restoring your data is the most important task that you need to be able to do. Having a good way to restore your data limits the impact of drastic problems (your MacBook not working anymore) and makes less significant problems (the accidental deletion of a file you need) trivial to solve.

  Once you have an automated backup system that updates your backups frequently and stores them in at least two ways (such as on an external hard drive and on DVD or iDisk), you are protected against loss of your data (see figure 16.1). Test your backup system periodically by restoring some files to make sure your backed-up data is ready when you need it (see Chapter 14 for more information about backing up).

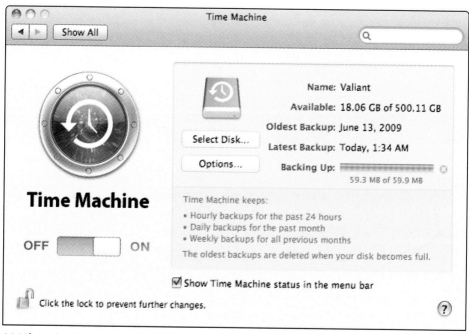

16.1 If your backup system includes Time Machine (which it should), the only data at risk is that which has changed since the last backup, which shouldn't be more than one hour ago.

- **Alternate startup disks.** Your MacBook startup disk is all important because that is where the OS is stored. If your startup disk or the system software it contains has a problem, you might not be able to start up, which reduces your MacBook to being a very cool-looking piece of technology art.

  Your toolkit should include an alternate startup disk that you can use to troubleshoot and solve problems that prevent your MacBook from starting up on its normal startup disk. Several possibilities exist for alternate startup volumes; you should maintain at least one, and preferably two, of the following options:

  - **A Mac OS X installation on an external hard drive.** You should install Mac OS X on an external hard drive so that you can start up your MacBook from that drive when you need to.

  - **Your Mac OS X installation disc.** You can use the software installation/recovery disc that contains the Mac OS X installer as a startup disk. It contains the basic software you need to start up your MacBook and accomplish a limited number of activities. Any updates you have applied to your primary system are not included in the version on the installation disc, so you have to use the version of Mac OS X that was current when the disc was produced. Because you can have the most current version of the OS installed on an external hard drive, you should keep the OS X disc to use if your hard drive is not available.

Genius

You should start up from your alternate startup disk and run Software Update periodically to keep the alternate startup volume's OS software current. Plus, this tests the drive to ensure that you can actually start up from that volume before you need to actually do so, such as when there is a problem with your primary startup volume.

  - **Third-party application discs.** Some third-party applications, such as disk maintenance, antivirus, and backup software, include discs that contain system software that you can use to start up your MacBook.

- **Alternate user accounts.** Because some problems can be related to preferences and other files that are specific to a user account, having an alternate user account is important during the troubleshooting process (see figure 16.2). If you haven't created an alternate test user account, you should do so now.

- **Mac OS X and application installers.** While you can start up from the Mac OS X software disc that was provided with your MacBook, you also need this disc to reinstall Mac OS X, so you should keep it in a place where you can find it when you need it. If you purchase an application on disc, keep the original discs where you can also access them when needed. If you purchase applications by downloading them from the Internet, burn the installer files that you download to a DVD or CD and keep those discs with your other installer discs.

Caution If you have to purchase upgrades to an application that you downloaded originally, be aware that the version you purchased might not always be available from the Web site from which you got it. So, if you lose the application because of a hardware or software problem, you might have to purchase it again or even purchase an upgrade again to be able to download it. Store application installers on a DVD or CD so you can return to them in the future.

16.2 A troubleshooting user account can help you identify a problem that is related to your primary user account.

● **Important information.** Consider devising some secure way to record passwords, user-names, serial numbers, and other critical data so you don't have to rely on memory to retrieve such information when you need it. Although keeping such information in hard copy is usually not advised, some people find it safer to develop and use some sort of code for this information and then have a hard copy of the encoded information handy.

You can also store this data in a keychain. If you allow Web site and other usernames and passwords to be remembered, this information gets stored in your keychain automati-cally. You can store application registration information as secure notes (see Chapter 14). Storing data in a keychain is good because this data is protected with your user account password. As long as you can get to your keychain, the information it contains is easily accessible. You should back up your keychains, too, to use for troubleshooting.

● **System profile.** Consider maintaining a system profile generated by the System Profiler application (see figure 16.3). This information can be very helpful when you are trouble-shooting problems.

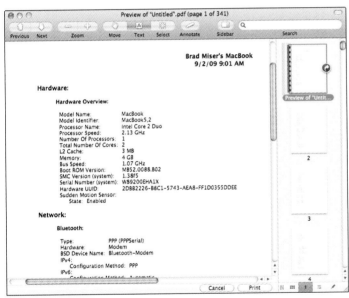

16.3 A detailed system profile can be useful when you are troubleshooting a problem.

Understanding and Describing Problems

When you start to troubleshoot, the most important thing you can do is to understand a problem in as much detail as possible. This understanding usually enables you to know what you need to do to correct the problem, or at least it gives you ideas of things you can try. As you gain insight into your problem, you should be able to describe it in detail, so you can get help from others if you are not able to solve it yourself.

Being able to recognize the symptoms of various kinds of problems helps you to identify what the problem likely is, which puts you in a position to try solutions.

Recognizing user errors

One common source of problems is our own mistaken actions or lack of proper actions. Recognizing a problem that you've caused is a bit tough, because user errors can have many consequences. The most common one is software or hardware not doing something as you expect it to; in such cases, a common cause is a failure to do things in the recommended way.

Some common user errors include the following:

- **Not following instructions.** Sometimes taking a few minutes to read them can save minutes or hours of troubleshooting time.

- **Not doing proper maintenance on your system.** The Mac OS X Software Update feature can help you to automatically keep your operating system and all your Apple applications current.

- **Not keeping enough free space on your hard drives.** If a drive is full, or very close to being full, you might have problems when you try to store more data on it.

Recognizing software problems

Software problems can manifest themselves in a number of ways, but the most common symptoms are hangs, unexpected quits, and unexpected behavior.

A hung application is one that has stopped responding to your commands and appears to be locked up. Hangs are usually accompanied by the spinning color wheel icon, which indicates that a lot of processor activity is happening, but the process being attempted isn't moving ahead. Fortunately, because Mac OS X has protected memory, a hung application usually affects only the application itself, and your other applications continue to work normally. You are likely to lose unsaved data in the hung application, but at least your losses are limited to changes you've made within a single application within the last hour (assuming you are using Time Machine to back up).

Caution When you force an application to quit, you lose any unsaved data with which you are working, and so you shouldn't do it until you're pretty sure the application is actually hung.

The only immediate solution to a hung application is to force it to quit. After forcing an application to quit, you should look for updates to the application in case the issues that caused it to hang have been solved.

Sometimes the application you are using suddenly quits. The application windows that were open simply disappear. That's bad enough, but the worst part is that you lose any unsaved data with which you were working, and there's nothing you can do about it.

Likely causes of unexpected quits are software bugs, conflicts between applications, or conflicts between applications and hardware. You should always restart your MacBook after an unexpected quit, and, like a hang, you should check to see if an update to the application is available.

Unexpected behavior is also easy to recognize because an application starts not doing what you are telling it to, or doing things you aren't telling it to. Likely causes of this problem are bugs or not using the application as it was intended. Internet attacks or viruses can also be the cause of unexpected behavior. When an application starts acting oddly, quit it and perform a restart of your MacBook. Then check for updates to the application that is misbehaving (see figure 16.4).

Genius Along with backing up your data, another good practice is to frequently save your documents. The time between saves is the amount of data that is at risk. So, if you save every 10 minutes, the most data you stand to lose is the last 10 minutes of work. Some applications have an autosave preference (Microsoft Office applications do) that you can set to automatically save your files at specified intervals. Other applications (such as Microsoft Office) will try to recover documents that were open when the application crashes, but this doesn't always capture the document as it was when the application crashed.

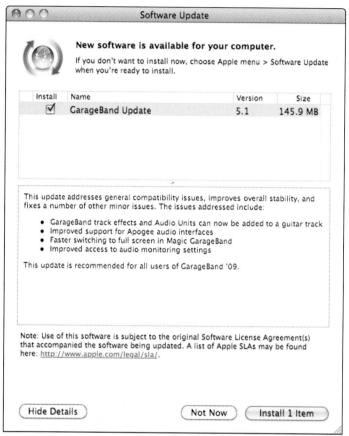

16.4 If you have a problem with an Apple application, run the Software Update application; an update might easily and immediately solve the problem.

Recognizing hardware problems

As odd as it might seem, the most unlikely cause of a problem is a hardware failure. Although hardware does fail now and again, it doesn't happen very often. Hardware failures are most likely to occur immediately after you start using a new piece of hardware or close to the end of its useful life. Sometimes you can induce a hardware failure when you upgrade a machine or perform some other type of maintenance on it.

Symptoms of a hardware problem are usually pretty much in your face. You have a piece of hardware that just won't work as you expect it to or won't work at all (hopefully, that hardware isn't your MacBook).

If the cause of a hardware problem is software, you can often solve the problem by updating the software associated with the device. If the problem is actually with the hardware itself, you'll probably need help to solve it, such as having the hardware repaired.

Describing problems

Being able to accurately describe a problem is one of the most fundamental skills for effective troubleshooting. In order to describe a problem accurately, you must take an in-depth look at the various aspects of the problem, which puts you in a better position to solve it. And if you need to get help, effectively describing your problem is critical to being able to help someone help you.

Following are some questions you need to answer:

- Which specific applications and processes were running (not only the particular one with which you were working)?
- What were you trying to do (for example, print, save, or format)?
- What specifically happened? Did an application unexpectedly quit or hang? Did you see an error message?
- Have you made any changes to the computer recently (for example, installed software or changed settings)?

The answers to these questions provide significant clues to help you figure out what is triggering the problem. And identifying the trigger goes a long way toward identifying a problem's cause.

As strange as this may sound, when a problem occurs, you should recover the best you can and then immediately try to make the problem happen again. Try to re-create everything that was happening when the problem appeared the first time. Have the same applications open and follow your trail the best you can, exactly as you did when the problem inserted itself into your life (see figure 16.5).

When you attempt to re-create a problem, there are two possible results — and both of them are good if you think about them correctly.

One result is that you can't make the problem happen again. In this case, about all you can do is to go on about your business and hope that you just got unlucky with some combination of events (if there is an underlying problem, don't worry about missing it because it will likely happen again at some point). This result is good because you can just move along.

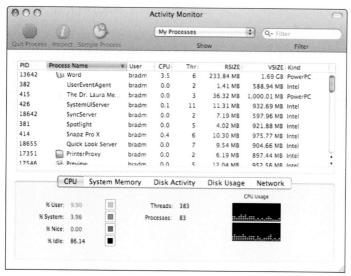

16.5 You can use the Activity Monitor application to see what processes are running at any point in time, such as when you are trying to re-create a problem.

The other result is that you are able to replicate a problem. While this is painful because you don't really want to be dealing with a problem, being able to replicate a problem makes figuring out what is happening much easier. (The hardest problems to fix are those that occur only occasionally or intermittently.) If you can re-create a problem, it is much easier to describe and it is also more likely that you'll be able to get help with it if you can't solve it on your own.

Trying Fast and Easy Solutions

For proper troubleshooting, you should learn to first recognize and describe problems. However, in reality, your first step in solving problems will often be one of the techniques described in this section, and in many cases, you'll just jump over describing a problem and get right to trying one of these fast and easy solutions. The amazing thing is that one of these will solve many of the more common problems you might encounter, at least temporarily. If the fast and easy solutions fail you, then you have to move into more complicated efforts.

For each of the solutions described in the following sections, you learn when to think about trying it and the steps you need to follow.

Forcing applications to quit

When to try: An application isn't responding to commands, and the spinning color wheel appears on the screen and remains there (the application is hung).

What it does: The command causes the OS to forcibly stop the application and its processes.

Cautions: You lose any unsaved data in the application that you force to quit.

1. **Activate the command by doing one of the following:**

   - Choose Apple menu ➪ Force Quit.

   - Press ⌘+Option+Esc.

   - Perform a secondary click on the hung application's Dock icon and select Force Quit.

   The Force Quit Applications dialog box appears. In this dialog box, you see the applications that are running. An application that is hung appears with red text and the text "(Not Responding)" next to it, so that you can easily identify the hung application.

2. **Select the hung application.**

3. **Click Force Quit.** The warning sheet appears.

4. **Click Force Quit.** The application is forced to quit and closes. If it doesn't work, try again; sometimes it can take a few times to get a hung application stopped. Forcing an application to quit leaves it unstable. Restart your MacBook before you continue working to minimize the chances of additional problems.

Forcing the Finder to relaunch

When to try: The Finder isn't responding to commands, and the spinning color wheel appears whenever you try to select or work with something on your desktop, such as a Finder window.

What it does: The command stops the Finder and starts it up again.

Cautions: Relaunching the Finder is a hit-or-miss proposition, so don't be too surprised if it doesn't work.

1. **Activate the command by doing one of the following:**

   - Choose Apple menu ➪ Force Quit.

   - Press ⌘+Option+Esc.

   - Perform a secondary click on the Finder's Dock icon and select Relaunch.

   The Force Quit Applications dialog box appears.

2. **Select the Finder.** If the Finder is hung, its name appears in red and the text "(Not Responding)" appears next to it. If it isn't in red, you don't need to relaunch it.

3. **Click Relaunch.** A warning sheet appears.

4. **Click Relaunch.** Your MacBook attempts to relaunch the Finder. Like a hung application, it can take a few tries to get the Finder to relaunch. If successful, you are able to work on the desktop again. If not, you'll need to perform the steps outlined later in this section. Forcing the Finder to relaunch leaves it in an unstable condition. Restart your MacBook before continuing to work.

Restarting

When to try: When your MacBook or an application isn't working the way you expect, or whenever you've forced an application to quit or the Finder to relaunch.

What it does: Shuts down all applications and processes on your MacBook, shuts the MacBook down, and restarts it.

1. **Perform one of the following:**

   - Choose Apple menu ⇨ Restart.

   - Press Ctrl+⌘+Power key.

   - Press the Power key once and click Restart.

2. **If the Restart dialog box appears, click Restart (see figure 16.6).** The MacBook shuts down and then restarts, and you can get back to work.

16.6 Restart your MacBook when applications aren't behaving themselves.

Genius

If a restart isn't the specific cure to a problem, it is almost always one step in the process. When in doubt, restart.

Shutting down soft

When to try: When your MacBook or an application isn't working the way you expect, or whenever you've forced an application to quit or the Finder to relaunch and normal behavior isn't restored with a Restart.

What it does: Shuts down all applications and processes on your MacBook and shuts the MacBook down.

1. **Perform one of the following:**

   - Choose Apple menu ⇨ Shut Down.

   - Press the Power key once and click Shut Down.

   - Press the Power key once and press the Return key.

2. **If the Shut Down dialog box appears, click Shut Down.** The MacBook shuts down.

Shutting down hard

When to try: When your MacBook appears to be locked up and doesn't respond to any of your commands.

What it does: Shuts down the MacBook, regardless of any running processes.

Cautions: You lose all unsaved data in all open applications.

1. **Press and hold down the Power key until the MacBook screen goes dark and you hear it stop running.** The MacBook turns off.

2. **Press the Power key again.** Your MacBook starts up.

Logging in under a troubleshooting user account

When to try: When an application isn't performing as you expect, and restarting your MacBook doesn't solve the problem.

What it does: Determines whether the problem is related to your specific user account or is more general.

Cautions: If you remove an application's preferences files, you have to re-create any preferences for the application. Make sure you have important information, such as registration information, backed up elsewhere.

1. **Perform one of the following:**

   - Choose Apple menu ⇨ Log Out *accountname*, where *accountname* is the currently logged-in account.

   - Press Shift+⌘+Q.

   The Log Out dialog box appears, and a 60-second countdown starts (the logout happens automatically when the timer counts down to zero).

2. **Click Log Out.** The Login window appears.

3. **Log in to your troubleshooting account.**

4. **Repeat what you were doing when you experienced the problem.** If the problem goes away, it is most likely related to the previous user account, which means, in most cases, that a preferences file has become corrupted.

5. **Log out of the troubleshooting account.**

6. **Log in to the previous account.**

7. **Quit the application that is having a problem.**

8. **Open the Preferences folder (Home ⇨ Library ⇨ Preferences).**

9. **Locate the preferences files for the application that has the problem.** Preferences files have the extension .plist and include the application's name somewhere in the file-name (see figure 16.7). Some preferences files are stored within the company's or application's folder within the Preferences folder.

16.7 Removing a preferences file can sometimes restore an application to normal behavior.

10. **Delete the preferences files for the application.**

Caution Deleting a preferences file can remove any personalized information that is stored in it, such as registration information. Make sure you have this information stored in another location before deleting an application's preferences files.

11. **Restart the application.**

12. **Reconfigure its preferences.** If the problem doesn't recur, you are good to go. If it does, you'll need to try one of the more drastic steps, such as reinstalling the application.

Repairing external hard drives

When to try: You see error messages relating to a hard drive, or you are unable to store data on it (and the drive isn't full).

What it does: Attempts to verify the drive's structure and repair any data problems.

1. **Quit all applications.**

2. **Launch Disk Utility (Applications ➪ Utilities).**

3. **Select the drive you want to check or repair.**

4. **Check the bottom of the Disk Utility window for information about the drive you selected.** You see the drive's type, connection bus (such as ATA for internal drives or FireWire for an external drive), connection type (internal or external), capacity, write status, S.M.A.R.T. status, and partition map scheme. If you select a partition on a drive, you see various data about the volume, such as its mount point (the path to it), format, whether owners are enabled, the number of folders it contains, its capacity, the amount of space available, the amount of space used, and the number of files it contains.

5. **Click the First Aid tab to see some information explaining how Disk Utility works.**

6. **Click Repair Disk.** The application checks the selected drive for problems and repairs any it finds. When the process is complete, a report of the results appears.

If Disk Utility is able to repair any problems it found, you're done and the drive should work normally. If the problems can't be fixed, you can try a different disk maintenance application. In some cases, you might need to reformat the drive, which erases all its data.

Repairing the internal hard drive

When to try: You see error messages relating to the internal hard drive, or you are unable to store data on it (and the drive isn't full).

What it does: Attempts to verify the drive's structure and repair any data problems.

1. **Start your MacBook from an alternate startup disk (more on this later in this section).**

2. **Select the MacBook internal hard drive in the Disk Utility application.**

3. **Follow the steps in the previous task to repair the drive.**

Repairing permissions

When to try: When you are getting error messages stating that you don't have permission to do something for which you should have permission or when you are experiencing unexpected behavior.

What it does: Repairs the security permissions associated with the files on a selected drive.

1. **Quit all applications.**
2. **Launch Disk Utility (Applications ⇨ Utilities).**
3. **Select the drive on which you want to repair permissions.**
4. **Click Repair Disk Permissions.** The application starts searching for permission problems and repairing those it finds. When the process is complete, you see the results in the Information window on the First Aid tab (see figure 16.8).

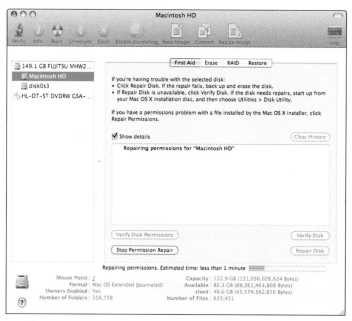

16.8 If you see odd security errors, try repairing a drive's permissions.

Reinstalling applications

When to try: An application isn't working correctly. You're sure you are using the current version (all patches and updates have been applied), and you've tried restarting and shutting down soft.

What it does: Restores the application to like-new condition.

Cautions: You lose any updates or patches that were released after the installer you have was produced; you may lose all your preferences for that application, including registration information, so make sure you have that information stored elsewhere.

1. **Delete the application by doing one of the following:**

   ○ Run the uninstallation application for the application you want to remove if one was provided.

   ○ Drag the application's files and its preferences files to the Trash; then empty the Trash.

Genius
You can reinstall many applications using the receipt that was created when you first installed it. To do this, open the following folder: *startupdisk*/Library/Receipts, where *startupdisk* is the name of your startup disk. To reinstall an application, double-click its PKG file in this folder.

2. **Run the application's installer (see figure 16.9).**

3. **Update the application to its latest version.**

4. **Reset your preferences.** If the application still doesn't work normally, the cause is likely a conflict between the application and the version of Mac OS X you are using or some other part of your system, or the application might just be buggy. Possible solutions are to use a different application, avoid the functionality of the application that causes the problem, or live with the problem until an update fixes it.

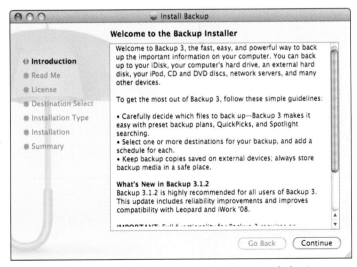

16.9 Reinstalling an application can restore it to its proper behavior.

Starting up from an alternate startup external drive

When to try: When you try to start up your MacBook, the normal startup sequence stops with a flashing folder icon on the screen, or when your MacBook is behaving oddly and you want to isolate the problem to your current startup disk.

What it does: Starts up your MacBook from the software installed on the external drive.

Cautions: You must have created an alternate startup disk (see Chapter 14); you'll use the version of the OS installed on the external drive, which might not be the latest version if you haven't kept it updated.

1. **Connect the external drive to your MacBook.**

2. **Restart your MacBook.**

3. **As it restarts, hold the Option key down.** After a few moments, each valid startup disk appears.

4. **Select the external hard drive from which you want to start up.**

5. **Click the arrow pointing to the drive you selected.** Your MacBook starts up, using the OS installed on the external drive.

6. **Use the MacBook.** If things work as expected, you know the problem is related to the previous startup disk, in which case, you'll have to take more drastic action, such as reinstalling Mac OS X on your normal startup disk. If the problem recurs, you know that it is related to a specific application, to a hardware device, or to the MacBook itself, in which case the likely solutions are to reinstall the application or to get help with the problem.

Genius

To set the default startup disk, open the System Preferences application and click the Startup Disk icon. Select the disk that you want to be the default startup disk. If you want to restart the MacBook from the disk, click Restart. If not, quit the System Preferences application and that disk will be used the next time you restart or start your MacBook. When it starts up, if the selected disk is not valid or has a problem, your MacBook selects one of the other valid disks to start up.

Note If you ever start up your MacBook and it stops with a flashing disk icon, it means that the computer can't find a valid startup disk. This either means there is a problem with the disk itself or something has happened to critical Mac OS X files, which prevent the system from operating. Try reinstalling Mac OS X. If it can't be reinstalled on the drive, the drive has a problem you'll have to fix.

Starting up from the Mac OS X installation disc

When to try: When you try to start up your MacBook, but the normal startup sequence stops with a flashing folder icon on the screen; when your MacBook is behaving oddly and you want to isolate the problem to your current startup disk; or when you want to reinstall Mac OS X.

What it does: Starts up your MacBook from the software installed on the installation disc.

Cautions: Only limited functionality is available, and the version of Mac OS X and its software is the one that was current when the disc was produced.

1. **Insert the Mac OS X installation or System restore disc.**

2. **Restart your MacBook.**

3. **As it restarts, hold down the C key.** The MacBook starts up from the software on the disc. Starting from the disc is slower than from a hard drive so continue to hold the key down until you see the language selection screen.

4. **Select your language.**

5. **Press Return.** You move to the Install Mac OS X screen, where you have limited access to the computer, mostly through the Mac OS X Installer menus. For example, you can open the Utilities menu to run the Disk Utility or run the installer to reinstall Mac OS X.

Getting Help with MacBook Problems

We all need a little help once in a while. When it comes to your MacBook, there's a wealth of assistance available to you.

Getting help from the Mac Help system

Mac OS X includes a sophisticated Help system that you can use to find solutions to problems you are experiencing, or to get help with a specific task. In addition to Mac OS X, many other applications also use the same Help system. To search for help, follow these steps:

1. **Choose Help.** The Help menu opens.

2. **Type the term for which you want to search in the Search box.** As you type, matches are shown on the menu. These are organized into two sections (see figure 16.10). In the Menu Items section, you see menu items related to your search. In the Help Topics section, you see links to articles about the topic.

3. **To see where a menu item is located, select it.** The menu opens and the item is highlighted (figure 16.10 shows the Empty Trash menu item being selected).

4. **To read an article, click its link.** The Help window opens, and you see the article in the window (figure 16.10 shows an article about removing files and folders from the Trash in the background).

Genius

When you move away from the Help window, it closes. However, your most recent search is saved so you can return to the results just by opening the menu again. To clear a search so you can perform a new one, click the Clear (x) button in the Search bar when it contains a search term.

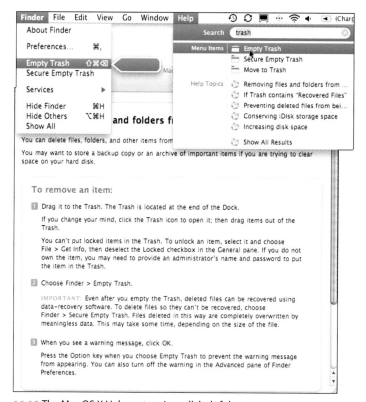

16.10 The Mac OS X Help system is, well, helpful.

Describing a problem in detail

If none of the fast and easy solutions presented earlier results in a problem being solved, you may have to create a more detailed description so that when you ask for help, you increase the odds that someone will be able to help you. In this section, you learn about some tools that can help you increase the level of detail in your problem descriptions.

Profiling a MacBook

Your MacBook is a complex system of hardware and software, in which each element has numerous technical specifications. Fortunately, you can use the System Profiler application to capture all the details about your system so that they are available to you when you need them, such as when you need to get help.

To create a profile for your MacBook, perform the following steps:

1. **Choose Apple menu ⇨ About This Mac.** The About This Mac window appears.

2. **Click More Info.** The System Profiler application appears. In the left pane, you see various categories of information about your MacBook, such as hardware components, network information, and software information.

3. **Select an area about which you want detailed information.** The details appear in the right pane of the window. With some categories, you see more options at the top of the window. For example, when you select USB, you see the various USB ports on your MacBook. You can select one of these to get more information about the device connected to it.

4. **When you see information you need, choose File ⇨ Print.** System Profiler builds a printable version of the profile.

Genius

The full profile is very long, sometimes 300 pages or so. You can create smaller versions of the profile to print by choosing View ⇨ Mini Profile or View ⇨ Basic Profile.

5. **When the Print dialog box appears, click PDF to open the PDF menu.**

6. **Choose Save as PDF.**

7. **Name the profile.**

8. **Choose a save location.**

9. **Click Save.** The profile is saved with the name and at the location you selected.

Monitoring a MacBook's activity

When a problem occurs, Mac OS X doesn't provide a lot of feedback directly. However, you can use the Activity Monitor application to get a closer look at what's happening in the background. Here's how:

1. **Open Activity Monitor (Utilities folder within the Applications folder).**

2. **Click the CPU tab.** In the upper part of the window, you see a list of all the processes running on the MacBook. For each process, you see a variety of information, such as how many CPU resources it is using and the amount of memory. At the bottom of the window, you see a graphical representation of the current thread and process activity in the processor (see figure 16.11).

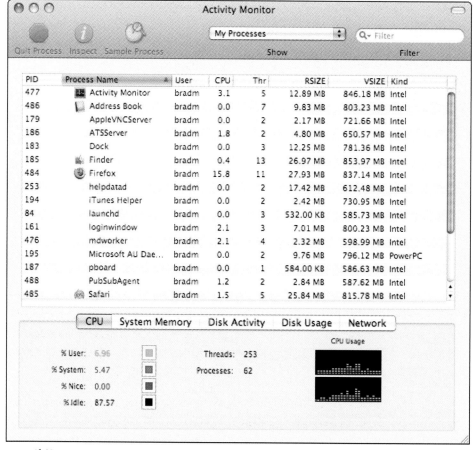

16.11 If CPU activity is maxed out for a long period of time, then a process is hung and you'll probably need to force it to quit and then restart your MacBook.

3. **Click the CPU column heading to sort the list of processes by the amount of processor activity.**

4. **Click the Sort triangle so it is pointing down indicating that the processes consuming more resources appear at the top of the list.** When a process is consuming a large amount of CPU resources or a lot of drive activity over a long period of time, it can indicate that the process is having a problem or is the cause of problems you are experiencing. In most cases, problems you are experiencing are caused by applications. You can limit the processes shown in the window to be just for applications, which can make the window's information easier to interpret.

5. **On the pop-up menu at the top of the window, select Windowed Processes.** The list is reduced so that it includes only processes associated with applications.

6. **Use the other tabs at the bottom of the window to explore other areas of the system.** You can use the Disk Usage tab to assess how much free space your drives have. You can use the System Memory tab to assess the status of your MacBook's RAM and its virtual memory.

Genius

Select a process and click the Inspect button. The Inspect window opens and you see several tabs providing information about various aspects of the process such as its memory use, statistics about how it is working, and the files and ports it has open. Sometimes this information is useful when doing detailed troubleshooting. For example, you see the number of recent hangs the process has experienced, which can tell you if the process is problematic, which can provide clues to help you solve its problems. You can also stop a process by selecting it and clicking the Quit Process button, which is similar to a force quit.

Capturing screenshots

When you experience a problem, being able to capture a screenshot is a great way to describe and document the problem. It's even more useful when you ask for help because you can provide the screenshots to the person from whom you're asking for help to give her detailed information she needs to help you. For example, if an error message appears on the screen, you can capture it in a screenshot.

There are two built-in ways to capture a screenshot in Mac OS X. You can use keyboard shortcuts or the Grab application. To use a keyboard shortcut to capture the screen, perform the following steps:

1. **When something appears on the screen that you want to capture and you want to capture the entire screen, press ⌘+Shift+3.** An image file is created on the desktop and you can skip to Step 4.

2. **When something appears on the screen that you want to capture and you want to capture part of the screen, press ⌘+Shift+4.**

3. **Drag over the area of the screen you want to capture and release the trackpad button when the area you want to capture is highlighted.** An image file is created on the desktop.

4. **Open the image file you created.** It is named Picture *X*, where *X* is a sequential number. The file opens in Preview and is ready for you to use for your own purposes or to provide to someone else when you ask for help.

Mac OS X includes the Grab application, which enables you to capture screenshots in a slightly more sophisticated manner. Here's how:

1. **Launch the Grab application by double-clicking its icon in the Utilities folder within the Applications folder.** The application opens, but you don't see any windows until you capture a screenshot. You do see the Grab menu.

2. **Choose Capture ⇨ Timed Screen.** The Timed Screen Grab dialog box appears.

3. **Organize the screen as you want to capture it.** For example, switch back to the Finder or other application that shows the message or window you want to capture and configure the windows as you want to capture them (see figure 16.12).

Genius In addition to the Timed Screen option on the Capture menu in Grab, you can use Selection to capture part of the desktop that you select by drawing a box around it; Window to capture the active window; or Screen to capture the entire desktop.

4. **Click Start Timer.** Grab's timer starts. After 10 seconds, the capture is taken.

5. **Save the image file.** The screen capture is ready for you to use for your own purposes or to provide to someone else when you ask for help.

Genius If you are serious about screenshots, you should consider using Ambrosia Software's Snapz Pro X, which was used for almost all the figures in this book. This application gives you lots of control over the screenshots you take and you can even capture motion so you can make movies of your desktop activities. To try Snapz Pro X, visit www.AmbrosiaSW.com/utilities/.

16.12 Once you click Start Timer, you have 10 seconds until the screen is captured.

Getting help from others

After you've tried the fast and easy solutions and the various Help systems on your MacBook, your next stop should be the Internet. Here are some places to try:

- **www.apple.com/support.** The Apple support pages are a great source of information, and you can also download updates to system and other software. Check out the Tech Info Library, which can search for specific problems. You can also read manuals and have discussions about problems in the forums that are available here. If the problem you are having seems to be related to the OS, Apple hardware, or an Apple application, this should be your first stop.

- **www.google.com.** Move to the Google search page and type a description of the problem you are having. The odds are good that someone else has had, and hopefully solved, the same problem. Explore the results until you find the help you need.

- **www.macfixit.com.** This is a good source of information related to solving Mac problems, because you can get help on just about every aspect of using a Mac. Most of the information comes from Mac users, and you can ask specific questions, although the answer to your question is probably already available.

- **www.macintouch.com.** This site offers a lot of news that can help you solve problems, especially if those problems are solved by a software update of which you might be unaware.

- **www.versiontracker.com.** You can quickly find out whether updates have been released for applications with which you are having trouble.

Note

If you do ask for help without doing the basics yourself, you might get the response RTFM. The "R" stands for "Read." The "T" stands for "The." The "M" stands for "Manual." I won't describe what the "F" stands for, but you can probably guess. If a quick search on the Apple Web site would find the help you need and it's clear you didn't even bother to do it, RTFM might be in your near future.

Genius

You can email me at bradmiser@me.com to ask for help, and I will do my best to provide a solution for you, or at least point you to a more helpful source if I can't help you directly.

Trying Harder or More Expensive Solutions

Hopefully, you'll never need to do any of the tasks described in this section, because they apply only when you have a significant problem. And they either take a lot of time and effort or can be expensive. Still, you have to do what you have to do.

Reinstalling Mac OS X

If you discover that your system has major problems, such as when your internal drive is no longer recognized as a valid startup drive, you might need to reinstall Mac OS X. Because it takes a while, and you might lose some of the installation and configuration you've done, you shouldn't make this decision lightly. If you determine that you do need to reinstall Mac OS X, here's how to go about it:

1. **Back up your data.**

2. **Make sure your data is backed up by trying to recover a file or two if you can (some problems will prevent this and you'll just have to trust that your backup system has worked).**

3. **Start up from the Mac OS X Installation disc.** After you've selected a language, you see the Install Mac OS X screen.

4. **Click Continue.**

5. **Agree to the license.** You move to the select a disk screen.

6. **Select your internal hard drive.**

7. **Click Install.**

8. **Follow the on-screen instructions to complete the installation.** When the process is complete, your MacBook restarts.

9. **Update your software (see Chapter 14).** In most cases, reinstalling Mac OS X from the disc moves you back to an earlier version so you want to make sure you update your operating system to the current version.

10. **Reinstall any applications that don't work correctly.** Mostly, these are applications that install software into the system; these need to be reinstalled because the software they installed was removed when Mac OS X was reinstalled.

Genius

When you install Mac OS X, you can click the Customize button to choose specific options to install. For example, to save some hard drive space, you can deselect languages that you don't use. When you've selected or deselected options, click OK and the files you excluded won't be installed.

Hopefully, your MacBook has returned to prime condition and is working like you expect. Because the installer doesn't change the contents of your Home folder, the data you had stored there should be intact, including your application preferences, iTunes content, and so on, so you can get back to what you were doing quickly. In rare cases, this data might have been disturbed, in which case you'll need to restore it from your backups.

Melting and repouring

Sometimes, things get so bad that you just need to start over. This goes even farther than simply reinstalling Mac OS X because you erase the internal hard drive, which means that all the data on it is deleted, including the system and all the files stored on it. This is drastic action, and should be taken only if you really need to do it. Also expect the initial process to take a long time.

Caution

If you follow these steps, all the data on your hard drive will be erased. If you don't have them backed up, they're gone forever. Don't do this unless you are sure your data is protected.

1. **Back up your data and test your backups to make sure they work if you can.** In some cases, you won't be able to do this, such as if you can't start up your computer, so you'll have to rely on your existing backups. If they are out of date, you don't want to perform these steps unless it is your last and only recourse.

2. **Start up from the Mac OS X Installation disc.** After you select a language, you see the Install Mac OS X screen.

3. **Choose Utilities ⇨ Disk Utility.** The Disk Utility application opens.

4. **Use Disk Utility to erase the internal hard drive (see Chapter 14 for the details).**

5. **When the process is complete, quit Disk Utility.** You move back into the Mac OS X installer.

6. **Click Continue.**

7. **Agree to the license.**

8. **Select your internal hard drive.**

9. **Click Install.**

10. **Follow the on-screen instructions to complete the installation.** When the process is complete, your MacBook restarts. When it does, your MacBook is in the same condition as when you first took it out of its box and turned it on.

11. **Follow the on-screen instructions to perform the initial configuration.** Again, this is just like the first time you started your MacBook.

12. **Create the user accounts you need (see Chapter 2).**

13. **Update your software (see Chapter 14).**

14. **Reinstall your applications.** If you installed Mac OS X from the software discs included with your computer, the iLife applications should have been installed, too, but you'll have to manually install all your third-party applications.

15. **Restore your data from your backups.** Your MacBook should be back to its old self, but without the problems you were having.

Genius

If you use Time Machine for your backups, you can restore your data into the appropriate user accounts.

Professional Repairs by Apple

If your MacBook has hardware problems, you'll probably need to have it repaired by Apple. You can do this by taking it to a local Apple Store or using Apple's Web site to arrange technical support. To get started with the Web approach, do the following:

1. **Move to www.apple.com/support and search for "repair."**

2. **Click the Online Service Assistant link.** You move to the Online Service Assistant Web page.

3. **Type your MacBook serial number.** This number is on the MacBook case and in your profile document. You can also get your serial number by opening the About This Mac window and clicking the Mac OS X version information twice.

4. **Select your country and click Continue.** On the resulting screen, you see warranty information about your MacBook, along with links to various resources you can use to have Apple repair it for you.

Index

The Genius is in.

Macs
PORTABLE GENIUS

978-0-470-29052-1

Mac OS X
Leopard
PORTABLE GENIUS

978-0-470-29050-7

iPhone 3G
PORTABLE GENIUS

978-0-470-42348-6

Final Cut Pro
PORTABLE GENIUS

978-0-470-38760-3

iMac
PORTABLE GENIUS

978-0-470-29061-3

MacBook Pro
PORTABLE GENIUS

978-0-470-29170-2

The essenti... ...on the go.
Designed for ... ...has all the
information y... ...nterior and
easy-to-naviga... ...nd tricks as
well as sa... ...ctivity.

WILEY
Now you know

Available whe...